AF381516

Frames of Anime

Frames of Anime

CULTURE and IMAGE-BUILDING

TZE-YUE G. HU

HKU PRESS
香港大學出版社

Hong Kong University Press
The University of Hong Kong
Pok Fu Lam Road
Hong Kong
https://hkupress.hku.hk

© 2010 Hong Kong University Press

ISBN 978-962-209-097-2 (*Hardback*)
ISBN 978-962-209-098-9 (*Paperback*)

British Library Cataloguing-in-Publication Data
A catalogue record for this book is available from the British Library.

Digitally printed

Contents

List of Illustrations

A Note to the Reader

All Japanese and Chinese names in this book are given in the following order: family names precede given names. For Japanese words, macrons are included. Where names have an established conventional spelling in English, I have retained the spelling (for example, Tokyo and Toei). The Chinese pinyin system is used except for internationally known names. All translations from Japanese and Chinese are the author's unless otherwise noted.

Acknowledgements

The writing of this book took place while I was a visiting scholar at the University of Oklahoma and more recently, a lecturer at the University's School of International and Area Studies. I thank the institution for providing me an anchoring place to complete the work. The University of Oklahoma allowed me access to its library facilities and other services. I resided in Ponca City for a while and would also like to thank Ponca City Library for their excellent inter-library loan assistance.

My inquiry into Japan's visual culture began when I was a graduate student in the Department of Comparative Literature at the University of Hong Kong. I would like to thank my supervisors Dr Patricia Erens and Dr Wimal Dissanayake for giving me the intellectual freedom to explore the subject. Former department chairs Professor Anthony Tatlow and Professor Jeremy Tambling had the imagination to consider my rather indefinite and unrefined proposal then. Through the years, I have silently saluted their far-sightedness and empathy toward my research. I am glad that they concurred with my desire to investigate a subject that has its roots in the Far East. I am grateful for their initial approval. My research path later matured steadily when I was a Japan Foundation fellow in the Division of Cinema and Theater Arts at Waseda University. This book would never have been possible without this prestigious fellowship. The institutional support "opened doors" for me; I was able to meet relevant people and travel to places for obtaining materials that enhanced my research immensely. I am especially grateful to Professors Iwamoto Kenji and Yokota Masao for making my fellowship at Waseda possible and for the time they spent on clarifying my ideas and commenting on my work. I take responsibility for any errors and oversights.

I am also indebted to the gracious friendship of Matsuoka Tamaki; words cannot express my gratitude. Many people have encouraged me along the way, some of whom I met at conferences, seminar presentations, film festivals, and animation studios. It would be impossible for me to name them all, but I would like to express specially my fond appreciation to retired animator Oda Katsuya for sharing generously his collections with me and the numerous discussions we had on animation. His ex-colleagues and friends in the industry had, in one way or another, contributed to my fieldwork and helped to deepen my knowledge of Japanese animation. Peer reviews are crucial to the improvement and honing of my work; members of the Society for Animation Studies, Japan Society for Animation Studies, and the editorial board of *Animation: An Interdisciplinary Journal* had at various stages read parts of my work and I appreciate their critical comments. I would also like to thank Ian Lok, former editor of Hong Kong University Press, for taking an interest in my manuscript initially. Michael Duckworth, publisher of the Press, was instrumental in finding anonymous reviewers who offered invaluable advice and suggestions that helped to refine and sharpen my ideas immensely. In the final preparation of this book, I was fortunate to have a lengthy discussion with Dr Sano Akiko and her generous offer of archival materials helped to further strengthen my work.

When the manuscript was ready for submission, Jaquine Hudson Bly appeared at the appropriate moment and became a much-appreciated editor-cum-mentor. I would also like to express my gratitude to an ex-colleague and friend, Waheeda Gapar, for editing my draft manuscript and to Connie Jeng and Sugawa-Shimada Akiko for their language assistance. When I encountered difficulties in my writing, Dr Fukushima Yoshiko offered me advice which helped to ease the writing process. I extend my sincere thanks to her. By chance, I met my undergraduate Chinese Studies professor, Kow Mei-kao, again at a conference. His encouragement was a source of strength. I also cherish the friendship of Ho Lai-aoe and Tham Wai-mum for their counsel and goodwill. I also want to thank Hong Kong University Press for their expertise and care in bringing this book to press.

I have presented portions of my work at various institutions over the years, and would like to thank my hosts, event organizers, and audiences at Sophia University, Anglo-Daiwa Foundation, Waseda University, Nihon University, the Japan Society of Image Arts and Sciences, University of Helsinki, National Chiaotung University, Academia Sinica, and Nanyang Technological University. I taught two semesters in the Japanese Studies Department of the National University of Singapore. The teaching experience led me further into adopting an interdisciplinary approach for my research. I benefited from various senior colleagues' expertise and the progressive courses that they created.

A journey of a thousand miles begins with a single step; it takes time, effort, and resources to study and explore a culture. I believe that in reaching out to understand the others, one learns to understand oneself and the discoveries are immeasurable. I hope that with the publication of this book, my family members will begin to see the fruits of my endeavor. Finally and yet most importantly, I am grateful to my parents and my late grandparents who showed their patience and compassion. Their experiences of history, of living in the East, of change and tradition, of war and peace times, and of life in specific terms, often run in the back of my mind as I work on my research.

Above all, I thank my husband Kenneth Ho for his spiritual support and our real-life animated companions Shiro and Aki, for their precious presence and trust and to whom this book is dedicated.

Introduction

In the beginning was the deed. The word followed as its phonetic shadow.

Leon Trotsky[1]

Do not loathe wordlessness, for it is expression par excellence.

Dōgen Kigen[2]

This book examines a late twentieth-century Japanese "invention" that fascinates and dominates the world. It does not come in a hard form, quantifiable, as in metal or in liquid state with tactile and tangible qualities. It is neither a Toyota nor a Honda over-2000 cc. sedan-car model; nor is it a cup of Nissin seafood noodles. It is a "toon product," which can also be broadly referred to as "cartoons." When specifically identified and defined, it is *anime*, the popular Japanese form of animation. The inquiring observation is why it has attained such a ubiquitous status despite the country's continuously stagnant economy amidst a worldwide perception that Japan has lost its attractiveness as an economic ideal. Less than two decades ago, it was remarkably known that the world's second largest economy was on a shopping spree, actively buying North American media corporations renowned for their supply of successful "software products," such as Hollywood films and pop stars, while from the other side of the Atlantic, water lilies and sunflowers painted by late master painters such as Claude Monet and Vincent van Gogh were eagerly sought after. Electronically, Japan had already made it at the time, creating and exporting just about everything that the wealthy industrialized world wanted, and by the 1980s, it was believed that Japan's technological prowess was required to expand into the creative arts world. Its corporate-made Walkmans, video players, high-tech television monitors, and the like, urgently required software contents to broadcast. It was thought that investing into the popular cultural haven of the West was a logical and viable move. Here, I am referring to the corporate world of Japan as it was increasingly known in the late 1970s onwards that the Japanese government worked closely with the nation's business sector in order to compete internationally. This corporate world has been nicknamed as "Japan Inc." One of the leaders of "Japan Inc." is Sony Corporation, a principal manufacturer of audio, video, communication and information technology products for the consumer and professional markets. In the late 1980s, American movie businesses such as Columbia Pictures and Tristar Pictures became subdivisions of Sony. Essentially, Sony wanted to change into a "science- and information-based company" in addition to their core business which was electronics (Harris, 1996). In other words, Sony wanted to tap into the creative enterprises of Hollywood; by owning part of Hollywood, it would help boost its worldwide business expansion.[3]

Little did Japan know then that it actually had more to offer to the West and the world (for example, the Pokemon craze among kids in the US from 1997 to 2000, and Miramax and Buena Vista Home Entertainment's courting of Studio Ghibli for worldwide distribution rights of its animated works); and, ideologically and materialistically, this "invention" thrives in a multidimensional world of imagination, technology, and corporate glamour. Up until the early 1990s, anime was still regarded as a cheap form of animation; its other known title was "limited animation," meaning that it was a budget constraint cel-based type of animation which could contain as few as two to three animated frames per second, as compared to an expected twenty-four frames per second in normal animation made for mass viewership. Around that time, it also acquired a new name, *japanimation*, which transformed its previous cutesy, *kawaii,* or lowly status connotation into something more imperative and expansionistic.

This book examines the fundamental expressive platform of anime. It analyzes in detail the historical growth of the medium-genre, its essential ties with an innate sociocultural environment from which it originates, and the internal and external agencies which interparticipate in advancing its popularity. It aims to place the medium-genre in relation to a "language-communicative" inquiry that is specific to this insular territory and its inhabitants' quest to meet and live in a new era. Other countries have embraced the animation medium and produced some of the finest work. They have contributed much to its industrial growth, but arguably, besides the United States, no other country in the world possesses that self-generative vast market in supporting such an infinite supply and demand of works produced.

By designating anime as a form of language-medium, I do not mean just the sound and words which the Japanese use for communication, but also denote a larger communicative system of signs. It is a new communicative medium that has arisen not only to surmount the age-old adopted Chinese writing system and the improvised phonetic symbols that cumbersomely spell out foreign-borrowed words, but also embodies a free interstellar space that allows the imaginative spirit to take flight. I also consider anime as a "medium-genre" because it has acquired unique recognizable characteristics. These characteristics can be denoted from the fields such as character design, background presentation, origins of storylines, production work practices, channels of distribution, and kinds of audienceship. Central to my thesis is the focus on the modernization experience of the Japanese which provides centrifugal force in nurturing the emergent strength of the medium-genre and its widespread acceptance and communicative usage within the Japanese society. However, the amplification of my standpoint retracks further back in time to the historic and cultural formations of the *wa*-people community, its once unabated centuries-old absorption of Chinese cultural practices and thought and — in contrast — the constant, inner, and reactionary realizations of its differential identity. Academically, this book intends to theorize the medium-genre's phenomenal existence by locating the discussion first from an Asian viewpoint and second, by tracing its layers of concentric radiation from an Asian territory.

This is not to say that pioneering works by historian Antonia Levi and Japanese literature specialist Susan Napier are irrelevant to my investigation of anime. On the contrary, their contributions open up new avenues of analysis and indicate the warm responsive dialogues which the medium-genre has already solicited from the West. Levi's book, *Samurai from Outer Space: Understanding Japanese Animation* (1996), spells out clearly the target readers, namely, the American *otaku*,[4] and her later paper, "The New American Hero: Made in Japan" (1998), explains the popularity of manga and anime heroes and heroines among fans and followers in the American scene. In the paper, she contends that the flawless male white heroes no longer hold the interest of viewers and readers as they are deemed to be "derivative and simplistic" and can only make the American comics genre appear as "light entertainment." Manga and anime characters open up a non-Judeo-Christian world in which other mythical possibilities are present. Moreover, values like righteousness and justice and an ultimate moral black-and-white solution are not overly emphasized in manga and anime; they hence widen the "depth and humanity" and the "diverse," "realistic" image of what a hero truly is. Napier's book, *Anime from Akira to Princess Mononoke: Experiencing Contemporary Japanese Animation* (2001a), covers in greater detail the character-heroes and heroines found in the better-known anime works. For example, adopting a gender-based approach, Napier compares and contrasts the distinctions of several anime heroines, thereby observing an array of changing identities among young Japanese females. Published in 1999 was Helen McCarthy's *Hayao Miyazaki: Master of Japanese Animation*. A British animation magazine editor, McCarthy wrote her book primarily for the English-speaking fans of Japan's currently most renowned animation director, Miyazaki Hayao.

In a journal paper, "Confronting Master Narratives: History as Vision in Miyazaki Hayao's Cinema of De-assurance" (2001b), Napier expounds positively on the more desirable and pluralistic worlds of Miyazaki's works as compared to the harmonious worldview of Disney's film productions, and praises the *kokusaika* ("internationalism") of the Japanese director. If "internationalism" can be seen from the director's choice and treatment of animated stories, then by what yardstick does one measure the meaning of Miyazaki's anime? Since the Disney-based productions are slighted as centrically American and closed-door as Napier has commented, might it be contradictory at the same time to shower accolades on the other side of the globe where collective works are being described as "exotic," "complex" and containing less of the "Japanese self," and yet, "exemplify more Western-type models of courage and heroism" (2001b: 474)? In other words, anime as exemplified by Miyazaki's animated works seems to live up to certain Western ideals of which, ironically, Western-made animation is incapable. Although it covers a wider repertoire of anime work including that of other directors, Napier's later book-length work (2001a) keeps the embryonic perspective rooted in a Western gaze and experience of anime, suggesting that anime is solely made for Japanese and Western viewers. In a way, her theorizing position cannot be faulted as it reflects and retracts an entrenched "legacy of Orientalism" with which the West perceives Japan (Treat, 1996: 1–14). Furthermore, the Oriental counterpart, Japan, has long perceived this legacy as a catalytic force which helps to motivate, maintain, and encourage existing and new orientalistic perspectives and projects. Japanese studies scholar Thomas Lamarre (2004/5: 179) aptly describes this dual courtship as "a well-established pattern of complicity between Western Orientalism and Japanese auto-orientalism. The Western Orientalist gaze thus becomes a source of self-identity for the non-Western position, which is made subject in its relation to that gaze."

For the subject of anime, the crux of the issue is a deeper dialectic concerning a distant Far East ethnic-territorial community's quest to project its identity onto the West. Geo-politically, the dialectic not only pertains to East-West dialogue in general. Specifically in the Japanese case, it also bears upon Japan's position in Asia — her given geographical roots versus her phantasmagorical *relocation* dreams, and her *other* occasionally higher aspirational status-intentions *in* Asia. Disney may have appropriated *other* stories to suit its global American agenda; that of the anime's *other* turns out to be mostly Western and Japanese in content. The latter's agenda needs more interrogation from a third-party perspective, and while undertaking this task, I am aware of my background. After all, my exposure to commercial animation also largely involves consumption of developed countries' animated feature films and television series. Moreover, I also come from a region which has become a subcontractual production center and which helps produce anime and other commercial animation from Japan, Western Europe, and North America. For example, in Taiwan, 90 percent of the nation's animation industry work comes from abroad (*Macroview Weekly*, November 15, 2006) and the well-known Japanese animation studio Toei already has a subsidiary animation studio in Manila, Toei Philippines, with a staff of over a hundred assisting project work from Tokyo. Cultural Studies scholar Meaghan Morris (1990: 41) once wrote about the complexity of social experience that surrounded academicians and how "the proliferation of different places in and between" might influence our learning, teaching and writing experiences and thus, our intellectual practice. I am therefore aware of my hermeneutical position. I am also of the view that diversification of knowledge cannot be emphasized enough if we would like to contribute to a world in which we can understand each other better. Pertaining to the subject of anime per se, I do not remember coming across any anime that depicts a Third World children's story, or folk legends from an underdeveloped country (that is, anime productions that show substantial investment of energy, time and money in promoting a non-Western story). In my subsequent review and research on the medium-genre, the fact remains the same although there are exceptional cases. This is where I begin.

The question is how and where to locate my research within current scholarship on Japanese animation, particularly the generic anime kind. Apart from the publications mentioned above, there are a number of contributory journals and chapters written within the scholarly framework of Japanese studies, cultural, feminist, and media studies. Some of the earlier works did not focus directly on the origins and characteristics of the medium-genre, or a particular animated work per se. Instead, they postulated insightfully on the positions of its creations in the wider cultural context of Japan. For example, Mark Siegel's journal article in *Science Fiction Studies*, "Foreigner as Alien in Japanese Science Fantasy" (1985), was among the first to valorize the cultural matrix of science fiction anime creations in an animated television series made in Japan. Ron Tanner's book chapter, "Mr. Atomic, Mr. Mercury and Chime Trooper: Japan's Answer to the American Dream" (1995), further analyzed the Japanese modern mindset in his discussion of the country's postwar industry of producing robot toys, which were mainly merchandized objects derived from anime science fiction characters.

In 1987, the Society for Animation Studies was founded by Harvey Deneroff and shortly after, in 1991 the *Animation Journal* was launched and the founding editor was Maureen Furniss. It was during this time that writing directly related to anime began to appear. David Vernal's "War and Peace in Japanese Science Fiction Animation: An Examination of *Mobile Suit Gundam* and *The Mobile Police Patlabor*" (1995) was drawn from his award-winning senior thesis, "The Power to Command: Society, Authority and the Individual in Japanese Science Fiction Comic Books and Animation" (East Asian Studies, Harvard University). More recent was William D. Routt's "Stillness and Style in *Neon Genesis Evangelion*" (2000). Vernal's research was largely thematic in its analysis of a highly popular form of anime which focused on a high-tech science fiction environment where robots played a substantial role in the narrative contents. Routt's analysis, on the other hand, highlighted the techniques of making anime and showed that stylistics could advance storytelling contents, especially when the direction was centered on the psychological states of the characters. A more recent journal, *Animation: An*

Interdisciplinary Journal (first issue, July 2006), edited by British scholar Suzanne Buchan, has a wide-ranging scope, which offers a diversity of approaches in examining all kinds of animation and beyond.

Other known published papers include Susan Napier's book chapter, "Panic States: The Japanese Imagination of Disaster from *Godzilla* to *Akira*," in *Contemporary Japan and Popular Culture* (1996), Isolde Standish's paper, "Akira, Postmodernism and Resistance," in *The Worlds of Japanese Popular Culture: Gender, Shifting Boundaries and Global Cultures* (1998), and Paul Wells's contribution, "Hayao Miyazaki Floating Worlds, Floating Signifiers," in the journal *Art and Design* (1997). Paul Wells is a British media studies scholar and his book, *Understanding Animation* (1998), was based on the animation studies course that he and his staff had developed at the School of Humanities, De Monfort University. The book provides theoretical analytical techniques in reading animated works and most of those are Western-based. Therefore, the above-mentioned journal article is Wells's other pioneering work on the subject of anime in which he introduces Jungian interpretations for analyzing some of the motifs found in Miyazaki's animated work. However, it was a working paper, judging from the brevity and its provocative and inspiring analysis. As the twentieth century came to a close, more scholarly writing on anime was published, such as *Japan Pop! : Inside the World of Japanese Popular Culture* (2000), edited by Timothy J. Craig, and *A Century of Popular Culture in Japan* (2000), edited by Douglas Slaymaker.

British writer Helen McCarthy has published several guidebooks on anime; they include *The Anime Movie Guide* (1997) and, together with Jonathan Clements, *The Erotic Anime Movie Guide* (1998), and *The Anime Encyclopedia: A Guide to Japanese Animation Since 1917* (2001). There are also other publications primarily written for fans, as their titles indicate clearly. These include, for example, *The Anime Companion* series by Gilles Poitras (1999 and 2005), and Patrick Drazen's *Anime Explosion! The What? Why? And Wow! Of Japanese Animation* (2003).

In Japan, academic research on animation studies is not entirely non-existent; in fact it has become popular in recent years. For example, the journal of the Japan Society of Image Arts and Sciences has published papers related to the subject. Moreover, with increasing foreign interest in anime, local psychology practitioners, graphic designers, and academicians have also begun to take more active interest in anime. The Japan Society for Animation Studies (JSAS) was established in 1998; it publishes its own journal, *The Japanese Journal of Animation Studies*. It provides a discussion platform for writers, researchers, animators, media specialists, aestheticians, and psychologists interested in the study of animation, where they share findings on anime, a "hot" topic that has been receiving a great deal of attention.[5] Critical writing on animated feature films can also be found in commercial cinema monthlies including the longstanding and reputable *Kinema Jūnpo* magazine. There is also vast literature in the market published for anime fans. Publications such as *The*

Super Robots Chronicles: The History of Japanese Super Robots Animations, 1963–1997 (1997) and *Otaku ni narenai anime suki no hon* (1997) are typical examples in which individual authors are not cited, as they are company publications designed for the *otaku* reading market or simply for those who are concerned with the subject of anime.

Japan has experienced several "anime booms" in its postwar cultural history, one being in the 1970s. The first serious publication documenting the rise of anime in Japan was *Nihon anime-shon eiga shi* (The history of Japanese animation, 1977) written by two freelance writers, Yamaguchi Katsunori and Watanabe Yasushi. There was another momentous 16 mm film project that pre-empted this printed publication, *Nihon manga eiga hattatsu* (1972) directed by Yabushita Taiji. Since then, publications written by veteran animators and directors such as Miyazaki Hayao (*Shuppatsuten*, 1996), Takahata Isao (*Eiga wo tsukuri nagara kangaetan koto I and II*, 1991 and 1999), and Otsuka Yasuo (*Sakuga asemamire*, 2001) have become popular reading materials for both anime fans and professionals working in the industry. In recent years, there have been more homegrown publications in the market that document and narrate the rise of Japanese animation, not only in Japan but also worldwide. Examples of these include *Nihon anime-shon no chikara* (2004), written by Tsugata Nobuyuki, a member of the Japan Society for Animation Studies, and *Nihon no anime zenshi* (2004), a collective book project edited by retired animation producer Yamaguchi Yasuo. Both books are about the history of Japanese animation and were written when anime gained increasing popularity around the world. Another prominent member of Japan Society for Animation Studies, psychology studies scholar Yokota Masao, has published papers in Japanese and other languages that focus on the social-psychological issues of anime, particularly the impact of the medium-genre on Japanese mental health. His latest work, *Anime-shon no rinshō shinrigaku* (2006), is critical of formulaic character design in many commercially made productions. The book cautions stereotypical representation of anime characters and advocates animated narratives that pay attention to not only the multifaceted aspects of individuals but also their external appearances and facades.

So where does my research lie? The present study intends to fill a gap by systematically tracing the cultural and historical contours of the medium-genre and in the process, it emphasizes its indigenousness and, especially, the "drive" of its existence. The underlying goal is to solve the mystery of its persuasive existence within Asian soil riding on the cheap labor and resources provided therein and to address the observation that, until now, none of these Asian sub-production centers have successfully built a similar or comparative domain that matches the medium-genre's reign on other shores. In other words, this research aims to broaden the intellectual inquiry of the subject matter and to carry out a more balanced discursive study of Japan and its intricate relationship with Asia and the West. My methodogical approach is interdisciplinary and transnational and I have also tried not to treat the subject matter in one compartmentalized setting. Moreover, in dealing with such a popular cultural subject, its heterogeneous and polymorphous background calls for a more rigorous and multisided examination.

The title, *Frames of Anime: Culture and Image-Building,* demonstrates my attempt to grasp this dynamic, pervasive, and yet fleeting medium-genre. In order to generalize, conceptualize, and show its multifaceted aspects, particularly its image-laden contents, this book calls forth a certain mode of action that is to pin it down onto a work-in-progress platform, giving it a physical constitution to begin with. On a literal level, a frame makes up a picture on a film; a series of frames, when animated, rolls the film into motion and a narrative is formed. Especially in cel animation, the two-dimensional background is the locus of intense work; in the case of anime, even up until today, ranging from Miyazaki Hayao's directorial works to contemporary manga-artist-turned-animator director, Kon Satoshi's filmic creation, *Tokyo Godfathers* (2003), the hands-on input is still laboriously practiced unimpeded.

It has been said that the cinematic film is an artifact of human labor. So what makes anime outstanding in comparison to other forms of cinema in Japan? First, my approach to studying anime from the framing perspective stems from my visits to animation studios in Japan and other parts of Asia during which I was exposed to the working environment of anime-making. In the course of my research, I came across many framed artworks that were of the anime kind. For example, a typical scenic background is layered with several individual cels, frame by frame. What then sets the Japanese cel-based animation apart from, or makes it similar to, say, the classic Disney form of animation (if I am also given the opportunity to encounter artworks that come from the Disney studio)? The materials used might be the same. However, it is essentially the cultural aspects of making that differentiate the tens of thousands of frames created and filmed. Moreover, I was caught by the "illusion" of the static frames presented, including the sheer volume of anime production in Japan. By "illusion," I refer to the way the framing creates space and time despite the images' basically immobile characteristics.

In live-action cinema, the material film reels contain photographic images of narrative, life-sized design sets, and storyboards prepared by the director and his or her production staff. In addition, the physical presence of human actors also contributes to what the film is all about. An animated film, especially the cel-based kind, is primarily a record of human drawings, colorings, special and skillful camera filming techniques and effects, and other activities such as sound projection and synchronization of lip movements. It would be intriguing *not* to regard the frames as merely technical. There is a human story within the frame just as there is a bigger and deeper cultural story within and outside the frame. In other words, my reading of anime frames is initially literal and later cultural. But circularly, the orientation of my cultural reading of anime is also guided and lured by the literal technical images presented within the frames.

For example, considering the usage of tools and equipment is one facet of understanding. The foundational core is the "blueprint" storyboard, and anime has a unique and supportive sponsor-medium which is manga. Thus, prior framing decisions vary from aesthetics to thematic contents and, in many instances, have already been pre-presented and premeditated. This research is interested in unmasking the *layers* of framing and, quintessentially, understanding the cultural mindset of their construction. Integral to this construction practice are the *interstices*: Why are they out-framed and not encompassed within? What roles (if any) do they play in this framing business? After all, the medium-genre gives rise to its own existence by means of framing, embellishing, and projecting primevally; it also lives in marginal space, which is seemingly free in spirit and matter but is constantly searching and affirming its identity.

In the course of my research, a variety of methods were employed including face-to-face interviews, on-site visits, and reading biographical writings of animators and professionals working in the industry. I am also interested in the native response to the anime phenomenon, intellectual and non-intellectual, *otaku* and non-*otaku*, and the types of discourses present. Thus, publications written by the Japanese analyzing their self-understanding of the medium-genre and its popularity are examined as are the numerous exhibitions celebrating its growth and its success. The bulk of the animated works which I have chosen and cited in this study are the commercially known ones measured by their popularity, or those that bear the weight of an authorial stamp already known for individual characteristics. Apart from those, I also introduce relatively unknown works which I have encountered and discovered, or works that have yet to be foregrounded in terms of their significant elements and contributions. Distinctive features of some of these works may have already been credited in Japanese and have not been made known to the English-speaking world. Obviously, it is impossible to cover all the anime works. The predilection is still guided by the interpretations and findings that I wish to put forward and the conclusions that can be derived.

Chapter 1 presents the theoretical basis of my inquiry of anime. It draws upon scholarly works that hypothesize the abstract existence of this language-stratum. In the history of Western thought, these works have built upon one another over the ages and can be traced back to Plato and his concept of "receptacle." As this research focuses on a contemporary medium and the significant developments of its phenomenal existence occurred during certain political and cultural epochs of Japanese history, the analysis is made in the light of international material developments as well. The theoretical concepts that are highlighted and discussed serve to provide an exploratory and explanatory account of my evaluation of the medium-genre. A portion of the chapter also pays attention to indigenous cultural thought and philosophical reflections, including nationalist thinking and the resistance to follow the "archetypal shadow" of China.

Chapter 2 introduces the wide array of art forms available in Japan and stresses their continuity over the years. It demonstrates that anime is part of this continuity and that, aesthetically, anime is also interrelated to traditional art forms. The chapter describes the "visualness" of Japanese art forms, and looks back in history at the sociopolitical environment in which these periodic art forms were produced, practiced, and consumed. It maintains that each historical art form sought to play a role in expressing the pathos and times of society. The stress on subjectivity and the penchant for realistic expression are given weight so as to contour the distinctive indigenous developments. However, there is a slight twist in this chapter. It cautions that nationalistic discourses praising the likeness and influences of traditional Japanese art forms on contemporary media such as cartoons, animation, or even cinema had already appeared in the early twentieth century. Imamura Taihei's *Manga eiga ron* is one of the most exemplary. In other words, the chapter implies that while it is possible to trace the traditional artistic links of anime, one must perceive the spontaneous nationalistic efforts to place rhetorical emphasis on the country's artistic heritage, to practically embody it or incorporate it into the newly found art form, animation. Examples can best be seen in Studio Ghibli's animated works which will be discussed in Chapter 6.

Chapter 3 surveys further the cultural thought of the Japanese and interrogates the country's depth of thinking in relation to its expressive visual self, natural or constructed, and in response to a larger long-running project — dialogue with the industrialized West. Firstly, the primary aspects of Shintoism are discussed; anti-Confucianist thought of a Tokugawa *shintō* advocate, Motoori Norinaga, is also analyzed in comparison to a similar trend of thinking that already existed in China and Korea at the time. Philosophical writings that appeared in the early twentieth century, especially the works of Nishida Kitarō, are also considered in order to show that anime lies at the heart of an extensive prolonged communication project. The country's subsequent turn to aggressive imperialistic activities and its defeat in the Second World War may have rendered all pre-1945 philosophical writings obsolete, worthless, and even nonsensical. Consequently, what the "body" could not achieve via the written word and its experimental adoption of the Western form of structured reasoning, its *other* steadfast, visual-making, bona fide side was left to rectify the inadequacy and eventually took an increasingly central role in reconstructing identity and in restoring a sense of equilibrium. In this chapter, the concept of image-building is introduced. It is described as an all-round activity that spans material construction, aesthetic representation, and philosophical thinking.

Chapter 4 traces the chronological development of Japanese animation from the early twentieth century and the subsequent industrialization of the medium during the Second World War. It stresses that the animation medium developed hand in hand with filmic technology advancement and experimentation in Japan. While magic lanterns served the Meiji era, animation was able to progressively fulfil the dual roles of education and commerce during the Taishō and Shōwa periods. The presence of homegrown talent and investors also helped to promote the medium as both an art form and a mass communication tool. The early experimental development of the medium soon blossomed into a historic industrial stage by the mid-1930s, particularly with the powerful support of the military. The chapter also highlights a letter of valuable exchange between the Japanese and the Chinese written at the height of the Second World War. It shows the admiration and concern with which the Japanese had viewed the Chinese production of *Princess Iron Fan* (1941), China's first feature animation film, and the box-office success it received both in China and other parts of Southeast Asia. This film increased the fervor and enthusiasm with which the Japanese authorities viewed the medium. It also led to the production of two wartime feature animated films, *Momotarō no umiwashi* (1943) and *Momotaro umi no shinpei* (1945).

Chapter 5 examines the performative role of animation in the nation-rebuilding efforts of Japan after the Second World War. Using the concept of "performativity," the analysis further theorizes the imaginative visual path which the country did not forsake even after the war. The founding of Toei Animation Studio and its determination to become Asia's largest studio is discussed in relation to the production of the first full-color animated feature film in Japan and possibly in Asia, *Hakujaden* (*White Snake Tale*, 1958). Apart from the commercial and institutional support of the medium, the rise of manga artist Tezuka Osamu and his ambition to become the "Disney of the Orient" were also significant factors that helped to advance postwar development of Japanese animation, which also led to the birth of anime. The final section of Chapter 5 explores the definition and reception of anime in Japan and I argue here that this special visual language is part of a cultural continuum and modernization experience of Japan.

Chapter 6 discusses at length the creative worlds of Miyazaki and Takahata, with an emphasis on the collective yet individualistic components of their animated works. The chapter discusses the national consciousness of their cinematic oeuvre which circulates atmospherically within their creative minds and that of the native audiences which hinges on a modernistic meta-discourse that anime is capable of generating. In discussing their works, other types of anime production are compared and contrasted, and attention is paid to the discourse of "high art versus low art commercial animation," which has surfaced in recent years through writings of veteran commercial animation directors.

The final chapter looks into the applications of the "anime model" in some Asian countries. These include, in particular, their efforts to build an animation industry and attempts to produce animations that are publicly and privately sponsored. The chapter is critical of such application and questions the validity of this infrastructural form of implementation. By taking into account the different pre-existing sociocultural and political environments, I argue that there are some *missing frames* and therefore the eligibility of the model is problematic in the larger Asiatic context. The discussion here also revisits the original premises of the medium-genre's existence and its native endeavor to forge a distinctive presence, however spectral it may be. In addition, the chapter discusses the discourses of cultural imperialism in relation to anime and its popularity in Asia, including commercial animation produced in the West, with particular emphasis on those from the United States. The chapter is critical of such discourses as there are other issues and factors affecting the growth of indigenous animation in various parts of Asia. The availability of high-tech animating tools and financial support may not be sufficient for the current situation because — culturally, socially, and politically — the "collective will" to create animated or pictorial narratives has to be actively present in the first place in order to stimulate a homegrown animation industry.

The first three chapters of the book cover a wide spectrum of theoretical analyses when discussing the emerging phenomenal status of anime. Convergently, the various proposed Western and Eastern theories gravitate toward a certain direction that questions the role of language: the world of words versus the more fluid, less formalized world of the unspeakable, the un-rhetorical, and the visual. It is impossible to weave every theoretical position introduced therein into the subsequent chapters. However, whenever elaboration is necessary, reflections and additional explorations of their applications are reviewed. In addition, each progressive chapter also explores specific theories relevant to the subject and chronological period concerned. Some of the later chapters (4 and 5 for example), may appear more descriptive and informative as they are necessary for charting the development of anime. However, what essentially runs implicitly in the later chapters is the association of pre-proposed theoretical perspectives described in the early chapters. This is to emphasize that the interweaving of different points of view produces composite understanding. But the tenor does not stray far from the original aim, which is to explore the communicative basis of anime and its phenomenal existence in the historical-cultural system of Japan, and to find what it has come to mean, and how it has been viewed in other parts of the world.

Ponder this question, "how on earth did animation become anime in Japan?"[6] Experiencing the visual prowess of Japanese culture is more than personal; the frame of analysis is dialectical and cultural.

Origins of the Japanese Art of Animating

> Film animation is a visual communication technique whose basic potential is to clarify the complex, to reveal the invisible, to teach quickly and concisely.
>
> John Halas, *Film Animation* (1976: 10)

Animation is a visual language and an act of communicating. Technically defined, it is a movement-based medium in which each image is captured through the camera in order to create a series of alleged movements. The image may be hand-drawn or computer-generated; the material-base may be a cel sheet (transparent celluloid), a glass pane or a platform of beach-sand. Other forms of traditional hand-manipulated images include the use of wood puppets, clay figures, and cut-out paper puppets. To animate is essentially to communicate, to tell a story for oneself or others or for both, via a chain of manipulated and designed images. This chapter begins to theorize the Japanese art of animating ("art" meaning the aptitude, skill and knowledge) and to radically reflect upon the "self-assertive" existential status of this visual language which the Japanese have excelled in utilizing and embodying.

Language Unspoken and Unwritten

Before dwelling on the details and lest I am accused of "essentializing" the Japanese experience of animation, I will first discuss some philosophical discourses about language and its processes that have been explored in the West. These discourses pertain to a certain dimension of language that is hidden, indirect, and marginal. In her work, *Revolution in Poetic Language* (1984), French philosopher Julia Kristeva foregrounds the "status of the subject" in social articulation. In discussing the realm of bodily rhythms and energies, she introduces the Platonic term "chora" to appellate a "totality" that is "full of movement," "instinctual drives," and "stases". Although

Kristeva accords the chora as "part of the discourse of representation that offers it as evidence," she concludes that it can never acquire an "axiomatic form." This is so as the receptacle-space is conditioned to be everywhere and yet nowhere. Because the forefront is occupied by a paternal functional symbolic where linguistic structures are the means and the make-up of its operational milieu, the chora is reduced to the semiotic realm where the psychical, rhythmic, and maternal are some of its salient characteristics. According to Kristeva, both the symbolic and the semiotic are in a dialectical relationship and the significance is in this heterogeneous process. Another French philosopher, Maurice Merleau-Ponty, proposes a "theory of reversibility" by which he stresses the intersubjectivity and interactiveness of human communication that are already set within a pre-established social-historical world. As language is already present when an infant is born, Merleau-Ponty argues that "the idea of complete expression is nonsensical" and language "is always limited only by more language" (1964a: 43 and 42). In contrast, he values the world of painters where the shades, the colors, the contours and the lines, speak as much. For him, we should consider the moments of silence and "signs" as "signs" lead us to the "vague life of colors" (1964a: 45).

> If we want to understand language as an originating operation, we must pretend to have never spoken, submit language to a reduction without which it would once more escape us by referring us to what it signifies for us, *look* at it as deaf people look at those who are speaking, compare the art of language to other arts of expression, and try to see it as one of these mute arts. (1964a: 46)

Merleau-Ponty's theory of reversibility is not unlike American linguist Benjamin Lee Whorf's "principle of linguistic relativity" (1962), which states that language is a cultural phenomenon and our perspective of the world is colored by our own linguistic background; we are, therefore, not "free" in interpreting the world, nor do we have "the same picture of the world," unless we share common linguistic antecedents. In comparison, Marxist language philosopher V. N. Volosinov was concerned with the verbal sign and considers the speech act as an active interactive-participation between the speaker and the hearer. He was interested in the transmission of meanings in direct and indirect discourses, especially the "ellipses," "omissions," and the "emotive-affective grounds" of utterances (1973: 129). In other words, the pictorial expressiveness of communication, whether visible or invisible, is of primary importance if we pay heed to the social context of the communicative event and the enclosed stylistic elements.

In Japanese indigenous thought, particularly Zen Buddhism, the oblique aspects of language are not neglected and are often brought to the forefront at the performing level (e.g. in *nō* theater and Japanese puppet theatre, *bunraku*). A well-known incident noted in Shakyamuni Buddha's teachings was that once Buddha held a flower silently as he sat and faced an assembly. This incident occurred after he had gained enlightenment and many human and non-human beings who heard of his enlightened presence came to listen to his teachings. But during that particular teaching session, Buddha did not utter a single word and simply held a flower in his hand. As the crowd became puzzled and restless, one of his disciples, Mahakashyapa, smiled, and with that he demonstrated that he had understood the meaning of Buddha's visual gesture. It was noted that at that moment, Mahakashyapa attained enlightenment. Although the teaching incident was recorded as a legend and no historical evidence exists to substantiate the account,[1] it marked the beginning of Chan (Zen) Buddhism in which the "unspoken" or that which is "understood" could be transmitted and contemplated under non-verbal and non-written circumstances.

Although Zen Buddhism has its origins from India and China, certain Buddhist texts are highly placed in Zen thinking and one of them is the *Lankavatara Sutra* (1932). It is no coincidence that the first English version of the sutra was translated by a Japanese and he was the well-known Buddhist scholar, Suzuki T. Daisetz (1870–1966). The *Lankavatara Sutra* main teachings focus on the experiential nature of human existence, and explain that mankind is born into a world of accumulated knowledge and the realm of words tie us to established notions and appearances. There are statements throughout the sutra that denigrate the spoken and written word:

> The Blessed One replied: Mahāmati, words are not the highest reality, nor is what is expressed in words the highest reality . . . And then, Mahāmati, words are subject to birth and destruction; they are unsteady, mutually conditioning, and are produced by the law of causation. (1932: 77)

> Words are not known in all the Buddha-lands; words, Mahāmati, are an artificial creation. In some Buddha-lands ideas are indicated by looking steadily, in others by gestures, in still others by a frown, by the movement of the eyes, by laughing, by yawning, or by the clearing of the throat, or by recollection, or by trembling. Mahāmati, for instance, in the worlds of the Steady-Looking and in those of Exquisite Odours, and in the Buddha-land of Samantabhadra the Tathagata, Arhat, Fully-Enlightened One, the Bodhisattva-Mahāsattvas by steadily looking without a wink attain the recognition of all things as unborn and also various most excellent Samādhis. For this reason, Mahāmati, the validity of all things has nothing to do with the reality of words. It is observed, Mahāmati, even in this world that in the kingdom of such special beings as ants, bees, etc., they carry on their work without words. (1932: 91)

The above projections of various philosophical thinking (both Eastern and Western) evaluate the limitations of language in particular, the entrenched mode of direct language both in the written and spoken forms. They serve to advance the premise that I propose in this chapter, that is, the visual functions of animation fulfill a reality, a reality that may not be rational, structured, stable, or even highly visible or audible. In Japanese animation, the particular kind of anime is laden with energy which flows from the hand that draws the frames and that meticulously tailors the pre-calculated movements. Equally energy-driven is the creative flow of stamina that visualizes the aesthetic background and an imagined subjective abode. Semiotically, the abundance of manga and manga-anime in Japan can be said to be a reaction to the rational scientific world of written symbols as well as its "preframing" of reality and truth. The response is the provision of alternatives and the portrayal of a multiplicity of answers and processes. In other words, these new forms of the visual language are able to give free rein to the *other* world of phenomena that are not already pre-arranged or pre-classified by an existing organized language.

The Imposition of a Foreign Paternal Script?

But why does Japan, more than any other nations, excel in creating and consuming animation? To be specific, its manga-based animation is incessantly in production and in circulation. For example, during every major holiday season in Japan, at least four to six manga-anime feature films are shown in commercial cinemas. This does not include many other independent animation films made for the public or for private consumption.[2] To date, no nation in the world has the means and the audience base to support such a generic sponsorship pattern. My next analysis hinges on a subject area that may provide another intriguing inquiry into the anime phenomenon in Japan.

Historically, one can argue that Japan's centuries-old cultural relationship with China has ceased to exist since the beginning of the Meiji Restoration in 1868. The inception of modern reforms based on Western models and the pace with which Japan industrialized itself in less than half a century were stunning in world civilization history. Despite fervent debates about the suitability of keeping Chinese characters in the modern Japanese language, the archaic apron-like linguistic connection was never really broken; in fact, intense efforts were made to introduce new *kanji*-word combinations based on the thousands of Chinese characters that were freely available. Furthermore, in order to overcome the shortage of vocabulary in response to modernization and Westernization, the nation diligently prowled through old and existing Chinese texts, Confucian, Daoist or Buddhist, to find the *kanji* that best represented Western concepts, scientific terms, and culture, such as "democracy," "modernization," "theory," "photography," "atom," "credit," "parliament," "reform," "vacuum," "zoology," and so forth (see H. Iida, 2002: 47–62; Liu, 1995). Later, when China became a republic in the early twentieth century, it acquired a number of newly constituted *kanji* word combinations from Japan, which were created more than forty years earlier, and incorporated them into a new set of vocabulary. Language historian Nanette Twine (1991) noted that the Japanese overcame "the problem of orthography" by limiting the number of *kanji* in writing but also accepted the conciseness of *kanji* in certain expressions. At the end of the day, it was the policy of modification that helped retain the visual directness of many Chinese characters in the newly reformed Japanese language and the delicate balance of incorporating native expressions into the lingua franca.

What I seek to postulate is that the new modern language might have met the demands of a new world order and a new era in light of the industrial progress and technological advancement, including the expanding stable of Western semantic terms that were being incorporated into the Japanese lingua franca. However, the lingering shadow of China and the rest of a colonized Asia formed a disconcerting schizophrenic dialectic with the newly found identity of the Japanese nation. Before I elaborate further on this viewpoint, I should single out David Pollack's *Fracture of Meaning* (1985) that deals with Japan's adoption of the Chinese script and the problematic alien-ness resulted from such incorporation.

Pollack asserts that throughout Japan's literary history there are signs of resistance towards the adopted continental written form, one of the earliest being the appearance of *Kojiki* (*Records of Ancients,* AD 712) which was written partly in Chinese and partly in Japanese.[3] Pollack sees *Kojiki* as an intermediary text written in a period when Japan "was still in transition between orality and literary" (1985: 40). Specifically, some of the Chinese characters used to represent phonetically the Japanese vocabulary when being read aloud proved to be awkward and unintelligible, and they also upset the syntactical flow of the text. Thus, Pollack is particularly concerned with the unreadable parts of *Kojiki*. Using the Chinese written script to record the origins of the Japanese state based on oratorical indigenous accounts posed profound problems, since the two languages have different linguistic structures. The Chinese language is monosyllabic and each written character has a self-contained meaning, while the Japanese counterpart is polysyllabic. Therefore, finding written symbols to match the oral part must have been a tedious, trial-and-error process. Specifically, Pollack is concerned with the superimposition of "an entire philosophy of thinking" over native modes of expression. His study also draws on various writings appeared throughout the ages that "lament" and "critique" the overutilization of the continental written script. In a sense, Pollack's argument resembles Kristeva's theorization of the external versus the maternal interior and the representations that resulted.

From the writings of Zen monks to those of the nativist philosophers such as Motoori Norinaga, Pollack shows that the monolithic world of the Chinese had been occasionally resisted due to its "centripetal" logical mentality and the overemphasis on the written script. The "silence" that could not be written led to the "fracture of meaning" and thus, the preference for certain styles of expression that has persisted throughout the centuries. To push his thesis further, Pollack also suggests that the "fracture of meaning" acquired another geo-political significance when China began to appear weak and unchanging, particularly in response to foreign invasion and threat in the nineteenth century. Less explicitly written is the present comparative status to America in which twentieth-century Japan had found itself. Briefly, Pollack describes the later relationship as a "disappointed truculence" (1985: 55). I shall elaborate on the chronological developments of Japanese animation in Chapter 4. Here I wish to state only the point that if the "fracture of meaning" conveys the complexities of linguistic adoption and utilization, then a second ideological understanding follows; that is, once the "meaning" is cracked or breached, a sense of marginality occurs, and in order to find outlets for this discounted disillusioned body to continue its existence and expression, a space has to be created — or "framed" — for its *being* and *becoming* and its own meaning of survival. This space to which I refer is that ever-expanding layer of Japanese animation that has emerged after the Second World War.

Pollack's "fracture of meaning" hypothesis could be traced to the Meiji period (1868–1912) in which the *kokugo* national language scholars denounced *kanji* as "an invader," "a language spoiler," "a major obstacle to the modernization of the Japanese language" (Koyasu, 2003), and so on. Contemporary cultural studies scholar Koyasu Nobukuni, in comparing and contrasting the various *kokugo* discourses about the "problem of *kanji*" in the Japanese language, explains that *kanji kanbun* (Chinese character and Chinese language) has helped to shape the development of the Japanese language. In highlighting the published work (*Kokugo e no michi*,1957) of a later *kokugo* Shōwa scholar Tokieda Motoki (1900–67),[4] Koyasu not only concludes that *kanji kanbun* is a catalyst in the development of the Japanese language and an important introspective tool in introducing the Japanese to the world of writing, but also indicates that it is "an unavoidable expressive medium" that brings to the surface the innate character of the Japanese language (2003: 194). Paralleling Tokieda's view that *kanji* is a reality of the country's national language (*kokugo no jijitsu*) and that it is not to be viewed as a foreign language, Koyasu is critical of the continual discourse that the adoption of *kanji* has obstructed the original development of the Japanese language, thus causing "psychological cultural trauma" to the Japanese and their search for authentic Japanese culture. It is difficult to say whether the "*kanji* problem" is a real or an illusionary one, or whether it is a constructed manifestation of the national identity issue among the Japanese. It is, in my opinion, a constant national "desire" to seek a referential space for self-understanding , self-projection and self-expression that has led to the discovery and application of a new medium in the twentieth century. This new medium has the flexible capability to embody all kinds of images — old and new, technological and artistic, the mute, the unsaid, including a layer of human feelings and the natural instinct to show and tell.

Given that Pollack's "fracture of meaning" hypothesis is not solely applicable to the Japanese language, one can imagine that it may apply to other cultures which at some point in history have acquired reified language structures due to contact with higher cultures that had the means and enlightened influence on the recipient native cultures. These include, for example, the influence of Greek and Latin on the languages of continental Europe, the appeal of the Chinese language and culture on Korea, Manchuria, Mongolia and Indo-China, and the cultural waves of Indianization and Islamization that flowed into Southeast Asia. The questions to ask, therefore, are: Have these cultures made an issue of the cultural interactions and interferences? Do they find ways to express the "fracture"? If so, what are the manifestations and representations resulted from such interactions? If not, why not? In the Japanese context, it can be argued that it is the "drive" that underlines the "fracture" in the first place and feeds its persuasive anarchical position.

The Japanese Modernization Experience

Facing the West

Most Asian countries did not embark fully on the modernization process until after the Second World War. This is not to say that Asian societies remained traditional, rural, and agrarian until then, but a general survey showed that the degree of intensification and active acceptance only took place after the Second World War. In contrast, "The Land of the Rising Sun," as its name signified, got on a pre-dawn modernization train at an early stage, so to speak, and along the journey, "paused" and "pondered" and managed to sort out a balance in its modernization goals.

During the Meiji period, despite the emphasis on industrial learning and the absorption of Western scientific knowledge, there were steps to curb the overprioritization of science and reason above art and culture. Thus, the premier modernization slogans of the era — *fukoku kyōhei* (enrich and strengthen the nation) and *sonnō jōi* (honor the Emperor and repel the barbarian)[5] — were counterbalanced by other modernization streams and movements, represented by such slogans as *bunmei kaika* (civilization and enlightenment) and *jiyū minkan* (freedom and popular rights). The underlying idealistic and positivistic working principle that cut across these seemingly "mismatched" or irreconcilable modernization policy-slogans was the *wakon yōsai* (Japanese spirit and Western knowledge) essence. Hence, traditional Japanese arts and crafts, including even *kabuki* theater, hitherto criticized as plebeian and unrefined at the end of the Edo period (1603–1868),[6] were later bestowed with a centering presence, elevated to shoulder the divine seat of the *yamato damashii* (the primal ancient Japanese soul/essence).[7] In other words, the enlightenment and fulfilment of a modern Japan should encompass existing native artistic productions and orientation, aesthetic sentiment, traditional cultural fundamentals, judgement, and taste. Gradually, self-critical assessment led to the preservation and liberalization of arts learning in Meiji Japan. By the mid-Meiji period, "the brush" was restored to its heritage status as evidenced by the founding of the Tokyo School of Art which concentrated on *nihonga* art education (Hane, 1986: 137). During the Edo period, although *rangaku* artist Shiba Kokan (1747–1818) incorporated European styles of painting into his illustrations, he also advocated a nationalistic theory of art which could serve practical purposes; that is, the paintings that could be "an instrument in the service of the nation" (Keene, 1969: 66).[8]

The crux of the matter is that anime did not appear all of a sudden in post-Second World War Japan. Its germination was imbued with a history of cultural nationalistic sentiment and a conviction to build a new world that matched the standards of the West at all levels. In less than half a century after the fall of the Tokugawa shogunate in 1867, the Meiji government succeeded in achieving its goals. As seen from the developments in education to those in military and national security, economic infrastructure, and even the daily living habits of its people, the modernization drive had been relentlessly defined and detailed.

The understated ideological imperative was to possess "what" the West had that made "them" noticeably different. In a nutshell, to the Japanese, Commodore Perry did not arrive empty-handed. Rather, he represented a culture of material wealth, especially of apparatus and equipment including steamships, railways, telegraphs, motor-cars, and the like. Not that Japan was "empty" or deprived of any traces of material civilization at that juncture, but that nationalistic-binary comparison mentality became a persistent self-propelling craving and a motive for both more material and symbolic acquisitions. One of the country's famous thinkers and writers, Fukuzawa Yukichi (1834–1901), put it this way:

> If we compare the knowledge of the Japanese and Westerners, in letters, in techniques, in commerce, or in industry, from the smallest to the largest matter … there is not one thing in which we excel … Who would compare our carts with their locomotives, our swords with their pistols? … We think we dwell on an immovable plain; they know that the earth is round and moves … there is nothing in which we make pride vis-á-vis the West.[9]

In all, the "Perry image" was intrusively feared and admired at the same time. Iida Harumi (2002: 8) noted that it was the prodigious baggage of "civilization equipment" (*bunmei no riki*) that accompanied Perry which caught the nation's attention. In other words, the native view of the arrival of Western foreign powers was not simply fixed in a defensive frame of mind. Wakabayashi termed the acceptance of Western culture as "pragmatic receptivity" and "a genuine respect for Western civilization"

(1998: 2–29). Hence, it did not take long for the Japanese to recognize the effective values of photography, a Western invention, and the role it would play in Japan's modernization.

Discovery of a new visual language

As I have mentioned earlier in this chapter, toward the beginning of the twentieth century, Japan found itself alone at the forefront when facing the tides of change that came from the West. From India to China, Korea to the Philippines, the outer region of Indo-China and Malaysia to Indonesia, all were under the veil of colonial advance and domination. The reality was made even clearer when the Japanese saw nearer to home that Hong Kong was ceded to the British.[10]

In the Japanese case at that time, photography as a visual language could undisputedly be regarded as an "objective transcript of visual reality"; that is a "reality *(jijitsu)* visual medium" that aptly complemented the political developments in Japan and China (Sino-Japanese War, 1894–95) and the Western nations' increasingly uneasy acceptance of Japan's rising as an industrial power and its imperial expansion (Russo-Japanese War, 1904–05). Photography arrived at a momentous juncture in realizing and reifying Japan's state of material and spiritual development. Firstly, the language was purely visual and it was a form of opportune "remedy" to the *kanji* problem found in the Japanese language. If the Japanese written script was fraught with Chinese characters and if the latter had brought much inhibition *(sogai)* to the growth of Japan's national language, it was plausible to conclude that the Japanese people's eventual highly enthusiastic embrace of this new visual language was due partly to the desire to represent itself as independent of its former Sino-centric cultural inclination and to display overtly the shaping of Japan on a Westernization path *(see* also Iwasaki, 1988). Moreover, the pre-embrace of this Western technological invention had already germinated during the *rangaku* period. I will return to this subject in the following chapter. What the Japanese saw in photography was "realism," a key aesthetic aspect of many Western paintings, its predecessor art form, which has become a salient artistic working principle in many well-known anime films such as *Akira* (1988), *Grave of the Fireflies* (1988), and *Princess Mononoke* (1997). For example, Kume Kunitake, one of the official members of the Iwakura Embassy (1871–73), wrote:

> The more we saw of the fantastic variations of Creation, the more
> astonished we were. Japanese painters all regard it as artistically
> elegant to use traditional Chinese techniques of landscape painting
> to depict the [folded] mountains of Japan, but in fact [their works]
> do not match paintings done in the Western style in the accurate
> representation of reality. This is because Japanese painters are

> unaware that Japanese mountains have different forms from those
> of China. Realistic Western paintings of mountains, water, trees and
> cattle reflect the true appearance of landscape, as well as the actual
> colors of the sky. As society progresses in enlightenment, painting,
> too, becomes more refined.[11]

To reflect reality of the times in which they lived, the nation found a new medium called photography, by which the realist moments of existence could be conveyed and captured at hand, preserved, and communicated privately and publicly. Like the realistic fiction that appeared during the Meiji period, photography could depict "the human psyche and environment" of a dynamic changing era all the more visually and directly (Twine, 1991: 133). Credited as Japan's most elderly Meiji photography scholar and critic, Ina Nobuo (1963: 14) lauded photography as a "public thing" (*daishu no mono*) that the "limitations of language could be overcome." It was also being described "as an art form, free of stylistic constraints … and the ability to communicate a sense of the times" (Ozawa, 2003: iv). This open reception of "things" Western was due to the framing of *seiyō* (the West) as a collective progressive civilization model to be followed. In those days, *seiyō* meant Europe (Conrad, 2000: 58–76) and almost all of the latest technological innovations originated from there, including photography, whose inventor was from France.[12] As mentioned earlier, the disconcerting schizophrenic dialectic was not only directed at Asia but also within the entire "optical field view" of a much further away Occidental land, Europe. That momentous fragmentary being of a photographic image was a gesture in framing an emerging identity amidst all the *korō* (the ignorance, ugliness, stubbornness, and so on)[13] by which Japan was surrounded. Najita and Harootunian (1998: 211) analyzed the "leaving Asia" — *datsu A* — thinking, which meant "principally the zone of Chinese civilization and 'entering Europe' — *nyū Ō* —." My argument is that while the intellectuals since the pre-Meiji times had attempted to separate, distinguish, and recuperate the authentic Japanese language, another more effective and direct new language had already taken root. To trace the genealogy of anime further, the earlier enthusiastic import of glass instruments from the Dutch and the resultant popular appeal of the magic lantern (a pre-camera optical device) was a notable indication of anime's prior inception and potential in the forging of a new symbolic identity of the Japanese from the late eighteenth century onwards. However fervently and laboriously the Japanese emphasized the material *yamato kotoba* (pure Japanese words) and the alien-ness of the Chinese language and, later, Western languages, and despite the amount of rebuttal in scholarly criticism that was showered on the myth of the Japanese language (see, for example, Miller, 1982, and Dale, 1986), they did not affect the development and deft utilization of a non-ideographic, non-alphabetic visual language that could better express the depth of Japanese modernity and its search for identity.

Today, digitalization of images has rendered the use of film stock almost obsolete. However, less than a hundred years ago, animation had relied on film and the camera for transferring visual images for screen display. Late Western animation artists such as Len Lye (1901–80) and Norman McClaren (1914–87) even preferred to paint directly on film stock (Bendazzi, 1994: 115). The success of Japan's homegrown photographic film industry in the 1930s resulted in a newfound confidence and the widespread acceptance of this new form of visual language even though it was of Western origin. Moreover, the growth of the photographic film language in Japan was phenomenal and was initially popularized by the educated and privileged classes and regarded as a "high culture symbol" (Tomaru, 1997: 127).

Animation as a latecomer industrial art had benefited from the growth of the country's photographic film industry. In short, photography as a new form of visual language was a forerunner of anime. If photography was able to testify to a changing era, animation and anime were able to excite the populace of Japan especially when the pictures were seen to be moving and the contents looked alive, vivid, graphically scenic, and invigoratingly inspiring. Photography offered realism and technology but the animation embodied more from the realms of art and fantasy.

The later zeal and appreciation for artistic skills that the Japanese have used in animation is not entirely geo-political, although I have tried to theorize and historize it in this chapter. The humankind's unceasing artistic spirit to create and communicate at all times is part of a narrative continuum of human existence. Closely connected to my research is the inquiry into the continuity of art forms in Japan: how, in each epoch of history, expressing the inexpressible can be seen through various art forms that have arisen, whether supported by aesthetic or other socio-political reasons, or a complexity of both. The following chapter thus explores this expressive continuum in Japanese cultural history and argues that anime is part of this ongoing process of artistic adoption and negotiation in response to the changing environment. More importantly, it is a means to maintain a differential identity and a way to express a self that is not immune to bodily functions and fantasies, and carnal and childlike behavior; and the innate need to chart a self-referential functional narrative sets upon a stage, within a screen, a constructed frame.

Continuity of Art Forms and Their Visualness

> I would be fascinated to talk with you about Japan for a moment.
> I am much interested in that extraordinary country, with so many
> curious aspects and artists.
>
> Camille Pissaro, *Monet and Japan* (2001: 65)

Every country has its own repository of art forms, but whether it takes pride and interest in preserving them, re-understanding the contexts of their production, or even has the means to constantly exhibit them worldwide is another matter. In Afghanistan and places that are situated on the western portions of the Silk Road, we hear of stories such as the one describing how colossal and cliff-sized sculptures of Buddha were destroyed and damaged due to warfare and religious reasons. In Japan, so far, despite the heated arguments about "*datsu –A–*," many of the imported art forms from Asia, particularly those from India and China, have remained to this day. If the *kanji* problem is a burden that hinders modernization of the country, what about the wide-ranging array of skills, crafts, art forms, and artifacts that equally and directly display the scale and depth of Indian, Chinese, and even Korean cultural influences? On the contrary, these foreign *kanji* (Chinese characters) and art forms are proudly entrenched in the Japanese art tradition and are much appreciated as part of the country's cultural heritage. In essence, the continuity of art forms in Japan today is due to a complexity of factors and the attitude with which the Japanese have rectified their modernization path.

This chapter introduces the "visual-ness" of Japanese art forms including anime and attempts to locate and conceive the twentieth-century medium-genre in a visual awareness tradition that exists within the mental make-up of an assimilating subject. Despite their similarities, there are differences between Chinese and Japanese arts, in terms of style and content, and there are also socio-political, artistic, and philosophical divergences. It was also the case with the animation creations that appeared in the second half of the twentieth century (see Chapters 4 and 7). Although anime can project an industrial high-tech image, it possesses features of traditional old art forms. In the following discussion, I distinguish a number of recurrent visual traits and put forward the view that these art forms are not simply "art for art's sake." They also play important narrative roles in describing the times and ethos in which they flourish. It is through these art forms that expressive subjectivity and a "free space" can be perceived and enlivened, indicating the interconnectedness among the artist, the spectator, and the environment.

Traditional Art Forms and Their Aesthetic Elements

Emakimono

The classic Japanese two-dimensional art forms, namely paintings and wood-prints, first appeared during the Asuka period (AD 593–710)[1] in which there was widespread absorption of Chinese culture. At that time, Buddhism was adopted as a new religion and was favored by the ruling class. It was not until the late Heian period, or from the turn of the eleventh century onward, that unusual stylistic elements began to appear and Japanese-style paintings became categorically termed as *yamato-e*. One distinctive type is the *emakimono* or picture-scroll. The genre became established during the Kamakura period (1185–1333). Originating from Tang-dynasty China, it assumed an altered form when expressed by the Japanese painters. It also acquired several names such as *monogatari-emaki, nikki-emaki, sōshi-emaki, e-kotoba, e-den,* and *engi* (Seckel, 1959: 38). When translated to English, they literally mean "narrative picture-scroll," "tale picture-scroll," "diary picture-scroll," "sketches and short writings picture-scroll," "drawings and phrases picture-scroll," "painting-tell picture scroll," and "cause/reason-origin picture scroll" consecutively. The subject matter and painting style were unique; they were not found in any art forms around the world. Firstly, its foremost typical emphasis was on the "realist" human world engulfed within the cyclic elements of life — youth, beauty, love, sickness, old age, spiritual enlightenment, labor, military warfare, power and intrigue, and death and grief. In short, they are about the ephemeral nature of existence.

Contained within the cosmic world of *emakimono* was also the acute effort to recognize particularities and emotional nuances of human conditions. As a result, these picture-scrolls did not only reflect the trends in medieval Japan but also provided a guiding window for us to understand the psychological and ideological perspectives of the artist and his spectatorship's aesthetic expectations. The main stylistic technique was the use of "hair-thin lines" through which human figures, trees, houses, and even rhythmic movements were outlined. Facial expressions were economically expressed in the single-stroke technique. For example, a straight line was used for the eye and a hook for the nose. In this way, the artist was freed from over-illustrative details (Munsterberg, 1957: 72–74). The technique resembles line-drawing process in cel animation, including the line-tracing technique. Thus, when the Japanese encountered animation in the early twentieth century, the medium was initially addressed as *senga eiga*, meaning line drawing film (see Chapter 5). In the animated film *My Neighbors the Yamadas* (1999), director Takahata Isao pays tribute to the *senga* world of animation in which the art of clear line illustration is foregrounded and set within a bland light-pastel art background. The film deliberately employs a design background which does not reflect a sophisticated multi-layered Disney-influenced kind of cel animation.[2]

Emakimono emphasized formalistic expressions and shapes. It allowed the artist to focus on narrative continuity, spatial perspective, and other decorative demands. Thus from a literary tale such as Lady Murasaki's *Genji monogatari,* to a narrative story about the founding of a famous temple or shrine *Kitano tenjin engi-emaki*, a miraculous tale of a monk *Shigisan engi emaki*, caricatures of animals and people in *Chōjū jinbutsu giga* (English title: *Animals at Play*), the viewer is drawn into the picture-telling world of *emakimono*. Other examples like the epic documentary recordings of court struggles, chaotic fiery scenes and battles in *Ban dainagon ekotoba* and the *Heiji monogatari emaki,* the travelogue of a priest and his preaching work in *Ippen shōnin eden*, activities of the working class in *Ishiyama tera engi emaki* — Seckel (1959: 64) describes that the *emakimono* "painter is always at pains to lead our eye in the main direction of the picture, to arouse expectation, produce lively rhythms, and ensure that a spark constantly leaps from figure to figure, shape to shape, and color to color."

Japanese art scholars and historians regard *emakimono* as "a form of painting where happenings and events are spoken through the act of illustrating; mood scenes are also expressed as a result, the tale could be furthermore comprehended and appreciated" (M. Sano, 1998: 81). Foreign scholars in general are attracted to the realist elements, especially when viewed in contrast with the objective and often emotionally remote Chinese scroll pictures which lack true-to-life sentiments and representations and a certain "direct instantaneous" visual appeal that attracts the attention of the viewer. This is the fundamental difference. In the history of Chinese art, realist, dynamic, rhythmic, and animated contents did appear. On the bronze vessels of the Zhou dynasty (sixth to third century BC) to the tomb paintings of the Han dynasty (the third century), there are vivid scenes of people showing them engaged in action (for example, hunting, leisure entertainment, and preparation of food and street processions). Sculptures depict the dynamic characteristics of the subjects concerned; they could be a pair of wrestlers in body-to-body contact (in the late Zhou dynasty), or a galloping horse in the Han and Tang dynasties. Sometimes, the subjects include lions and tigers in their ferocious regal poses. Paintings also showcase everyday lives of ordinary people; the most representative is *The Qing-ming Festival on the River*, which was drawn during the early part of the twelfth century. However, these close-to-life illustrative traits somehow faded and are not so much valued in Chinese art memory and reproduction. Or, if more of these art examples are available and if they are still around, they are not displayed or promoted adequately in public. In addition, if such artifacts are mentioned or focused upon, especially when the contents feature rich narratives favored by the Mongol and Qing rulers (e.g. paintings of hunting trips and warfare), they tend to be dismissed as "in foreign taste."[3]

Whereas in the case of Japan, despite the absence of precious and aggrandized materials such as gold, bronze, jade stones, ivory, and bricks such realist narratives survive, and many can still be found in monochromatic ink and paper and some in wood.[4] Today, this direct and informative trait of *emakimono* is embodied in countless manga works and their co-animated creations. Another unique feature of *emakimono* is the artist's slightly elevated optical view of his painting subjects. The narrative contents are often "rooflessly" illustrated; that is, the viewer can have a broader multidimensional sense of the painted story despite the presence of "doors" as privacy markers. In other words, like manga and anime, *emakimono* fulfils a storytelling role besides its two-dimensional illustrative presentation.

Regarding technique, *emakimono* seems to possess the rudiments required of a drawn animated film. For example, one of its important stylistic feature is its focus on the mannerism and facial expressions of each figure drawn. Although the drawn figures might look alike from afar, the *emakimono* artist was also mindful of the characteristics of each drawn figure, be it an ox or a deity messenger. For example, an ox was represented in an *emakimono*-like panel screen by Tawaraya Sotatsu (1589–1651?), which depicts a scene from *Genji monogatari*. The animal's uneasy pose and restlessness subtly reveals the romantic tension between two static lovers; in the story, Prince Genji steals a chance to meet his long-lost lover Lady Utsusemi.[5] Another example is the deity messenger in the *Shigisan engi emaki*. He is illustrated in a spinning motion while running an errand in the sky, and is hurrying in the spectator's direction. His action seemingly sweeps across a cinematic screen (Seckel, 1959: 125). From a twenty-first-century perspective, one cannot help but be reminded of cartoon characters such as the Road Runner who beeps at top speed, or Doraemon, the robot-cat who accelerates in haste to rescue the ever accident-prone Nobita.[6]

Imamura Taihei, a film critic and one of Japan's pioneering animation theoreticians, argues in his book *Manga eiga ron* (1941) that animation (which he calls *manga eiga*, meaning "manga film") has its roots in Japanese traditional arts (*kako no nihon geijitsu*), the earliest being *emakimono*. His book has been reprinted by several publishers after the war; a recent one is the edition published by Iwanami

Shōten in 1992. Imamura notes that while every "filmic shot" gives birth to a moving perspective, in *emakimono* (as painted multi-perspectives are present) the viewer's gaze moves too (*idō de aru*). Moreover, the near-and-far ways of viewing are no less lacking and hence "various conceptual ways of viewing are active" (*kannen tekina*) (1992: 126–127). He also states that while the film camera persistently causes movement, the *emakimono* artist merely changes his position in order to paint and express an endless flow of perspectives (1992: 131).

Citing *Ban dainagon ekotoba* as an example, Imamura praises the detective value of *emakimono* viewing, as the art form allows room for free interpretation, and the imaginative way of storytelling (*kūsōka no hōhō*) is just as fresh and vivid. As introduced above, *Ban dainagon ekotoba* features contents of court intrigue and struggle between rival political forces within the Imperial Palace during the Heian period. Produced in the late twelfth century by court painter Tokiwa Mitsunaga, the picture scroll reveals the artist's attempt at objectivity in spite of his sense of uncertainty in documenting the historical event.[7] Among other picture scrolls that are mentioned, *Chōjū jinbutsu giga* is singled out by Imamura for its comic satirical representations of monks and aristocrats during the late Heian period and its portrayal of their corrupted lifestyles. The picture scroll does not carry any literary descriptions; the artist simply lets the visual representations tell the story. For example, one scene features a frog posed as Buddha. It sits in a meditative position on an altar and a monkey clad in a Buddhist clergy robe kneels in submission and puffs out "sutra chants." A group of animals dressed in mourning clothes sit at the side. Further front is another group of chanting animal monks whose frolicking behavior seems incongruent with the solemn occasion. Positioned behind the ceremonial frog is an owl perched upon a tree branch. The owl is watching the scene with a cold, nonchalant expression.

On a side note, Imamura's *Manga eiga ron* can be categorized as a form of nationalistic discourse not unlike the philosophical writings of Nishida Kitarō and other earlier *kokugaku* thinkers. The description of *emakimono* contents by Imamura above serves to weave in the viewpoint that a Japanese art form such as *emakimono* is equally effective in creating an imaginative world of storytelling, *kūsō no geijutsu* (1992: 141). However, in tracing the visual-likeness and influences of traditional Japanese art forms on animation, one must also be aware that there is an accompanying conscious effort to promote, draw, and articulate their visual qualities rhetorically. At this juncture, the reader should be reminded to consider the rest of this chapter as an introduction to Japanese traditional art forms and their visual connections to Japanese animation. One needs to keep in mind the underlying nationalistic discourse and its persuasive weight on the subsequent progressive developments of Japanese artistic thought and production, especially from the mid-eighteenth century onward.

Chinzō

Apart from *emakimono*, portrait painting is another example of two-dimensional art that displays the realist tradition. Originating from Southern Song China (1127–1279), such works hailed from the Kamakura period and became highly popular during the Muromachi period (1333–1573), and were heavily influenced by Zen Buddhism. In Zen portrait painting, Zen masters became the reflective subject matter for illustration. As Zen stressed the value of intuitive enlightenment and prolonged guidance of a Zen master, portraits of living Zen masters (*chinzō*) became important and commemorative images for disciples. This led to an evolution of an artistic tradition which demanded acute observational skills of the painter. The result was that such portraits were often realistic images bearing unique and individualistic characteristics of the Zen master. From background setting to posture, dress details to facial expressions, each portrait painting depicted a powerful psychological presence which could be regarded as the early genealogical images of manga/anime characters, which also included the *ukiyo-e* courtesan and *kabuki* character prints that appeared during the Edo period.

In relation to anime, especially of the manga-anime kind, the appeal of the character-design is one vital feature that draws the reader-cum-viewer to the narrative. However, equally important is the psychological representation of the character concerned, that is, the ability of the author-illustrator, and later the animation director, to describe the mental state of the character that lies behind the external facade. In other words, character portrayal makes an equally lasting impression on the reader and viewer besides the storyline, and it is not too far-fetched to compare contemporary popular anime character designs with those of Zen master portrait-paintings, particularly the facial features and expressions. For example, the hanging scroll painting of the Zen priest Ikkyū is comparable to the anime character Hana in director Kon Satoshi's film, *Tokyo Godfathers* (2003). Both present certain psychological tension and anxiety set within their portrayal frames.[8]

Although Zen portrait paintings were meant as contemplative wall paintings, anime characters were created for popular consumption in the late twentieth century. They may have originated from a different time and space, but the approach with which the "author-illustrator" portrays the character is fundamentally the same. It is highly observational, at times almost caricature-like, and psychologically inclined. The only difference is that in animation, realism is further enhanced with sound expressions and rhythmic movements that encapsulate a better portrayal of the drawn character.

Shōhekiga[9]

While *emakimono* has certain distinctive aristocratic origins, there were several interior design developments during the latter half of the Muromachi period, namely, the introduction of tatami flooring, Zen study-rooms (*shoin*), *shōji* sliding door, colorful *fusuma* panel doors, and folding screens. They eventually became an archetypal interior design style that can still be seen in many Japanese homes today.[10] The Japanese have maintained the tradition of sitting and even sleeping on the floor, and thus majestic-sized furniture and its decorative elements have no interior architectural purpose. During the Muromachi period, because of the growing interest in tea-drinking (*chanoyu*) and the introduction of the Zen-influenced *wabi-sabi* aesthetic,[11] folding screens and wall-panel paintings became visual-oriented frameworks.

During the Azuchi-Momoyama period (1573–1603), golden background panel works were also present. Brilliant flowers, pine trees, birds, and prancing lions were featured with gold-dusted finishing and there was a newly-found interest in a polychromatic world. However, Zen-like monochromatic artworks did not disappear. They too manifested poetically as they still played the dual visual role of describing and evoking a meditative sense of nature. These wooden structures may be statically placed but they are removable partitions and the framing of an enclosed space is a flexible option.

The movable characteristic of Japanese sliding doors prompted the late independent Japanese animator, Kinoshita Renzo (1936–97), to use it ingeniously as a framing technique in his award-winning animated film, *Made in Japan* (1972). Caricaturing Japanese society in the late 1960s and early 1970s, the film contains such characters as a politician, a street protester, and a *sarari-man* (company employee). Other illustrations include Japanese characters who are dressed in traditional attire and sometimes in Western clothing, scenes depicting the affluence of Japanese gastronomic tastes (for example, the amount and variety of food being consumed and later regurgitated), routine-like sexual romping, and other juxtaposed images of a very much industrialized Japan and its seemingly traditional side. While Barthes (1982) interpreted Japanese signs and symbols as "emptiness," a native insider such as Kinoshita self-questioned the post-Second World War state of Japanese society through his animated multiframes, denoting a listless semiotic Japan and its puppet-like inhabitants.[12] Technique-wise, Kinoshita's rendering of a single condensed cel-world of a tatami-spaced room and the skill with which he interchanged the "frames" of action and contents practically reflect the flexibility of Japanese interior design.

Chinese people basically regard folding screens or screen-doors (*byōbu*) as a means to protect privacy and to block wind (*dang feng*). These devices may often have *fengshui* meanings in its construction and location. The Japanese, however, tend to value such structures more for their decorative and informative elements in addition to its flexible architectural functions. Thus, we find images of street parades, crowd-gathering festivals, and also plain images of working-class people engaged in everyday activities being featured on folding screens. In other words, the informative realist trait of *emakimono* is also demonstratively seen in the above-mentioned interior designs of pre-modern Japan.[13]

Ukiyo-e

Although ostentatious and Zen-influenced wooden panel artworks could only be afforded by the rising merchant class and the upper class (the samurai and the court nobles), *ukiyo-e*, or wood-block prints, was produced abundantly for the masses. Meaning "paintings of the floating world" or "paintings of the drifting world," both titles refer to a principal Buddhist terminology used for describing the passing pleasures and sorrows of the living sphere. During the Edo period, *ukiyo-e* was made for the rising middle-class to satisfy their plebian taste for genre-paintings. The subject matter was focused on entertainment and the everyday world.

Buddhist wood-block prints from Tang China first reached Japan during the Nara period (710–794) and were basically religious iconographic prints designed in graphic or word form. Their contents included mainly sutra teachings and doctrines (Swann, 1966: 199). During the seventeenth century, while the Chinese also printed erotic novels and pictures in wood-print, the Edo craftsmen further developed the technique into a decorative art form which eventually became well-known in the West. It was a prolific art product that called for a co-ordinated division of labor — painter, wood engraver, printer/colorist, and publisher. It was similar to postwar manga-anime production in which specialization of labor was the main practice. Produced in bulk, *ukiyo-e* satisfied the growing urban populace's indulgence with "fashionable" objects. Initially, *kabuki* actors and courtesans were illustrated abundantly; later editions included colorful travel guide books and landscape prints that depicted changing atmospheric moods with sensitive color shades and graduation (e.g. the works of Hokusai and Hiroshige), thus giving a touch of realism to the representations.

The "realist approach" re-surfaced again in *ukiyo-e*. Not that it had disappeared from the repertory of Japanese paintings since the onset of the *emakimono* during the medieval periods; in fact, it seems to be the constant matrix countenancing the hallmark of *yamato-e*. For example, the drawing lines of *ukiyo-e* are essentially prototypes of the fine wire-like lines found in *emakimono*. The basic difference is that they are bolder in strength and length due to the contents portrayed. When one glances at Kitagawa Utamaro's (1753–1806) masterpiece, *Woman Bathing*, the sleek linear profile of a fully nude female body provides a faint and yet powerful matching remembrance of the lady robot in director Oshii Mamoru anime film, *Ghost in the Shell* (1995), whose perfect-10 naked anatomy, complete with muscles and sinews, stretches the "realist approach" to the maximum.

Emakimono had been in existence for over 250 years (from the early Kamakura period). It had been patronized by courtly circles and the lesser nobility and the samurai. *Ukiyo-e* also reigned comparatively supreme throughout the Edo period before it declined in popularity during the Meiji period (1868–1912). Each picture-art form has dominated different historical periods; in post-Second World War industrial Japan, the dominating art form is undoubtedly anime, in particular, the manga-anime kind.

Kabuki *and* Bunraku, Nō *and* Kyōgen

Japanese traditional performing arts had strong historical links with China, Korea, and North and West Asia. Scholars have discussed the similarities which they share with some of the old traditions of Southeast Asian minority populations. The subsequent developments nurtured and perfected by the Japanese themselves have, however, led to the development of new genres and artistic achievements. One primary example is *nōgaku*, which is a general term for *nō* and *kyōgen* stage-acting. Dating back to the mid-fourteenth century, it was originally a form of entertainment for the aristocratic class, namely the shogunate and its imperial court nobles (Yoshinobu, 1971: 84). Two other equally rich and magnificent theater arts are *bunraku* and *kabuki*, which became highly popular among the urban populace and the affluent merchant class residing in Edo and Osaka during the Edo period.

They have often been called the four great traditional performing arts of Japan because of their historical evolvement and the important roles they played in the social milieu of Japanese lives from the mid-fourteenth century to the Edo period. Except for *kabuki*, which had tried to adapt to Western influences during the Meiji period, the rest have remained true to their classic theatrical forms to this day, and have continued to support the multilayered cultural environment of industrial Japan. *Bunraku,* or puppet theater (its older title name, *jōruri*),[14] entertains audiences with skillful combination of verbal narration and puppet body manipulation. Its calculated human-like movements are particularly attractive to the spectators. In addition, the narrative tales are *jojishi*, or epic heroic poems that document the rise and fall of ruling houses.[15] Among the puppet theatrical arts in the world, the Japanese variety is the most unusual. This is because the spectators can see the puppet master at work, although he or she is dressed in black. This odd theatrical element has led Barthes (1982) to question the absence of the "antinomy" principle of animating as the supposedly unseen backstage actions can be viewed openly. In other words, it pertains to the ideological framing dimension which I will discuss further in Chapter 3.

In relation to aesthetics and the Japanese world-view of narrative drama, one significant characteristic is performing the mental state of the protagonist, especially in *nō*. The masked actor playing the sole *shite* role (the protagonist) first "identifies himself with the true essence of the whole role" (Ortolani, 1995: 112 and 121) and in the process genuinely expresses the mind and body of the soul-role he plays. The imitative act becomes truthful, real-life, and natural, which entices the audience to identify and experience with him the "inner essence" of the object-role.

On a different plane, Japanese animation at times possesses this profound quality. This is especially so when the animated character is directed by strong auteur directors such as Miyazaki Hayao, Takahata Isao, and manga-artist Tezuka Osamu. The imitative actions become true to the protagonist animated character and are not found within the realms of gag, slapstick, and forceful motion. The late manga-artist Tezuka Osamu was known to have told his team of animators that even though his *Astro Boy* had limited animated movements, the storytelling process would succeed so long as the audience could identify with the protagonist and experience his mental world.[16] As for Miyazaki's and Takahata's animated works, the audience is also emotionally drawn into the "innermost world" of the animated characters in films such as *Nausicaä of the Valley of the Wind, My Neighbor Totoro, Grave of the Fireflies* and *Only Yesterday*.

Another *nō* element which can be found in the cinema of Miyazaki and Takahata is the moments of non-action, rest, pause, feelings of space and time, intervals between events, and "silent breath" of the protagonist. In *nō*, these dimensions are known as "the art of *ma*," signifying the science of time and space in storytelling (Komparu, 1983: 70). *Nō*'s foremost aesthetic theoretician and playwright-artist, Zeami (1363–1443), once wrote that "what [the actor] does *not* do is of interest" (1983: 73) and, as a result, such silent *ma* moments moved the audience mutually to experience his contemplative world.

Pauses can occasionally be found in the animation cinema of Miyazaki and Takahata. They can last for five seconds or more without any apparent movement, music, or background sound. For example in *My Neighbor Totoro*, the scenes of *furusato* (hometown) and summer-time seem to operate on the *nō*'s *mugen-kaisō-ho*, that is, the "reflection-in-vision method" (Komparu, 1983: 75),[17] which transports the spectator back to Japan in the 1950s and the "real" rustic experiences could be recollected and enjoyed before one's eyes. While Zeami's metaphysical concept *kokoro* (Ortolani, 1995: 123) describes the highest levels of *nō* performance, in the cinema of Miyazaki and Takahata it could be translated as a collective cultural will to arouse reminiscences (*kaisō*) of pre-industrial Japan. In short, their films have a certain directional aim to achieve "in remembrance of things past." They draw the spectator into a spiritual reunion with the former poetic self of old Japan. In other words, the masks which actors wear in *nō* theater are essential artistic narrative devices; they allow the actors to assume the "living space" of the characters and to draw the audience's attention. In anime, the drawn characters and the background are "art surfaces" upon which the audience may dwell and further reflect.

The colorful and idiosyncratic components of *kabuki* theater could also be perceived in contemporary Japanese animation, especially of the manga-anime kind. While *nō* lends spiritual silence and poetic elegance, *kabuki* allows connection to the loud and spectacular world which the urban populace experiences every day. Attending a *kabuki* play is like experiencing a manga-anime being screened; the stage décor and design are architecturally built so as to create progressive and regressive frames of view. Revolving stage, roof and floor traps, the versatile *hanamichi*[18] situated at the side of the theater, realistic composition of scene design, backdrop decorations, and the complex lighting plot (in the past, candles were used) are all spellbinding. In addition, the bizarre costumes and stylistic facial make-up further exaggerate the visual appeal. Closest to the animation method of metamorphosis is the actor's quick change of costumes before the audience and his magical ability to change forms and move with agility. Heroic feats, dramatic poses and gestures, candle-lit faces, and the tangling rope that the hero or villain uses to fly across or vanish into darkness, are further reflections, allusions, and associated reminders of kinetic energies found in manga-anime.

Performance Studies scholar Fukushima Yoshiko (2003), while researching on the impact of manga stories on *shōgekijō* (little theater performance troupes that have risen in post-Second World War Japan) and the appeal of manga among Japanese youths, has argued for the influence of early Japanese literary genres and theater on Japanese popular culture. In examining the multiple codes and signs found in playwright Noda Hideki's works, she asserts that there is a "much longer tradition" fundamentally supporting, distributing, producing, and recreating an extant circulatory cultural and social system. In my opinion, Japanese animation, particularly the manga-adapted anime works, simply metamorphoses into silhouette cinema and television images. The visual and playful elements in *kabuki* are in turn embodied in a "toon" form.

Edo Period and Discovery of the West

Flourishing of popular arts and period of social order

The Edo period or the Tokugawa period (1603–1868) has gained considerable attention from researchers and scholars recently. They are anxious to recoup its rich past despite its feudalistic foundations. The rise of Japan as a major economic superpower in the 1970s is one of the reasons that prompts more foreign scholars to study Japan's pre-modern past. Japanese scholars have also begun to see the Edo period in a new sympathetic light in comparison to the imperialistic Meiji era and the problems of post-Second World War industrial Japan.

This sub-section aims to give a descriptive account of the Edo period as there are striking resemblances between popular culture of present-day Tokyo and the flourishing arts scene in the Edo period. In fact, Tokyo is not much different from its feudal urban past; it is as much an "embryonic capital" as Edo was (Coaldrake, 1981: 235–284). For example, land is still constantly being reclaimed to make space for residential and economic activities and transportation networks are being maintained, rebuilt, and expanded to provide the "salaried men" easy access to the city. In the Edo period, apart from the city of Edo, the other important urban centers included Osaka, Kyoto, and Nagoya. In present-day Japan, these urban centers have retained many of their historical characteristics but Tokyo is still taking the lead in setting trends and fads and the city continues to attract talents from other parts of the country.

Under the Tokugawa government, regular attendance of vassals was required at the city of Edo. As a result, there was a regular flow of powerful samurai families into the city; it was alternated at times when wives and children were taken hostage in the city while the men returned to their fiefs. Their periods of residence lasted for months and the cycle was repeated every other year. Hence, the concentration of samurai in Edo led to a large demand for commodities, ranging from food supplies to entertainment. Merchants and artisans flocked to the city to supply goods and services. Roving samurai, who had lost their lords in power struggles with the Tokugawa, also arrived at the city to look for jobs and opportunities. As discussed earlier, popular art forms such as *ukiyo-e* and *kabuki* were the evolved cultural output of a growing consumer capital city. By 1700, the population of Edo had grown to a million and Edo had become the largest city in the world. In the beginning there were two major strands of culture. One was the warrior culture that mimicked the aristocratic court culture of Kyoto and the other was the commoner culture which tried to take part in the cultural pursuits practiced by the warrior class. Eventually, a common mass culture appeared as both the warriors and commoners shared the everyday familiarities of urban living; that is, the sights, sounds, and ethos of an urban consumer society.

As a result of the emergence of market centers such as Edo and Osaka, the country's rural economy gradually developed into a capitalist market economy which in turn propelled new popular arts that had appeared in the cities. One interesting example is the wood-block *emaki*; it was not unusual for a publisher to print a minimum run of 10,000 copies to satisfy consumer demands and to meet his production costs. This genre was also known as *kiroku-ga* (meaning "painting as record-keeping") and the works were often commissioned by rich merchants and *daimyō* ("feudal lords") who wished to record spectacular events. One could also argue that the genre is a form of pre-modern manga-anime as the painted contents show meticulous details of Edo city life. For example, when recording the splendid parades of foreign embassy missions sent from Korea and Ryukyu (Okinawa), the artist also paid minute attention to a samurai policeman who fell asleep at his post, or the "finger-pointing and laughing crowd" who were enjoying the carnival event

(Toby, 1986: 425). In comparison, a number of post-Second World War manga-anime works also amplify the urban aspects of Tokyo, the most notable of which is Ōtomo Katsuhiro's *Akira* (1988) with its realistic portrayal of highways and fast cars including a prophetic scene of a cult-like Shinto priest/priestess parading with his/her followers on the streets of Tokyo.[19]

The Edo period also saw the expansion of the publishing industry; millions of books were printed for the increasingly literate public. The published books were often bestsellers as the populace was hungry for information due to the period of peace and social order. The books covered a wide range of subjects including *nō* and *kabuki* plays, poems, erotic literature, translated books from China and Holland, local travel guides, and even novelization of peasant uprisings (e.g. the *Sakura Sōgoro Story*; see Walthall, 1991: 37) and other actual events that involved the samurai class (e.g. the play, *Chūshingura*).[20] In short, the Tokugawa government's censorship policies had not been overtly strict and thus, popular culture flourished.

The historical roots of Japan's contemporary advertising industry could be traced to the Edo period. For example, *ukiyo-e* artists were often admitted to *kabuki* rehearsals. This gave them time to prepare new billboards and posters that advertised the new plays to the public. In addition, *kabuki* actors were known to insert subtle, and at times quite obvious, advertising lines in their scripts. By doing so, they directly or indirectly helped to promote new products that were available in town. These included fashionable rice crackers or delicious *udon* noodles. Edo studies scholar Nishiyama (1997) recounts that these advertisement insertions were meant to provide comic relief, especially during moments of high tension in the plays. Similarly, present-day television also seizes upon such moments when goods such as candies, lunch boxes, video games, and toys are endorsed and advertised by the manga-anime characters when their programs are on air. The animation cinema of Miyazaki and Takahata does not escape from such advertising ties either. For example, the release of *Laputa* (1986) directed by Miyazaki was linked with the electronics brand Toshiba and the food maker Ajinomoto. Takahata's film, *Only Yesterday* (1991), had tie-in promotions with the tomato sauce brand, Kagome. Toy lunch sets for children produced by Kagome were launched when the film was released.[21]

A description of Edo's popular arts scene would not be complete without taking into account the tradition of narrative arts, which encompassed a great variety in the early nineteenth century. Oral narratives in Japan became popular during the Heian period (794–1185), especially after the fall of Taira House in its battle with the Minamoto clan. Known as the *Heike monogatari*, blind priests and lost samurai began to narrate ballads about the Taira-Minamoto power struggles accompanied by the *biwa* and later the *shamisen* (both are stringed instruments). These tales were often tragic in content and were later expanded into stories about other social classes. As a result of such an expansion, they reflected the values and feelings of the commoners. During the Edo period, narrative art forms included punch-line stories, riddle improvisation, topic-of-the day stories, battle narratives, *jōruri* (song recitation), comic stories, impersonations of famous people, and gesture. They were often performed with musical instruments, masks, or mechanical contraptions when required. Such arts relied on a master-apprentice relationship for the learning and performance of skills. Today, more than a century later, many of these narrative arts can still be seen in television variety shows and live performances held in city and provincial halls. It is also common today to find such performing artists lending their voices to manga-anime characters. At the Into-Animation II Festival held in Tokyo in 1999,[22] two animators acted as stand-up comedians to host some of the screening events; this stamps an indigenous Japanese touch that is in sharp contrast to many bureaucratic-like international animation festivals held elsewhere.

Contact with the West and Western influences

Japan's first contact with the West was with the Portuguese in the mid-sixteenth century, and subsequent contacts were made with the Spaniards, the English, and the Dutch. The Ainu people living in Hokkaido were also in contact with the Russians who arrived from the northern waters. Among them, the Portuguese (particularly the Jesuit missionaries) and the Dutch traders were instrumental in introducing Western culture to the Japanese, and the fruits of their work can still be felt and seen in present-day Japan. Through the Portuguese and the Jesuit missionaries, Christianity, Western astronomy, medicine, cartography, painting, and copper-plate engraving were introduced. Their influences were religious, political, economic, and cultural. For a while, Portuguese learning was fashionably known as *namban bunka* (meaning "Southern Barbarian Culture"). In this section, emphasis is put on this cultural category, especially in the field of two-dimensional art.

First, there is the uniquely identifiable *namban byōbu*, "Southern barbarian folding screen-paintings," which are about the Portuguese missions in Japan, their meetings with the Japanese, their gestures, dress, and activities. Painted by artists commissioned by the ruling class or the rich merchants, these screens displayed an early panoramic insight into Japanese impressions of Westerners. The majority were faithfully executed with attention to detail. For example, one shows a well-dressed Caucasian man posing with his Negro slaves. It shows subtly the clothes they wore and the roles they played before their master. Although the materials used are expensive (gold leaf background, paint powders of malachite, lapis-lazuli, and so on; see illustration example in Boxer, 1979: 113), the element of fantasy is absent in the execution of the subject's characteristics. This is in stark contrast with many manga-anime of today in which portrayals of Western characters are usually exaggerated with large sparkling eyes. However, one distinguishable legacy remains; that is the minute attention paid to clothing which could be discerned in many European-based manga-anime-films created after the Second World War. For example, Ikeda Ryoko's manga, *The Rose of Versailles*, which first appeared as a weekly *manga* story in the early 1970s, was known for its lavish costume design and the historical detail that the artist paid to the French setting.[23] European-inspired oil paintings were also introduced by the Portuguese, and the subject matters of these paintings were often biblical stories. According to Boxer (1979: 110–124), most of the paintings and folding screens produced at that time were copies of European originals, as the Jesuits taught the Japanese Christian converts to acquire the styles of Renaissance art. Boxer also notes that some of these paintings were done with a mix of Japanese and European materials. For example, oil paints were often used for painting the figures and Japanese paints were used for the background.

Early scholars had attributed to the Portuguese the introduction of the more efficient movable-type printing press in Japan, which replaced the old Chinese method of block printing and in addition to the existing "Korean tradition of movable type,"[24] which led to a publishing boom during the Edo period. As mentioned earlier, from the mid-eighteenth century, tens of thousands of *ukiyo-e* were sold, as were other reading materials such as novels, plays, and travel guides. Twine (1991: 29) notes the existence of large publishing houses that employed professional writers and illustrators. There were hundreds of libraries just in Edo alone. The Edo townspeople's insatiable appetite for reading has never been curbed since then. Today, when traveling by trains and subways, or sitting in cafés, many salaried men and women read manga books which are thick like phonebooks (although more men seem to be reading manga than women), or they read pocket-sized script books. The popular attraction to the "visual effect" (illustrations) in books can be traced to this period. I will return to this characteristic in Chapter 5.

Due to the missionary activities of the Portuguese, their contacts with Japan were gradually banned from the 1610s onward. Replacing them were the Dutch traders. The Tokugawa shogunate granted them the special privilege of limited residency on the offshore island of Dejima which faced the coastal city, Nagasaki. Hence, for the next two hundred years (1640–1853), *rangaku* (Dutch learning) became a popular subject. It even captured the special attention of Shogun Yoshimune (1684–1751; see Goodman, 1986: 49). While the Jesuits set up missionary schools, orphanages, and hospitals to spread Western learning and culture, the Dutch did not have the means or the zeal to pursue such activities. It was the Japanese themselves who took the opportunity and approached the confined Dutchmen, who numbered no more than twenty on Dejima island, for tutorials on subjects ranging from mathematics and botany, to surgery, language, and art. Semi-private schools were also set up by feudal lords to acquire Dutch learning. Later, more private schools were established by individuals to research and disseminate *rangaku*.

Japanese artists began to study European paintings seriously; this time around they did not just copy but also innovated and paid particular attention to the realism of European still-life paintings. Eventually, the concept of *chiaroscuro* was grasped. *Rangaku* enthusiasts such as Honda Toshiaki (1744–1821) observed that

> European paintings are executed in great detail, with the intention of having them resemble exactly the objects portrayed so that they will serve some useful function. There are rules of painting that enable one to achieve this effect. The Europeans observe the division of sunlight into light and shade, and also what are called the rules of perspective. For example, if one wished to draw a person's nose from the front, there would be no way in Japanese art to represent the central line of the nose. In the European style, shading is used on the sides of the nose, and one may thereby perceive its height. (Keene, 1969: 63)

Scholar Ōtsuki Gentaku (1757–1827) praised Dutch still-life painting:

> In the shapes of the flowers, the forms of the fruits, and the design of the birds and insects, there is such realism in the colors, such precision in the positions, such brilliance, that one feels exactly as if one were seated in some celebrated garden whose exquisite perfumes scented one's sleeves. Ah, the skill with which life has been copied may indeed be called robbing the art of the Creator. (Keene, 1969: 63)

Among the *rangaku* artists, Shiba Kokan (1747–1818) stood out not only for his innovative work but also for his theoretical beliefs in painting realistic images of Japan. His works like *Daruma* and *Waterfowl and Willow Tree* (Lee, 1983: 188–191) are interesting hybrids of Japanese and European styles and demonstrate his creative attempts to break new ground. Art historian Sherman E. Lee notes that Shiba's work displays "tensions" as he tried to combine the flatness of Oriental painting in opposition to a Western dimension where a vanishing-point perspective abides.

Another Western influence on Japanese art painting could be seen in Maruyama Ōkyo's (1733–95) folding screens that depict pine trees in snow. This renowned piece is known for its astonishingly life-like elements that exhibit fine details and moods. Maruyama's work is said to be influenced by contemporary Ming Chinese realist painting techniques at the time and he had also adopted a Western form of naturalism into his innovative style of painting. When viewed today, it is still astoundingly life-like and photographic. His sketches of flora, fauna, and animal figures are meticulously executed and reflect a strong awareness of Western scientific interest.[25] Such evidence of a Japanese inclination to absorb new techniques of art is indisputable.

The question to ponder is whether realism appeals to the Japanese artist to innovate and to portray the "physically visual" in a realist manner. Dutch paintings produced from the sixteenth to the eighteenth centuries have been known for their "realist strategies" (Westermann, 2004) in depicting the life and the newly-found independence of the Dutch Republic.[26] The rise of Dutch trading power had indeed brought Dutch art to the shores of Japan and in the process heightened the Japanese awareness of realism in illustration, but, as I have shown in preceding sections of this chapter, there already existed indigenously a keen visual observation of life as reflected in the *emakimono* illustrations. The artistic realist trait is still in force today and is evident in contemporary anime cinema. It can be found in, for example, the animated films directed by Miyazaki Hayao, Takahata Isao, Ōtomo Katsuhiro, Oshii Mamoru, and Kon Satoshi. The emphasis on realism still prevails today as seen in many contemporary anime works. The thematic trait of realism will be progressively examined in the following chapters because it is unique to the Japanese representation of art and the experience of the visual and real.

Last but not least was the Japanese craving for Western goods during the Edo period. Engelbert Kaempfer (1651–1716), a physician-scholar who visited Japan during the years 1690–92, wrote that the Japanese liked "new and rare curiosities" and such items became "extremely profitable" due to the small quantities brought in by the Dutch traders. Although Chinese silk and Indian spices still commanded the main bulk of the goods imported to Japan, the Dutch realized that the Japanese had developed a fondness for their manufactured goods, especially "coral, amber, rough molten glass, used for coloring porcelain, mirrors (which are broken here and used for telescopes, magnifying glasses and spectacles)" (1999: 209).[27] An illustrated example of "an early Japanese use of a European invention" could be seen in Ihara Saikaku's bestselling novel, *The Man Who Spent His Life in Love* (1682), in which the protagonist Yonosuke was seen on a rooftop and was using the telescope deftly to watch a woman in her bath.[28] C. R. Boxer, in his study of the Jan Campagnie (Dutch East Indian Company) in Japan, also notes the "fleeting fancies" of Japanese officials when goods such as colored glasses and clocks were presented to the shogun, and they gradually became regular items for trade with the Japanese (Boxer, 1979: 159–160). Indeed, a glance at the various lists of imported goods from 1672 to 1674 testifies to the Japanese fondness for "glass products," including glass bottles, telescopes, perspective glasses, and even pieces of broken glass. They arrived in boxes and chests among other exotic goods from the Middle East, India, Southeast Asia, and China.

The Japanese form of magic lantern, utsushi-e

The Japanese were fascinated by the visual images which the "glass products" could provide. They also liked glasses with painted images. By the turn of the nineteenth century, the Japanese form of magic lantern appeared and was known as *utsushi-e*. This visual instrument was to become one of the colorful exhibits of the Edo period, especially for the entertainment it could present. Edo historians have generally termed an *utsushi-e* show as a *misemono* show because of its appeal to the masses or the townspeople, and also because such show was often held in a crowded bazaar, a festival event, or a theater-hall designed for such visual treats.

There were other subordinate glass-lenses exhibitions during the Edo period. One was the experience of peeping wood-block prints and pictures through a smudged lens (Markus, 1985). This was known as *megane-e* or *karakuri-e* (meaning "show box") where paintings and woodcut prints of famous places like Kyoto and sceneries of China and Holland could be viewed through the lens (Tamon, 1964: 160). Another was the experience of seeing through a telescope for a small fee. The fourth was the *nozōki* show ("peep" or "visual" show, another variation of *karakuri-e*) designed at the waist-level with portholes for the spectator to view images enhanced by Western lenses. An operator managed the show and provided some musical background as the images changed.

In contrast, an *utsushi-e* show was held indoors and in a dark environment. This was because the images were projected on a white-cloth screen, manually operated by a master-artist, who also designed and painted the narrative lenses and directed the theatrical performance. Accompanied by the singing narrative voice of a *shamisen* artist and his musical instrument, the *utsushi-e* master, helped by two or more assistants, worked behind the screen. His work included the fast change of lenses to create new images or movements. Utmost care was given to the candle which was lit within the wooden device. Through the candlelight, images were projected onto the white screen (which was about the size of a wall of an average bedroom) and the image created a flickering, eerie atmosphere. Most of the narratives were samurai tales and ghost stories; they exuded an indigenous touch, despite the use of an essentially Western invention. Most of the stories were also adapted from *kabuki* and *bunraku* plays. However, it is likely that erotic stories were shown possibly to an adult audience.

European magic lanterns were metal-plated, steam-powered, and imprinted with decorative designs. The Japanese magic lantern was made of wood only and could be handled easily by the user. It was possible that due to the shogunate's general distrust of Western imports and learning, the *utsushi-e* master learned to convert the European device into a Japanese-made *mono* (thing). The adaptation allowed him to make a living as he demonstrated the right skills. There were other probable reasons; for example, steam technology, electricity, and metal-plate making were still being studied and were not manufactured industrially. Beasley (1995: 49–50) records that such technological activities only began to take place in the mid-nineteenth century when small industrial complexes were set up by the feudal lords living far from the central Edo region. In a television documentary made some time ago about a master *utsushi-e* artist,[29] the master demonstrated his skills in making his own glass panes and lenses in his own laboratory. At a talk and live demonstration sponsored by the Chiba City Museum of Art entitled *Edo Anime* (August 21, 1999), one of the surviving disciples of a master artist said that the earliest images of *utsushi-e* were largely scenic pictures of Amsterdam and Holland that were shown to an avid audience who was curious about a Dutchman's fatherland.

In general, Japanese animation scholars, teachers, and film historians acknowledge *utsushi-e* as Edo's form of anime (or simply called "Edo anime"), one of the pre-modern ancestors of today's Japanese anime. Copies of this original Japanese-made camera obscura device are still being kept in several city museums today. To sum up, Edo's cultural heritage was overwhelmingly rich in material and spirit although it was a feudalistic and hierarchical society with Western "barbarian" elements. More importantly, the remnants of its popular culture have been carried over into modern Japan, including its ideological life force and outlook, and have been further augmented and flavored by the advance of a new century of Westernization and a newly-found national identity. Whether traditional or modern, one cannot ignore the historical development of Japanese art forms when exploring the aesthetic, performing, and ideological frameworks of Japanese animation.

The theme of realism is interpreted graphically and ideologically in this chapter. Graphically, it is seen from the pictorial texts in which storytelling is expressed without words, as though words are considered to be incapable of expressing what ought to be said or to be paid attention to. Ideologically, the theme of realism shows a tendency toward details and facts, even to the extent of transcribing visual reality as perceived by the naked eye. Partly due to Japan's response to industrialization, we see deliberate efforts to adopt and apply Western forms of painting practically in the later periods of Japanese history. This differs from the traditional world of Chinese painting, where in general there are not too many realist pictorial elements. Rather, it is the psychological and emotional dimensions of the pictorial background, or *qing diao,* that grasp attention. The parameter of appreciation is subjective and abstract, and it depends on how much the beholder can identify with the connotations of the pictorial or the painter's communicative background world, or *yi jing*.[30]

How anime incorporates realism into animated storytelling will be further explored in the following chapters.

3

Cultural Thought, Expressing the Self, and Image-Building

> Now it happens in this country (Japan) the empire of signifiers is so immense, so in excess of speech, that the exchange of signs remains of a fascinating riches, mobility, and subtlety, despite the opacity of the language, sometimes even as a consequence of that opacity. The reason for this is that in Japan the body exists, acts, shows itself, gives itself, without hysteria, without narcissism, but according to a pure — though subtly discontinuous — erotic project. It is not the voice ... but the whole body (eyes, smile, hair, gestures, clothing) which sustains with you a sort of babble that the perfect domination of codes strips of all regressive, infantile character...
>
> Barthes (1982: 9–10)

At the turn of the 1970s, Japan, the country which Barthes subsequently summed up as an "Empire of Signs," was seen as devoid of a center, from fragmentary bits of food, mechanical pachinko games, nameless streets, and spiritually empty train stations, to the packaging of a gift, the cursiveness of a calligraphy painting, the theatrics of *bunraku*, and the brevity of *haiku*-writing. Barthes was critical of image-laden Japan. In reality, he had encountered a different environmental system of aesthetics and semiotics while living in a far-eastern land.

We have often heard this statement being made about Japan, "the Japanese are good at imitating." Derogatorily, it implies a centerless self which simply exists to absorb and metamorphose others' inventions. However, one can also argue that even though that self is centerless, its subjective presence is more than enough to denote its sense of survival and existential source. Treading along Barthes's same mode of thought on Japan, I recall a mainland Chinese student once remarked to me that "the quantity and the taste of Japanese food do not make up for the initial aesthetic appeal." By this she meant that the fragmentary aesthetic presentations of nicely arranged dishes and their accompanying tableware were merely exterior, but in realistic and quantitative terms, it did not fulfill her gastronomic wants satisfactorily.

Historically, it was common to place bits of food in compartmentalized lacquerware and rustic ceramic ware. This Japanese etiquette is in fact influenced by a Zen or Chan aristocratic approach to food consumption and presentation which stresses austerity, blandness, and a certain sense of quiet contemplation and self-containment when having a daily meal. In the Japanese context, somehow the nobility's sense of decorum and dining etiquette are filtered into the rest of society whereby the aesthetic and spiritual aspects of dining are emphasized in addition to the basic needs to satisfy hunger.

Then, on another occasion, in comparing food culture of both countries, a Japanese friend said that she preferred the straightforward presentation of a Chinese meal; by that she meant the substantial portions of food served and the open collective way of dining at a round table. In other words, she was critical of the Japanese fragmentary and cel-like way of dining in contrast to the practical fullness of a Chinese meal experience. In my opinion, the differences in food presentation and ways of dining between the two cultures lie in the dimension of cultural practices. Japan's deft selection of cultural imports from China affects its distinctive native approach to everyday living, and the country's subsequent eventful encounters with the West is just as important.

This chapter further studies anime in the midst of the so-called "hybrid culture" and its "pure culture" matrix environment. It investigates and hypothesizes the productive spirit of anime as a whole in relation to the underlying native philosophical inclinations and cultural thought. My discussion aims to put forward the viewpoint that the present ubiquitousness of the medium-genre is primarily founded on deep-seated dialectical discourses between a being "self" and a counterpart "other."

Shintoism and the Supernatural

It can be said that anime is one of the most contemporary crystallized ornaments of an ever-visual-growing Japan. Upon close examination, its motley of images and narratives, detailed expressions and momentary pauses, transformations of time and space, childlike sounds and voices, and added energy and movements, speak of another world of fantasy and a rather untold living world. While Walt Disney, the late founder of the commercial animation empire in America, relied on "a European inheritance" for literary inspiration and graphic representations (Allan, 1999), in the Japanese context the impetus originates from Shintoism, an indigenous folk system of beliefs, customs, and reactionary responses to an implemented social mode of thought and practices.

With reference to the Japanese title of George Sansom's well-known work on Japanese cultural history, *Nihon: sono bunka no ayumi* (1931), the progressive "footsteps" of Japanese cultural tradition cannot be said to be a monolithic development, because each consecutive footstep carries with it native antecedents despite the external embellishment of a rationalistic and orderly appearance. As stated in Chapter 1, the "drive" to be different or the inability to "mask" the genesis self completely, stems from the presence of a reflective "other" which hosts antithetical qualities. To begin with, Confucianism principally concerns the human world, the affairs of the human realm, in particular the various kinds of relationships among humans. Not that the sage Confucius disregards the supernatural world completely but, first and foremost, he places "man" at the center of the universe, responsible for earthly events and the moral good. He teaches that the cultivated man, *junzhi*, should act according to the virtues of good behavior, for example, in his relationship to the emperor, to his parents, siblings, colleagues, friends, and so on. In *The Analects of Confucius* (Soothill, 1968: 353), it is stated that "[t]he Master would not discuss prodigies, prowess, lawlessness, or the supernatural." In other words, what matters most are earthly rational affairs. Those pertaining to heroic feats, the extraordinary, and the supernatural are insignificant and should not be regarded with gravity and concern in comparison to the civilized world of humankind.

Hence, in reality, the core of Confucianism runs antithetical to Shintoism. Yet, it was the very means by which the Japanese court in the fifth century AD strove to build a ruling code and established a viable government. Official adoptions of the Chinese calendar, writing, music, medicine, architecture, and the like, were implemented. However, *shintō*, or the way of the gods, ranks *kami* (gods/spirits) as upper beings who have the power to invoke respect and fear. They include all aspects of nature and can be a tidal wave, a cave, a tree, a crow, a waterfall and even a human being that has awesome qualities. Animistic it may seem, it is not unlike past Chinese folk beliefs in which reverence was paid to a certain spirit of a knife or that of a broom when one uses it, or to a butterfly gracing one's home. Such practice is similar to those of many other ethnic groups, which had harbored such animistic notions and ways of thinking in the earlier ages. However, in Japan, *shintō* had long been incorporated in the cultural polity of the nation-state and reached its zenith during the Second World War. It was not a distant past; it was only a few decades ago. During the Meiji period (1868–1912), in face of urgent nation-building purposes, *shintō* became more coalesced and instituted at the official level; the selfless duty to the emperor at that time was akin to that to the Sun Goddess who designated the emperor as a direct descendent. The emperor in turn presided over his subjects. The gradual stages of national institutionalization and the continuous and spontaneous habitual beliefs practiced at the folk level helped to maintain the mythical dimension of the supernatural. Furthermore, geography assists in augmenting such animistic thinking. The elongated island-country strides the crossroads of colliding volcanic planes and it stretches from the subtropics in the south to the temperate region in the north. In effect, flat monotonous land is scarce while mountains and rivers are abundant; and so are caves, rapid waterfalls, forests and mineral-rich hot springs.

In short, Japan is surrounded by nature and periodically experiences its wrath and beauty. Naturally, mythical narratives run abound even to the extent of adapting fables and legends from continental China to suit the native comprehension and experience.

As introduced in Chapter 1, the *Kojiki* contains not only accounts of deities, semi-gods, human beings and their legend-making stories, but also stories of love and passion entangled in the cyclic struggle of right and wrong. There was also an account of the Sun Goddess who went into seclusion due to the playful offense of her brother, Susa-no-wo. As darkness prevailed upon earth, the deities gathered to persuade and coax the Sun Goddess out of the rock cave. Finally, a mimic indecent dance did the trick and lured the curious Sun-Goddess out of the cave. Dutch historian, Johan Huizanga (1970: 218) laments the lack of the play factor in nineteenth-century Europe and assesses that play is an "integral part of culture as such" and that it "lies at the heart of all ritual and religion." Indeed, in all seasons and at different locations in present-day Japan, *matsuri*, or festival, is often held to appease a *kami*; offerings of food, objects, music, and dancing are part of the carnivalistic ritual. In parts of Southeast Asia, festive occasions are still being organized in accordance with folk beliefs, but whether such dynamic forms of childlike leisure, rapture movement, thrill, mirth, freedom, and fantasy (in reference to Huizanga's explanation of the play concept) do carry forward and manifest into productive national cultures through the medium of animation (as in the case of Japan), poses a vital inquiry. I will return to this discussion in Chapters 6 and 7.

Expressing and Producing the Self

Central to Shintoism are the pristine virtues of creativity (vitality) and fertility. *Shintō* scholar Muraoka Tsunetsugu identifies the creative *musubi kami* with "the power of growth and reproduction" (1964: 55) and tells us that the pre-Confucius period in Japan was an age of "naturalism and non-interference." The dichotomy of good and evil, and right or wrong, is not a cardinal point of activity. In actuality, it can be said that the processes of good and evil interflow "flexibly." Citing and studying the main works of three leading *shintō* thinkers including Kamo Mabuchi (1697–1769), Motoori Norinaga (1730–1801), and Hirata Atsutane (1776–1843), Muraoka explains that the *shintō* world is one in which morality is deemed to be irrelevant and even non-existent. What matters are natural laws and forces where characteristics such as "innocence, beauty, and strength are innate to that antiquated age" (1964: 60).

Muraoka's work on Shintoism spans several decades (from the 1900s to the 1940s). Throughout that period, his work might have served the imperialists and easily came under the academic umbrella of *kokugaku*, or national learning.

Interpreting Shintoism in view of the supernatural world, supernatural elements are so much a part of anime (a late twentieth-century Japanese medium-genre), one must draw the conclusion that while Shintoist rituals are being practiced daily by the Japanese (for example, visiting the shrines, participating in *matsuri* and purification matters such as taking hot baths), a large portion of Shintoist thought is in fact being marginalized to the psychological recesses of the populace. Hence, that mind frame of supernaturalism has sought a medium to survive and thrive, and it has found one that aptly gratifies its naturalistic instincts and tendencies, at least in a silhouette form.

Metamorphically, the *shintō* body of nature worship, with the chief characteristics of "creativity" and "fertility" rooted at its religious base, is best manifested by the endless production of anime and animated images in Japan, even to the magnitude of enlisting offshore cheap labor to help the productive process (see Chapter 7). On a brighter note, it can be said that the country's diminishing birth rate is offset by the prolific and generative anime realm in which the number of lively figures and characters is growing and has popularly been remembered and revived. For example, Tezuka Osamu's *Tetsuwan Atomu* (*Astro Boy*) television series, which debuted in 1963, has in recent years been animated again and rescreened in full color on national television, and *Hello Kitty* makeshift shrines are occasionally erected in department stores for shoppers to say a prayer or two in the hustle and bustle of material living and in memory of the sweet innocent world of its childlike characters.[1] For good or for worse, the flighty moment-oriented medium of animation is an expanding freedom oasis in which the Japanese may take refuge, however airy-fairy or immaterial it may seem.

The "frames" of Shintoism are said to have derived basically from two prescriptive orders. One is "visible and open" *kenro*, and the other is "concealed and mysterious" *yūmei* (Muraoka, 1964: 175).[2] Each is governed by a *kami*. Symbolically, the hidden order constitutes what forms a larger part of anime. After all, anime is best viewed in a dark room manifested by frame-by-frame viewing, which communicates to the deep psychological wants of the viewer. This is not to say that anime, or animation as a whole, is a "dark" form of communication tool which the Japanese regularly employ. Rather, the country exalts at its manifestative abilities including the bright, the colorful, and the liveliness of an illustrative world. In other words, it is a marginal space world (*senkai*), a literally "in-between living frame" in which one can relax and reside. It is similar to an antiquated *shintō* condition in which emotions and sentiments such as *kanji, shinjō,* and *jōmi* matter. It is a condition in which "there is not even writing" and the mind is not directed by the call of rationality; it is simply left "smoothly flowing with no sharp edges, and directed by nature" (Muraoka, 1964: 122). After Japan had lost in the Second World War, and the Anpo protests[3] and advocation of socialist ideals from the late 1950s to the early 1970s failed, this "imaginative space frame" became a refugee cavern in which fantasy, memories, and lost hopes could be individually and collectively deposited, re-invented and contemplated.

This refugee cavern may sound like Plato's "underground cave" in which the residents regarded the shadows as the reality (Plato, 1941: 222–230). On the contrary, the "imaginative space frame" which I theorize above is essentially buoyant and active. Plato's cave of residents referred to prisoners who moved in one direction, but the cavernous space of anime is inflated with performance energies and one-track thinking is virtually non-existent. Both the creators and the audiences are instinctively aware of the reflective shadows; in fact, the negative meanings of the word "illusion" bear little or no significance in the Japanese cognitive world of anime shadows. The framing of an anime shadow or projection marks the spatial separateness of the "other." This is a differential ground where the goal of creation and imagination is not to be curtailed. The rule is "not to spoil" the voluntary activity (not unlike the idea of Huizanga's play concept). This is why in the cosmic space of anime, even the subjects of sex, pornography, and violence are embraced intensely and vividly without exception or strict censorship, literally far more *momentarily*[4] and voluminously produced than the static erotic prints of *ukiyoe* or the Chinese-origin wood-block erotic print, *shunga*.[5]

Emphasizing the emotionality and sentimentality of Shintoism, Motoori identifies *mono no aware* as an aesthetic value and singles out the eleventh-century novel, *The Tale of Genji* as a principal literary work that embodies this indigenous form of Japanese aesthetics. *Aware* carries sentiments of sadness, sorrow, and pitifulness. *Mono* refers to an object. In brief, *mono no aware* means the "pathos of existence." It could refer to a wilting flower, the passing of a season, the loss of a loved one, or simply feeling sensibly the existential struggle of the other party. Time and again, Motoori is critical of the "Confucius canons of emotional restraint" (Tsunoda, 1958: 535). The concept of *mono no aware* can also be regarded as a Buddhist spiritual value, as Buddhism also stresses compassion and sympathy for the sufferings of others. In fact, the theme of suffering *dukkha* was the chief concern of Prince Siddhartha in his search for the spiritual liberation path.[6] The Buddhist doctrine of compassion for all beings is not solely for the human realm; all creatures whether living, moving, still, seen, unseen, existing, and coming into being, are all included in the Dharma world. In Buddhist sutras, one often encounters the phrase, "in everything, there will be kindness," especially when one pertains to the great vows to help deliver all beings from sufferings. The difference is that *mono mo aware* tends to project an atmosphere of resignation and empathy, which it is, at best, an aesthetic experience. In Buddhism, there is a pro-active desire and conviction to relieve the sufferings of others rather than merely dwelling on sympathetic sentiments or empathizing with the sufferings of others.

In the later half of the Ming dynasty (1368–1644) in China, there existed a liberal thinker, Li Zhi (1527–1602), who opposed the controlling mindset of

Confucianism and its practices of decorum, restraint, conformity, and hierarchy. To him, dealing with the daily life of the common folk was a more realistic approach. For example, matters concerning health, trading and commerce, working in the fields, and other related agricultural activities should be seriously considered. His aesthetic perspective centered on the value of *tongxin,* meaning "child's heart", or the purity and naturalness of a child's heart. In his view, each individual has a different temperament, upbringing, and way of living. Li Zhi believed that too much rote learning of Confucian teachings would lead to the formation of a *jia ren,* meaning "false human being," as a person tends to lose the "child's heart" of natural and spontaneous expression. For example, when a human being becomes a "false human being", he or she may not speak the truth, things that he or she does may not be truthful including his or her commitment to writing the truth. Li's radical and rebellious worldviews were obviously rejected by the feudalistic establishment and he died in prison (Ye, 1985: 336–356).

It is not known whether Motoori was acquainted with such anti-Confucius writings from China because Li Zhi's work was not exceptional. There were other late Ming and early Qing scholars who were critical of the authoritarian, bureaucratic, and increasingly corrupt culture that permeated throughout the Chinese society at the time. During the Edo period, epic novels such as *Water Margin* that features outlaws and their heroic adventures, *Golden Lotus* that depicts everyday lives of women and their families (including pornographic episodes), and such collections of supernatural tales as *Strange Tales from a Chinese Studio*, were readily translated and introduced into the literary world of urban Japan. Similarly, in Korea, apart from the above-mentioned anti-Confucius writings, other literary works from China were introduced. Through the tributary missions to Beijing, Chinese translated books on Western learning and Christianity were brought back to Korea and also from contacts with the Jesuit missionaries who were living in Beijing.[7] During the mid-fifteenth century, there was an intellectual movement known as "Practical Learning" in Korea. According to Li (2003), Korean intellectuals were exposed to Chinese literature that advocated anti-Confucian doctrines. While the ad hoc appearance of anti-Confucius works (as represented by the intellectual writings and literary works mentioned above) did not lead to any intellectual practical movement in China, it took an independent development in Korea. From the promotion of the spoken Korean language to the more widespread usage of *han'gŭl* (Korean alphabets), or from the recuperation of Korean native poetry and stories with the emphasis on human wants and desires (for example, sexuality, emotion, and material satisfaction) to the growing interest in innovative learning and science, they were all in a collective movement against the rationalistic and antiquated constraints of Confucianism (Fairbank et al., 1989: 319–321). Thus, the Japanese reactionary distaste for an imported ideology was not an exclusive and prodigal pre-occupation. As we will see later, the geographical positioning and the oncoming tides of history eventually propelled Japan to take a much farther course than its continental neighbors, especially in the field of aesthetic expansion and political prominence at the global level.

Image-Building and Living the Present

Iwamoto Kenji's work on Japan's pre-filmic era (*Gentō no seiki*, 2002) documentarily traces the country's sense of visual consciousness during the late Edo period. As mentioned in Chapter 2, the Japanese began to design and manufacture its own form of magic lantern when this Western import proved to be increasingly popular. According to Iwamoto, by the early Meiji period, magic lanterns were categorized into *utsushi-e* and *gentō*. *Utsushi-e* was regarded as a performance and entertainment art while *gentō* played a more specific role in education (knowledge) and entertainment. The *gentō* later became an important tool of national education and knowledge enrichment for the populace, especially with the recognized support of the *Monbushō*, Ministry of Education (2002: 126). From public health education, population control, civil consciousness education, reports on world events, information about renowned bureaucrats and military heroes including past historical figures, the latest information on Western knowledge, and even information about the revision of the national language pertaining to new terminology and grammar to acquire, *gentō* was much valued as a *bunmei kaikan* instrument.

Furthermore, this late nineteeth-century medium was not solely a public domain tool because it was also a *minkan no yūgu* or a *katei no yūgu*, meaning people's or family leisure tool (2002: 146). It demonstrated the consciousness of a new living age where active production and participation was also a consuming affair. When a mass communication event was called for, apart from the occasional use of candles, more expensive fuel materials like petroleum, gas, and electricity were readily utilized and they were generously sponsored by the government in order to achieve the best visual and communicative effects. This was a phenomenon hardly matched by other Asian countries at that time. To better understand the Japanese experience in "receiving" the realism of the new age, one has to question how much the practice of image-building played in the modernization of Japan.

As it has been partly covered in the preceding chapters, a subjective consciousness had always been present as represented by the artistic expressions and literary forms produced in the pre-modern times. Later, the consolidation of a samurai culture and the incessant military maneuvers it generated had driven the populace to the spiritual comfort and enlightenment of Buddhist teachings. It was particularly because of the religion's emphasis on compassion and the impermanence of life. Although not all members of the populace became ardent Buddhists eventually, nor did all members understand the deeper spiritual and philosophical aspects of Buddhism, the swiftness with which the Japanese rose to cope with the stark reality of a fast-changing era during the nineteenth century seemed to have a touch of Buddhist pragmatism. Renunciation of a painful era could not have driven so many devotees to take up a monastic life. Neither could negation of current developments and responsibilities drive so many people to take drugs, such as opium-smoking, as could be seen in the case of millions of Chinese during that time. What prevailed was the adoption of a Buddhist practice of literally *living the present* in the hope that a promising future was already in the making if one was living in a most meaningful and healthy way. It certainly provided a more empirical and counteractive way of coping with a new age. Thus, the *framing of oneself* in observing the images of others was a powerful act of differentiation and embellishment especially when an anchoring position had been established, and further identity development could be constructed and improved.

From a broader perspective, the larger image-building process of Japan was not a one-sided affair. Quilted within was the West's desire to preserve a Japan that was "still unaltered by Western influence" (Banta, 1988: 15). From the aficionado collection of *ukiyo-e* prints (the often exotic photographic shots of Japan), the call for the preservation of traditional arts and crafts, to the lauding of the uniqueness of Japanese *haiku* poetry, Japan was urged to cling to its Eastern roots in face of the overriding modern condition. Scholars such as Karatani Kojin and Shirane Haruo[8] have discerned this Western desire to recuperate "things Japanese" as a complicity of romanticist and Orientalist gestures in view of a self-aware over-advancing West and its self-reflective nostalgia for a fast disappearing pastoral and unindustrialized Europe. At home, this "East meets West" image-building process was further complicated by the lack of success in convincing the established political world order of the rise of a newly industrialized nation and its pursuit for recognition and frontal placement at the global arena.[9]

Image-building in the Japanese context was not just producing visual images per se. Real-life material structures that were engineered and majestically built, such as steel bridges, street lamps, shipyards, Victorian-inspired train stations, and other constructions, were on the menu. More persuasive and critical were publications of developing trends of thought in acknowledgement of its newly found identity and self-status. Nishida Kitarō's (1870–1945) philosophical works were ranked among the leading ones. Up to this point, in examining the subject of anime, I have put up a concourse of overlapping concentric ideas, concepts, and events in comprehending the background of its widespread existence in the Japanese environment. Image-wise, anime belongs indisputably to the visual category. However, in the world of Japanese cultural thought, a tendency toward aesthetic concepts and intentions has always prevailed. It is also precisely its aesthetic appearance and bent that make scholars, both local and foreign, question its philosophical foundations. What was in question again was the "imported, imitated" aspect (Blocker and Starling, 2001: 1); ranging from ancient to modern times, the body of philosophical writings was regarded as mere variations and re-interpretations. Blocker and Starling (2001: 18) argue that despite the borrowing of Indian, Chinese, and Western thought in Japanese philosophy, "how Japanese philosophers interpreted, criticized, modified, developed, and used imported ideas and methods" is itself a challenge worth studying, as it reverts back to the basic traditions of reasoning and re-reasoning, debates and starting afresh. My point is that the Japanese incessant drive toward self-image-building was all-rounded and peculiar and, even in the field of modern philosophical writing that arose since the Meiji period, we can see a deliberate "performance stance" in applying a Western mode of reasoning in presenting essentially Eastern ideas and concepts.

During the Meiji period, a number of American and European scholars were invited to take up prestigious teaching positions at the Tokyo Imperial University, and many Japanese scholars on their own accord traveled afar to the West in order to acquire knowledge of Western thought and sciences. Nishida Kitarō was one of the intellectuals who became well-known during that era. Although he did not travel abroad, he studied under Western professors at Tokyo Imperial University and even taught German after he graduated (Piovesana, 1963: 86). His series of writings, *A Study of the Good* (1911), *Art and Morality* (1923), and essays like *The Intelligible World* and *Unity of Opposites* (1943),[10] gave testimony to the country's long-laboring project to speak and to present to the Western world, using the West's required standard of logical reason and philosophy. Citing the works of Greek thinkers (pre-Socrates and after), mystical Christian thinkers, and later German philosophers, and with occasional reference to Buddhist and Confucian writings, Nishida aimed to *show* the reading world that Eastern thought was not as irrational and impenetrable as it seemed, the core of its depth was essentially universal, as methodically demonstrated by his exposition and reference to a trail of Western thinkers.

Still his roundabout methodical way of writings was meditative and repetitive. The gist of his rhetoric was largely Buddhist-influenced and was particularly of the Mahayana kind in which an active involvement in the *samsara*[11] world was called for, rather than a Hinayana approach which practiced withdrawal from society and individualistic self-attainment of enlightenment. Religion scholar Bernard Faure (1995: 263) warned that the misunderstanding of Zen/Chan Buddhist teachings might have been resulted from the philosophical writings of Nishida and other related studies representative of the Kyoto School which he founded. He was critical of the Buddhist concepts that were selectively employed and interpreted to represent to the West that the Eastern traditions were reducibly rationalistic, and alarmingly, to show that the "syncretism" of East and West thinking was achievable through a Japanese endeavor. What is telling is that Nishida's meditative writings speak reflectively of the nation's state of development and political and cultural thinking at that time. The fact that his works proved to be popular also shows that his fellowmen were in sync with his line of exposition.

Through the selective adoption and adjustment of certain Buddhist concepts, Nishida further augmented the "philosophy" of the age which, in my view, is "to live in momentum with reality." Phrases found in his writings include:

> ... reality is moving and is a continuation of events which do not stand still even for a second ... (1960:57)

> We know reality through moving ... (1973: 206)

> The world of reality is a world where things are acting on things ... (1958: 163)

> Reality is that in which we behave acting-reflecting ... (1958: 170)

> We act through seeing, and we see through acting ... (1958: 174)

> In order to survive, the subject must, again and again, begin a new life ... (1958: 185)

> We form the world by acts of expression ... (1958: 197)

> Life is an infinite moving by itself. There are always infinite directions, and infinite possibilities of [imaginary] illusion ... (1958: 208)

All those phrases suggested the animated inclinations of the existential self. He used the term "historical world" in his writings to denote the environment in which the historicity of the environment makes the self as much as the self acts on the environment. Definitively, he used the key term, *poiesis*.

Nishida demonstrated his knowledge of Western philosophy by using discursive writing. This indicates his attempt to understand Western methodological thought. The free adoption of European terms further demonstrates his willingness to assimilate Western classic philosophical terminology into his developmental blend of Japanese philosophy. The Greek term, *poiesis,* is one of them. Written in *katakana, poieshisu,* according to Nishida, does not exist in the animal world because the animal world lacks this creative power of making. Man, however, is not only biologically bound to this world but also possesses, historically, this "action-intuition" (*kōiteki chokkanteki*) to act and to create. The word *kōiteki* also means action or behavior in which a sense of thought and intention is included.[12] What Nishida meant to say is that as we are "bodies" living in the historical world, we are constantly conflicted with the tasks to live on, to produce, and to create, even to the extent of facing contradictions that are inevitable. Viewed from a practical Buddhist perspective, Nishida's thought is *un-Buddhistic* at its core. This is so as the Dharma world, which is the religious world order of Buddhism, is filled with compassion, charity, and equanimity. Within this context, one is encouraged to take a moderate middle-path; it is far from a world where the only prescription is to partake actively in its intense volition.

Nishida writes in his *A Study of Good* (1960: 85),

> As I have said before, since spirit is the unifying function of reality
> and since great spirit is the becoming one with nature, when we
> construct a self with a small self, pain is great, but as the self enlarges
> and becomes one with objective nature, we become happy.

What is the "enlarged self" that Nishida is referring to? Is he invoking an emerging political collective self that his countrymen must somehow be ingested into its construction? This analysis is not intended to vilify or criticize unreasonably Nishida's philosophical works but, rather, aims to highlight the thinking of his works, particularly their dialectical relationship with the West, and, specifically, the "historicity" of his own creative philosophy within the spatial–temporal frame of an expansionistic Japan. Nationally, his contributions did not go unnoticed by the government — he was awarded the Cultural Medal of Honor in 1940.

In this regard, what emerged in Nishida's writings and in their political-spiritual dimension was a tilted tinge of Shintoist thinking where conforming to the will of the times or an imperialistic *kamisama*, even to the extent of committing heinous heroic crimes on a massive scale, was deemed dynamically correct and selfless.[13] Thus, despite Nishida's being often lauded as the first leading Japanese philosopher "spanning the East and West" (Piovesana, 1963: 85), one could not overlook the imperialistic political environment within which his philosophical ideas surfaced and should be cautious of his contributions. However, the endeavor to persuade and reason with the West is best exemplified by his maiden concept of "pure experience" in which he philosophized as a unity of the subject and object where both recognized each other as one of the other and "to consider these as mutually independent realities is nothing more than an arbitrary assertion" (1960: 33). He also stated that

> Only when subject and object are mutually submerged, the thing and
> the self are mutually forgotten, and one arrives at a state wherein
> there is only the activity of a single reality in heaven and earth, does
> one first attain to the consummation of good behavior. (1960:145)

Who or what was the "subject" and "object" that Nishida was referring to? Why did this macroscopic attempt to find "similarities" in Western thinking that correlated with the Eastern side appear? Who were his target readerships? Could he be making an understatement in his work so as to plead and convince the West that just as the West had experienced the "Age of Enlightenment" at a much earlier time, the East was capable of attaining that experience too? Both the so-called divided and irreconcilable entities were essentially one and the same, and the sphere of subjectivity need not be wholly static or permanently geographical, if the Western notion of subject-object dichotomy was helpful at all in achieving universal good and world peace. Implicated within this grand geo-political narrative posited an

Eastern country which had come of age and maturity deserving recognition and concessions and was expressive of its desire to reconcile opposing cultures and frames of perspectives.

It may seem that I have diverged by venturing into the murky waters of politics, history, and philosophy, and thus opened a Pandora's box of problematic issues and discourses. However, the study of anime has to be examined from a cluster of interdisciplinary resources and with a conviction to unmask the many layers of frames that are buried or concealed. This chapter tries in part to discern the various cultural placements of Japanese indigenous thought and to bring to light the interlocking and overlaying of imported thought and invented local thinking that occurred at certain junctures of history. The power and appeal of anime in present-day Japan is supported by an indigenous pro-aesthetic cultural constitution. In short, the animating language continues to express the ebb and flow of hidden wants and desires and the ongoing unfulfilled aspects of corporate self-building and personal self-making in Japan.

Animation Studies scholar Alan Cholodenko (1991: 15), in examining the horizon of definitions given by the Webster Dictionary on the subject of animation and its related terms, narrows two definitive ways of "thinking about animation in play." One is

> ... endowing with *life* (be the enlivening agency, substance and that
> which is enlived material or immaterial)

and another is

> ... endowing with *movement* (be the pulsion and what is moved or
> altered in its movement material or immaterial).

In other words, animation in all cases predicates potentiality, materiality and actuality, and that in theorizing the medium, it cannot be divorced from investigating the areas of "being and becoming, time, space, motion and change ..." (1991: 15). Insomuch as post-Second World War anime is concerned, the medium-genre also carries with it, the aforementioned Meiji grand narrative, unfinished and disenfranchised. Given the nature of the medium-genre, energies are repetitively harnessed to generate new images, some self-critical and internally monologic, while others continue to consciously or subconsciously cross-entice geo-politically in the hope to be embraced by the other. Indeed, the "Empire of Signs" cannot cease to reproduce and to reconstruct images. The following chapter will focus on the industrial development of Japanese animation in the twentieth century and Japan's collaboration with other parties to become the "Disney of Asia."

Figure 1   Toei Animation Phils., Inc., a 100-percent subsidiary of Toei Animation Co. Ltd., Japan. Reprinted by permission from Toei Animation Co.

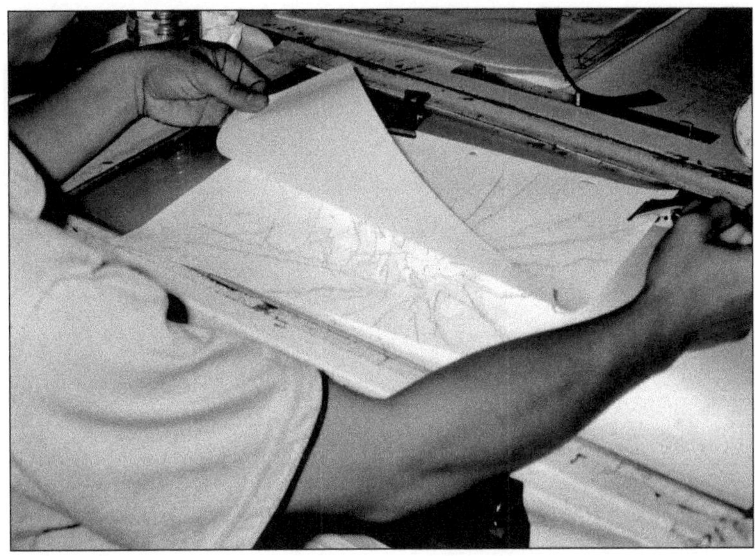

Figure 2   Frame-by-frame hand-drawing by a Filipino animator. Reprinted by permission from Toei Animation Co.

Figure 3   Digital line drawing by a Filipino animator. Reprinted by permission from Toei Animation Co.

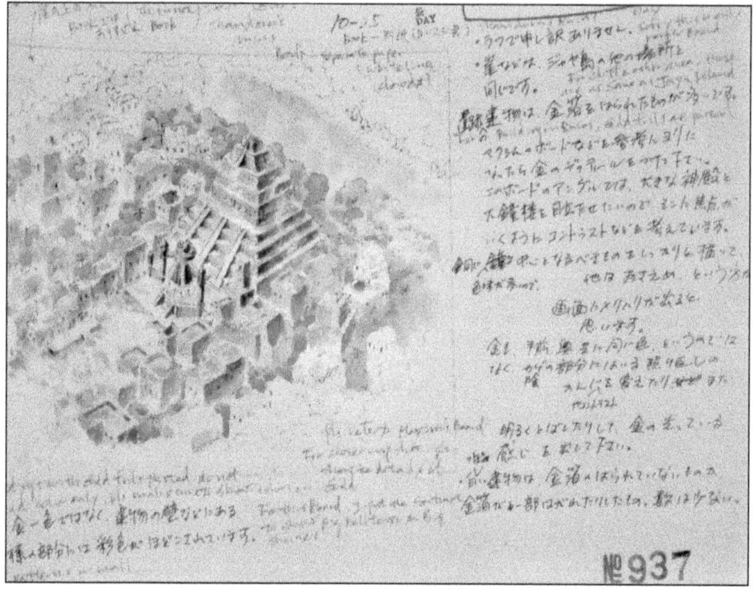

Figure 4   Instructions in both Japanese and English for overseas sub-contractual animation staff to follow. Reprinted by permission from Toei Animation Co.

Figure 5   A multi-plane camera at work. Reprinted by permission from Toei Animation Co.

Figure 6   *Taro, the Dragon Boy* (1979). Reprinted by permission from Toei Animation Co.

Figure 7   *White Snake Tale* (1958). Reprinted by permission from Toei Animation Co.

Figure 8   *Made in Japan* (1972), directed by Kinoshita Renzo. Reprinted by permission from Studio Lotus.

Figure 9   A younger Miyazaki Hayao (second from left), participating in a *matsuri*. Courtesy of Oda Katsuya.

Figure 10   Takahata Isao at the 10th JSAS Annual Conference 2008 in Japan. Photograph by Tze-yue G. Hu.

Figure 11   Pioneer Japanese animation historian, Watanabe Yasushi. Photograph by Tze-yue G. Hu.

Figure 12   Retired Toei animators, Oda Katsuya (left) and Kotabe Yōichi at an exhibition of Kotabe's *Heidi: Girl of the Alps* (1974) drawings. Photograph by Tze-yue G. Hu.

Figure 13   An animated storyboard in *Prokino,* May Issue, 1932.

Figure 14

One of the many promotional pamphlets distributed in Japan about the Chinese animated film, *Princess Iron Fan* (1941). Courtesy of Watanabe Yasushi.

Figure 15

Top: *It Was Night Before Christmas* (1974); middle: *The First Easter Rabbit* (1975); bottom: *Frosty's Winter Wonderland* (1976). Courtesy of Hara Toru.

Figure 16   A Meiji postcard dated 1911 juxtaposing a photo print of Mount Fuji and *emakimono*'s traditional line-drawn characters. Author's collection.

Figure 17   A Taishō postcard illustrating Tokyo on fire after the 1923 earthquake; see the realistic portrayal. Author's collection.

Figure 18

An illustration of a *nō* figure from an undated early twentieth-century postcard. Author's collection.

Figure 19

An undated early twentieth-century postcard featuring a woodblock print image (*ukiyo-e*) by Kitagawa Utamaro (1753–1806), who is known for his illustrations of Edo's women. Author's collection.

Figure 20

An undated early twentieth-century postcard featuring a color print image of a young girl with big eyes. Notice the *shiroi ten*, "sparkle" of her eyes. The artist was Nakahara Junichi (1913–88), who is known for his illustrations of fashionable young girls (*shōjo*). His manga-like drawings of female faces preceded postwar Japanese *shōjo* manga in which female and male characters often have big starry eyes. Author's collection.

Figure 21   An animated feature film made in Hong Kong, *A Chinese Ghost Story* (1997). Reprinted by permission from Film Workshop Co. Ltd.

Figure 22   An assortment of magazines in Taiwan promoting Japanese manga and anime. Photograph by Tze-yue G. Hu.

Figure 23   At the Comic Market event in the summer of 1999, Tokyo; see the human traffic. Photograph by Tze-yue G. Hu.

Figure 24

At the Comic Market event in the summer of 1999, Tokyo; an amateur manga artist or a manga-anime fan dressing up as a specific story character. Such dramatic dressing is called *cosplay* ("costume play"). Photograph by Tze-yue G. Hu.

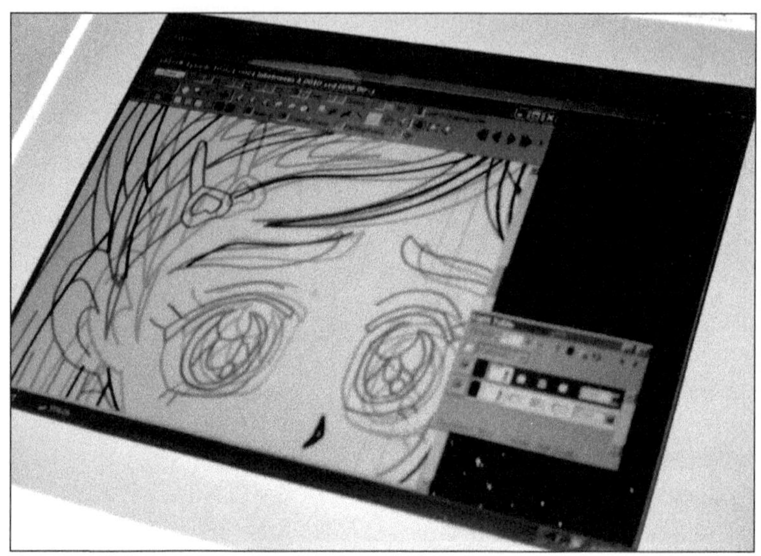

Figure 25   A work-in-progress anime character; see the focus on the big eyes. Photograph by Tze-yue G. Hu.

Figure 26   An illustration of *Heidi: Girl of the Alps* (1974) by Kotabe Yōichi. Author's collection.

 4

Development of Japanese Animation up to the End of the Second World War

> The various countries of the world are perhaps aware that our country is proud of her old civilization of two thousand six hundred years and is at the same time showing brilliantly swift progress in modern civilization, but it is a matter for regret that, due to the peculiar character of our language, customs, etc., the opportunities of having them made accurately known in foreign countries are lacking.
>
> With regard to the motion pictures of Japan, too, notwithstanding they can be compared with those of other countries so far as skill and efficiency of production are concerned, it is exceedingly regrettable that for the same reason the opportunities of having them presented and enjoyed in foreign countries are lacking. However, at the present time, the trend of sending them abroad has at last developed, and we believe that at no distant date in the future they will become a topic in the world market.
>
> Kokusai Eiga Kyōkai
(International Cinema Association of Japan, 1937)[1]

It really did not take long for this country in the Far East to find its film image, which was "a topic in the world market." While the 1937 Year Book does not place all emphasis on the medium of animation (others that were categorically discussed in detail include the fictional live-action films, documentaries, and news-report films), which was only classified as "cartoon" under the "Documentary Film" category, it shows that the medium had not been neglected at the time when the country tried to develop its motion picture industry. Today, global commercial animation producers, well-known independent animation directors, "wannabe" animation investors, and in-progress nationalistic industry builders such as those in China, Taiwan, and South Korea, may be envious and are inspired by the international awards upon which anime has been bestowed in recent years.[2] It is true that the success of the Japanese story cannot be measured merely by the state's initial financial support and sustainment. The private sector and the populace at large play equally significant roles in nurturing the growth of the medium as a whole. This chapter discusses and charts the development and the rise of Japanese animation in the twentieth century, and argues that the "exhibiting and performing" subject persevered despite wartime difficulties and the lack of initial technical know-how.

Beginnings of Japanese Animation

Early years and continuous growth

G. Bendazzi notes in his monumental book, *Cartoons: One Hundred Years of Cinema Animation*, that soon after the introduction of American cartoons on Japanese cinema screens, "around 1910, some local artists wanted to try their own skills as animators" (1994: 103). Taiwanese filmmaker and scholar Fan Jian-you (1997: 115) also points out that, besides the American cartoons, it was France's first animation film *Fantasmagorie* (1908) by Émile Cohl, with its emphasis on graphical changes, that made the Japanese realize the potential of "animating pictures on screen," or *dōga*, written in *kanji*. However, Yamaguchi and Watanabe (1977) and Tsugata (2004) are of the view that, from a Japanese perspective, the new medium is merely an old art form and that the Japanese are already familiar with it. The medium is simply a form of "lines" (*sen*) and "pictures" (*e*) that move and in the past it had already been incorporated into *utsushi-e* and other native techniques of art drawing. Film Studies scholar Sano Akiko (2006: 100) writes that during that period the Japanese were exposed to different kinds of European animation, for example, the works of Oskar Fischinger, Lotte Reiniger, and Ladislas Starewich. As a result, animation was also addressed as *zenei eiga* (avant garde film), *kyoiku eiga* (education film), *ongaku eiga* (music film), and *bunka eiga* (culture film).

The founding pioneers of Japanese animation were Shimokawa Oūten (1886–1970), Kōuchi Junichi (1892–1973), and Kitayama Seitarō (1888–1945). Each personally completed his first animated film in 1917. Shimokawa was a satirist cartoonist, Kouchi was a political cartoonist, and Kitayama was an artist trained in the Western tradition. Although coincidentally they completed their first animation films around the same time, each experimented and created on his own, working according to his own artistic instincts. The contributions of the trio, including those of their future apprentices and disciples, went on to propel the development of Japanese animation. For example, Kitayama managed to persuade Nikkatsu Film Company (one of the earliest film companies in Japan, founded at the turn of the twentieth century) to set up an animation film department, and he also opened his own studio later and worked with a variety of techniques. Among Kōuchi's apprentices was Ofuji Noburo (1900–61) who pioneered the use of special translucent Japanese paper and animating cut figurines on the screen. Ofuji's animated films were popular in Europe in the late 1920s (Bendazzi, 1994: 104) and attracted the attention of cinema-goers there. Shimokawa, because of his cartoonist background, was often commissioned to produce animation for various film companies, although it is not known clearly whether the apprentices who had worked with him made significant contributions to Japanese animation later. Kitayama was the youngest among the three; yet, his enthusiasm for the medium was tremendous. Apart from publishing a book, *How to Make Animated Films,* in 1930, his studio worked on all kinds of animation projects as "he produced a series of works to order for clients" (Tsugata, 2003: 24).[3] They included propaganda and science education films, commercial shorts, animated tales for children, and animated shots that were interposed onto live-action films.

One of his apprentices was Yamamoto Sanae (1898–1981), who went on to become a prolific creator of animated films. He later worked with Yabushita Taiji (1901–86), who was one of the key production members of Toei Animation Company founded in the mid-1950s. It is beyond the resources of this book to accurately draw an animation genealogy tree that shows the various master-disciple relationships and cross-joint productions that existed before the Second World War. However, it would not be implausible to say that some talented animation artists who made their debut later had worked with a master-animator before. They were either colleagues of the masters, or their junior staff members. For example, Seo Mitsuyo (1911–), director of the wartime *Momotaro* film series, was an apprentice of Masaoka Kenzō (1898–1989), who was an experienced filmmaker and self-taught animator. Masaoka had worked with several film studios, including Nikkatsu, before establishing his own animation studio during the early Shōwa period (1926–89). Another animator whose work had often received official commendation or seal of approval from the Ministry of Education was Murata Yasuji (1896–1966). Murata first acquired his animating skills from a childhood friend, Yamamoto Sanae. Tracing "Who's Who" in the Japanese pre-war animation industry might seem irrelevant and "ancient" for contemporary concerns, but it is not exaggerating to say that the existence of such a network of development relationships helps buttress the growth of Japanese animation. It became a most converging reason when the management of the later-founded Toei Animation Company sought to gather and employ the nation's best teacher-animators.[4]

Home-grown film technology and leftist cinema

Central to the development of the medium was the concurrent innovation and research on Western film technology. Although research materials related to this aspect of Japanese image-building are scarce and information-gathering is still ongoing, historical records show that the earliest Japan-made film projector (*wasei eishaki*) was manufactured in 1901–02 (*The Japanese Film Heritage: From the Non-film Collection of the National Film Center*, 2002: 131). It was said that three years earlier, in 1898, experiments were being carried out in the making of a home-made film camera (*The Japanese Film Heritage*, 2002: 62). During the 1918–19 period, with the establishment of an industrial company Takamitsu Kōjō (later renamed Takamitsu Kōgyu), Japan's film mechanical engineering began to take off. Film cameras were manufactured and they were modeled after the German-made ones. The first Japan-made film projector called the *Royal* was also launched (*The Japanese Film Heritage*, 2002: 62). Advancements in engineering design were complemented by diligent research on film material development and production. In 1924, a group of industrialists cum film development researchers approached the American Eastman Kodak Company for advice and assistance. However, they were "eminently" insulted and rebuffed by Kodak's conclusive report that "Japan was not geographically suitable" for establishing a photographic film industry, *nihon ni tekichinashi* (*Sōgyō nijūnen no arumi,* 1960: 6).[5] Between 1919 and 1922, the manufacture of dry plates was already in progress. The development and improvement was then hindered by the 1923 Kanto earthquake. As far as the celluloid industry was concerned, it was obvious that the Japanese wanted very much to master the production skills so that they could manufacture a full range of photography-related materials including print papers, chemicals, glass plates, and negative films. Photography historian Ina Nobuo (1963: 10) notes that by 1924 the state imposed heavy taxes on imported products in order to reduce the country's demand for foreign goods, which included filmic-based materials. This increased demands for homegrown celluloid products.[6]

As I have mentioned in the preceding sections, the country's media innovativeness from the Meiji period onward had been intricately supported by an indigenous web of relationships among the private enterprises, the public sector, and the demands of the populace at large. The founding of Fuji Film Company in 1934 (formerly known as Dai Nippon Ceruroido) was another achievement in Japan's modernization. It indicated the country's quest to "visually" realize itself: first, by acquiring the technological know-how; second, to utilize the knowledge to fulfill the new age's aesthetic aspirations; and lastly, to contribute and to meet the demands of other relevant industrial developments. In the field of animation, Yamaguchi and Watanabe (1977) note that by 1932 the audiences had become increasingly discontented with "just moving only" (*ukoku take*) silent films and craved for pictures that incorporated sound as well. Yamaguchi (2004: 59) reports that by the late 1920s the Japanese audiences looked for better forms of cinematic entertainment and were charmed by Disney-produced animated works that had sound effects. Until then, animation was regarded as a low-cost visual medium and was generally recognized as a one-person production effort. With the advent of sound effects, many animators began to ponder over the increased cost of production involving music composition and performance, sound recording and editing, as well as the search for sound specialists in animation filming. At that time, it was estimated that it would take three to four months to complete an animated film with full sound effects while a silent animated film required only a month. As cinema operators and animators tried to come to terms with the contemporary demands of the audiences, the continuing success and appeal of Disney-made animation in Japanese cinemas awakened the animation film producers to new possibilities of the medium. Yamaguchi (2004: 59) sees the highly-popular *Silly Symphonies* series[7] as a catalyst in influencing the future ambitions of the animators. Instead of merely producing for the local market, the Japanese animators realized that by broadening and distributing their works abroad, it would help to defray the costs of production. The *idea of export* of Japanese-made animation was thus germinated, and it was believed that domestically made animation would have market support in foreign lands; in Yamaguchi's and Watanabe's (1977: 27) description, "because they can be sold" (*uran ga tame*), it added an enterprising energy to the animators' efforts in promoting the medium.

The accelerating pace with which the photographic film industry developed also coincided with the growing power of the pro-militant government. In 1933, there was direct injection of monetary support from the government. The success of Fuji Film Company was supported by a sponsorship fund, stipulating the firm's continual research on developing film-related materials. The initial amount received in 1933 was 1.2 million yen (*Sōgyō nijūnen no arumi*, 1960: 17). The military support of film technology research was recorded in several accounts by Fuji's former key employees and others in *Nihon shashinshi e shōgen*, edited by Kamei Takeshi (1997, *gekan* "Part Two"). Through reminiscences of the participants who once worked directly on projects related to such research activities, the collection of articles reveal the extensive length and breadth of military support in nurturing the industry, and how the military government helped place great importance on film technology advancements in Japan. In particular, the articles highlight "photography as part of the military menu," *shashin heiki no chūmon* (1997: 58). All divisions of the military — land, sea and air — needed progressive improvements in specialist cameras, glass lenses, X-ray films, and the like, for warfare combat and espionage. They were in such great demand that one account encapsulates the period as "a dark age" of film technology development in Japanese history (1997: 112). In other words, it understates the inglorious beginnings of Japanese film technology and the chaotic vicissitudes it had undergone in face of its *other* softer dream role, which was to serve the entertainment world.

According to Yamaguchi and Watanabe (1977: 28), the Japanese only started to use celluloid (also known as cel) as drawing material around 1928. Although it was very expensive, the animators quickly became accustomed to using cel drawing for animating movements and they re-used the precious imported celluloid material by washing them repeatedly. In terms of artistic experimentation and output, although a number of earlier animated works were unfortunately lost or destroyed in the Kanto earthquake in 1923, those that have been recovered so far (dated from 1924 to 1930) show progressive attempts in experimenting with the medium as both a children's and an adult's genre. For example, Kouchi's political cartoon film *Eigaenzetsu: Seji no ronrika* (1926), is a classic piece of animated narrative where a chain of textual typography and illustration is intermingled to represent the identity crisis that Japan was facing at the beginning of the Shōwa period (circa 1926). The 32-minute film playfully reads out the undecided state of the country's future direction, self-questioning such schizophrenic geo-political maxims like

> Japan's Japan (*Nippon no Nippon*)
> World's Japan (*Seikai no Nippon*)
> Japan's World (Nippon no Seikai)[8]

The narrative at times pokes fun at politicians' and intellectuals' rhetoric and satirizes that newly-formed political parties at the time were in fact "re-clothed" from old ones. Other images include a sinking ship not knowing where to navigate in the Pacific Ocean, which portrays the fear of Japan. In a string of illustrations largely composed of texts and pictures obtained from other printed materials, the film powerfully spells out the political state of Japan at that time. Other innovative animated works that hardly touched on politics and current affairs include those directed by Ofuji Noburo known as *chiyogami eiga* (using special paper as an animating technique). For example, his animated film, the highly acclaimed *Kojira* (1927), is exemplary of that experimental period during which artistic achievements were valued as much as the ideal of freedom of expression.

That enthusiastic "free" germinating period of Japanese animation can be explained from a historic time of Japanese modernization. The Taishō period (1912–26) has been regarded as a "renaissance age" in all aspects of Japanese society. Although short-lived, the wide array of democratic thought and activities that surfaced evidenced a period of open-minded modernity. The medium of animation benefited from the "currents of cosmopolitanism" (Jansen, 2000: 537–575)[9] that graced the era.

Remnants of the "Taishō spirit" also spilled into the period of 1929–1933 when the rise of proletarian art and cinema also contributed to the visual variety of modern Japan. In order to raise public awareness of the influential ideological power of mass media, the leftist advocates had not neglected the animation medium from the beginning. While recognizing the work of other leftist artists, musicians, and writers in their respective fields (called The All Japan Federation of Proletarian Arts), in February 1929, Nihon Poroletaria Eiga Dōmei (*Prokino*, Proletarian Film League of Japan) announced its cultural activities through the monthly publication of the journal *Shinkō eiga* (later renamed *Poroletaria eiga* and *Prokino*).[10] In one of the memoirs published in 1981, it states that the proletariat film-journal was resolute in paying attention to different categories of film-making, including documentary films, live-action films, and animation films (see *Shōwa shoki sayoku eiga zasshi betsukan*, 1981: 70).[11] In particular, attention was paid to films that depicted the average working Japanese (*shōshimin*) and the increasingly anxious (*fuan*) social conditions of Japan brought by the Sino-Japanese War. As a result, one memorable anti-war film was made, *Entotsuya pero* (*Chimney Sweeper, Pero*). Directed by Tanaka Yoshitsugu, the film was made in 1930 by Dōei Sha which supported the proletarian movement at that time. The message is the fruitlessness of warfare, as the common folk suffer the most. The animated film uses paper-cut and shadow imagery to illustrate the movement and scene design. While the narrative is based on a faraway land in Europe, it is obvious that the message is allusive of political developments in Japan at the time (Yamaguchi and Watanabe, 1977: 23).[12] The film begins with a young adolescent, Pero, who is in awe of an imperial personality riding in a limousine. Like everybody watching the parade, Pero supports the ongoing war that involves his country and another country. Later, Pero receives an award for detecting the arrival of the enemy forces. But Pero does not know that his own country has started the war in the first place, and has ravaged the enemy's lands and killed civilians. When the war ends, Pero returns home but finds his home village in ruins. It is then that Pero realizes the cruelties of war and finds himself shouting the slogan, "*Teikoku shugi sen niwa hantai shiro.*" The slogan means "objection to imperialistic war ideology." In the 1930 June issue of *Shinkō eiga*, a synopsis of the animated film written by one of the production members, Matsuzaki Keiji, was also published. Since the film had a strong anti-war message, it was listed as "a wanted film" by the police. It was reported that when the animated film was shown in Tokyo in 1930, the hall was packed with spectators and many more were standing outside the screening hall waiting to be admitted. "Toward the end of the film, the audience's cheers and applause filled the arena and naturally, demonstrations were carried out and the atmosphere was energetic and lively" (*Shōwa shoki sayoku eiga zasshi betsukan*, 1981: 10). However, another report disclosed that as the film had caught the attention of the state police, its later screenings in other parts of Japan were conducted under difficult circumstances amidst the surveillance of the authorities. During one of the screenings, the police charged in and disrupted the session. As a result, the film-reels were said to be damaged and lost. The reels resurfaced in 1986 and a four-minute segment of the film censored by the authorities due to its anti-war message was restored in 1987 (see note 12). The publication *Prokino*'s support of the animation medium could be seen from one of its issues (1932, May) in which an animated storyboard appeared at the top of the printed pages, gracing the important sections of the issue.

First Industrial Development

The development of the animation medium did not suffer much hindrance even though in 1934 a Motion Picture Control Committee was set up and put film under government control. The country gradually became more disciplined and militant when "military officers, civilian and ultranationalist groups, in a series of events, took control of the government" (Fairbank et al., 1989: 710). The tide of political change also led to the intensification of political activities, assassinations, and coups during the period of 1931–34. Both external and internal political developments contributed to the change. Domestically, there were mounting economic problems caused partly by the world depression which began to affect people's confidence in democratic parliamentary government, and there was also the growing Marxist movement which called for an equalitarian form of government that would pay attention to the peasants' and urban workers' interests, as well as children's and women's welfare. Abroad, the Sino-Japanese War accelerated at an alarming pace due to the rise of Chinese nationalism. The rise of fascism in Italy and Germany also gained popular support among the rightist militant factions of the Japanese government. Above all, Japan as a whole was unsure of its own geo-political position on the world stage. Thus, debates on Pan-Asianism[13] and Japan's unequal status as a world leader continued unabated as the country struggled to decide its future political course.[14]

With the establishment of the Motion Picture Committee, more theaters screened war-related films as foreign films were gradually banned from being shown in public. As a result, the sudden increase of screening space gave public exposure to more locally produced short films, among which were short animated film features. Fan (1997: 117) notes that it was "momentous" for Japanese animators to be at work during that period. He cites an example for this. Prior to government intervention, individual animators could only experiment and work on the craft during night-time when electricity was more readily available. Another coincidental development, mentioned earlier, was that by 1934 Fuji Film Company had successfully manufactured its own brand of negative film. Under the directives of the government, the Monbushō (Ministry of Education), and the newly-established *bunka eigabu* (Culture Film Division), educational films were actively promoted and, naturally, animation was regarded as one of the most suitable media for disseminating educational messages. This period also saw the establishment of two prominent animation studios, P.C.L. (Photo Chemical Laboratories, Shashin Kagaku Kenkyūsho) and J.O. Company. Both were attracted to the new governmental direction in promoting educational films and the increased amount of public funds were made available for producing non live-action films.[15] In the *Cinema Year Book of Japan* (1938), which was also prepared especially for overseas distribution, the government proudly presented statistical data on its growing film industry. For example, a total of 558 films were made in 1936, an almost 40-percent increase, as compared to 1934 when 399 films were made (Iwamoto, 2004: 19).

However, a general survey of the short animated films made before 1934 showed that, increasingly, the contents of the films already carried propaganda narratives of the military and rightist sections of the government. In addition, one salient feature prevailed: a number of the films, either serialized or singularly realized, often depicted the unity of a group of animals warding off other groups of animals. Other foreign-made animated films had also adopted such an "animistic strategy" in their war propaganda efforts,[16] but in the Japanese case, the consistency and the quantity produced were breath-taking and impressive, even to the point of having a banal effect on the audiences.[17]

It was impressive that the medium was portrayed as a "universal space" for Mother Nature where different kinds of creatures (four-legged, eight-legged, feathery, shelled, and so on) could project their affinities and oppositions onto the animated frames. Often, sports such as soccer, baseball, and Olympic events provided the best competitive scenarios for featuring unity, strength, and ingenuity. The cuteness and innocence of the members of the animal kingdom, however, did not hide a larger and darker message that loomed behind the frames. This was so as, inadvertently, the *Hinomaru* national flag frequently appeared in the background, either discreetly placed at the beginning of the film narrative or toward the end of the film, when the champion animal would often be seen to be carrying it with pride. For example, in the short animated film entitled *Manga shinsarukani kassen* (1939, 11-minute, 35 mm), a group of crabs, insects, and beetles unite in fighting the bully monkey and the *Hinomaru* flag is waved in the background by one of the creatures.[18] The flag appears again in a Shochiku-made production, *Tōkyūniku dansen* (1943, 15-minute, 16 mm), in which two groups of dogs and monkeys compete in a rugby match. The monkeys are at first portrayed as smart and chic as they possess machines and equipment such as cars and bombs. The dogs, on the other hand, rely on their hard work and united strength. The "underdogs" in the end win the rugby match. Some animated films made at that time were also specifically direct in the portrayal of the enemy. One example is an eight-minute film made by J.O. Studio, *Picture Book, Momotarō vs. Mickey Mouse* (*Omochabako shiriizu daisanwa*, 1934). It features Japanese folk heroes emerging from a picture book to help save helpless animals and dolls who have found their island invaded by a group of mice.[19]

The titles and the number of animated films made also revealed that the bulk of monetary support came from the military. As explained above, while the establishment of Fuji Film Company was due to the timely injection of funds from the military, the military's ongoing and enthusiastic support of the animation medium from the 1930s to the early 1940s could also be regarded as the impetus for the first industrial development of Japanese animation. Animation film critic Mori Takuga (2004: 13) put it aptly that many of the animated films made before and during the Second World War were 35 mm films and they demonstrated the status of the animation medium in the film industry of Japan at that time. Mori was commenting on the breadth and length and of the "A History of Japanese Animation" program held at the National Film Center in Tokyo, July 6–August 29, 2004.

Leading the list of animated films that show animals in military attire taking up arms is the country's first animated feature film *Momotarō no umiwashi* (1943).[20] It is a 37-minute feature film using animal-like characters. It also features the Japanese military as the incoming savior of the Pacific Islands' colonized natives.[21] Directed by Seo Mitsuyo, metaphorically speaking, Momotarō was Japan's silhouette wartime mascot as opposed to America's Mickey Mouse.[22] The sequel, *Momotarō umi no shinpei* (translated as *Momotarō's Divine Army* or its known English title, *Momotarō — Divine Troops of the Ocean*, 1945) carried the biggest investment of time, energy, and monetary support. It is a 75-minute animated feature film which engaged over 50 staff at the time and a large orchestra of background musicians for its production. However, records show that not many Tokyoites had seen the film as it was screened toward the end of the war and by then many had fled to the countryside.[23]

Ironically, the director of both films was a former staff member of the black-listed proletariat publication, *Prokino*. In 1984, Seo revealed that the strength of his initial staff later diminished as both the male and female staff members were called upon to serve in the front lines or in war factories as there was an increasing shortage of labor. He never saw them again as many died on duty (Mori, 2004: 14). The director also revealed in a television interview decades later that the 1945-made animated film had caught the complimentary notice of the Imperial House. Seo's reposition to work for the rightist government was not unusual in Japan at that time. A number of writers, artists, and filmmakers did the same for survival and other reasons. Another ex-*Prokino* member Tanaka Yoshitsugu, who directed the risk-taking *Entotsuya pero*, later joined J.O. Studio and helped create *Omochabako shiri-zu daisanwa* (1934, see note 19), an evidently militaristic propaganda film entirely contradictory to the film he made in 1930.

Others tried to take advantage of the period to satisfy both their own artistic inclinations and the military-sponsored demands. Director Masaoka Kenzō's film, *Kumo to chūrippu* (1943), was based partly on a literary work by an award-winning female writer, Yokoyama Michiko. The film's narrative does not stray away from the main plot of the original story which is about the cunning Spider pursuing the innocent adolescent Lady Bug. Although it had been categorized as a racist film, it was a welcome change from the blatantly militaristic animated films being shown at the time. Masaoka was also credited for introducing new artistic and experimental techniques in animating the narrative, and the film exudes a sense of realist lyricism unseen in other animated works during that period. In an interview conducted years after the war, Masaoka revealed that the creative inspiration for the film dated back to the days when he was a student. During that time, he came across the artistic works of León Bakst (1866–1924) and the ballet production works of Sergei Diaghilev (1872–1929) (Matsunomoto and Ostuka, 2004: 28–29).[24] Both were innovative Russian artists who founded the *Mir iskusstva* [World of Art] magazine. This was the product of an art movement at the turn of the twentieth century which advocated individualistic artistic expression and the return to folklore and previous European art traditions (for example, eighteenth-century rococo). The movement's artistic aegis includes elements of self-parody, carnivalistic art, and marionette and puppet theatre (see Read, 1994: 28, 379; Petrov, 1997).

The movement was focally neo-romanticist in its artistic inclinations and it explains why Masaoka's animated film exudes a rather Western puppetry/marionette spectacle, including the mask-like behavior of the character Spider and the carefully designed stagelit backdrop. Masaoka also revealed that the filming process was affected by the shortage of electricity during the war and his poor eyesight due to malnutrition. Ironically, these circumstances may have contributed to the dreamy yet realistic effects of the film that were in line with the carnival-like and folkloric-forest tale elements. Although the production of the film was originally supported by Monbushō, the film did not receive its official special recommendation in the end. It was because the animated film storyline was said to have featured the black spider as the "native" who turned malicious toward the "colonist" white female bug. Thus, it did not fit into the ideological framework of the country's imperialistic Greater East Asia Co-Prosperity Sphere interests (Yamaguchi and Watanabe, 1977: 42). The artistic treatment of the film, the lighting, music, delicate animated movements, and background designs are all excellently presented. However, the emotive aspects of the film betray its simple storyline narration and are reflective of the wartime tensions that prevailed during the period.

Princess Iron Fan versus the *Momotarō* film series

The determination and support that the Japanese military government had given to the production of the *Momotarō* film series was not without a hidden impetus. On the surface, Momotarō as a wartime mascot that represented a leading liberating hero against the foreign Allied Forces, which were symbolically represented by America's popular cartoons, Mickey Mouse and his friends. However, the tenacity to produce and complete the making of the sequel, *Momotarō umi no shinpei*, was driven by a darker historical shadow situated geographically nearby.

Imperialistic Japan viewed China with disdain and there was a generally heavy sense of dismal hopelessness about the country, especially because of its incapabilities to deal with the advancing West and its ongoing warlordism and disorder at home. China, however, produced arguably the first animated feature film in Asia in 1941.

Even though the Wan brothers of China did not have technological assistance from abroad,[25] and they also lacked knowledge of other advanced filmmaking techniques, and had only little financial support at the beginning of their career, they still succeeded in making *Princess Iron Fan* (in Chinese, *Tie shan gong zhu*, in Japanese, *Tetsusen kōshu*). The film was shown to appreciative audiences in China and parts of Southeast Asia. The narrative of the film was based on a traditional Chinese folk legend, *Journey to the West*, and the tale of *Princess Iron Fan* was extracted from parts of the beloved folk narrative.

Critics and film reviewers have tended to emphasize the anti-Japanese war elements embedded in the film. However, at that time the film was not so much directed at the Japanese than at the Chinese audiences themselves; quintessentially, it aimed to instill the Chinese with the spirit of unity and unselfishness in face of adversity. By using the animation medium as a platform for artistic expressions, the film displays an "Eastern answer" to Disney-influenced type of animation. In an article published in 1936, the Wan brothers had already stressed the importance of utilizing "Chinese traditions and stories, consistent with our sense of sensibility and sense of humour …" (Quiquimelle, 1991: 178). In the article, the Wan brothers paid tribute to American cartoons and even admitted that their work had been influenced by Max and Dave Fleischer's animated works. However, they also expressed admiration for animated works from other countries, notably the German and Russian productions. As Quiquimelle has pointed out, the Wan brothers were conscious of aesthetic matters pertaining to "ethnicity," that is, works that authentically bore the stamp of a culture, be it American, German, Chinese, or Russian. In a rare and unusual letter written by the Wan brothers to the Japanese in 1942, again the animators stressed that

> We always had this notion that the Eastern art of film-making should embody Eastern color and taste and it should not imitate and follow wholly the style of Hollywood. Thus, based on this creative aspiration, as seen from the characteristics of *Princess Iron Fan*, in the areas of facial make-up, fashion, action and line-drawing, they all yield originally to traditional Chinese art.

The letter was dated September 13, 1942. The existence of the letter and the fact that the addressee and the requesting party were Japanese speak volume for the status of the film in the eyes the Japanese (see Appendix 1 for the author's translation of the letter in English). Written at the height of the Second Sino-Japanese War (1937–45) when many parts of China including Southeast Asia were under the control of the Japanese military forces, it is strange that the letter does not mention a word about the war or even make indirect reference to the decades-long warfare between the two countries. What the Wan brothers provided in the letter was exactly what the counterpart wanted to know, that is, the production process of Princess Iron

Fan, the creative and economic problems encountered, and the attempts that were made in overcoming them. The entire letter was transcribed into Japanese by the late film critic Shimizu Akira and was published in a film journal *Eiga Hyōron* in the December issue, 1942. In the introduction to the article, Shimizu reported the tremendous response that the film received in China and the astonishing news that even with such a limited market (*shijō ga semaku*), the film in Shanghai alone could be screened in two cinemas at one time.[26] In Japan, the film was also released in thirty theaters. Since it was *manga eiga* ("comic film")[27] and was made in such tough economic times, it was necessary to understand the circumstances under which it was made and the hardship the artists had gone through. Image-wise, Shimizu saw it as a "dream" (*yume*) that had come true and one that had taken place in "inland" (*naichi*, meaning China).[28]

Ironically, the *other* proved to be ahead in the quest for a different kind of animation that was imbued with cultural pride and representation. From basic drawing techniques to background artistic direction, clay model preparation to animators' drawings, coloring, quality control, filming, sound recording, and even issues concerning the health of the staff, the Wan brothers described in as much detail as they could. They showed no intention of hiding any ugly facts or presenting an illusionary "all was well" picture of their production process. The letter ends with a cautionary note; that is, their *Princess Iron Fan* was nothing to be envious about and, in fact, the animators would rather welcome comments and advice from the "Eastern people" (*dongfang renshi*). The names of Wan Laiming and Wan Guchan then appear at the end of the letter.[29]

It is interesting to note that the Wan brothers did not address the obvious reader as Japanese (*riben renshi*) but chose an accommodating broad-based term, "Eastern people," and it corresponded with the earlier part of the letter which stressed the indigenous development of "Eastern filmmaking" as opposed to the American approach. What the Wan brothers did not reveal in the letter was the great inconvenience and hardship which the animators faced in recruiting and managing production staff members due to the invasion of the Japanese military forces in the Jiangsu region. Before the making of *Princess Iron Fan*, the Wan brothers were already engaged in making short animated film series that contained patriotic messages, calling for all Chinese to rise against the invading enemy. Animation historian Bendazzi (1994: 182) writes that the brothers moved around the region so as to produce their animated works.[30] Anticipating that the Japanese military forces would pursue them due to the nationalistic message of their work, the Wan brothers operated in studios situated in Wuhan, Chongqing, and Shanghai. They escaped whenever the advancing Japanese military forces moved near. Later, it was reported that the production of *Princess Iron Fan* was in the French Concession part of Shanghai. Shimizu's article praised the Wan brothers' perseverance in managing two animation studios during the making of *Princess Iron Fan*, one in Shanghai and another in Suzhou. In other words, it is likely that the film was made in several places under difficult circumstances during the war. Moreover, the Wan brothers revealed in the letter that the film project lasted three years, contrary to the common belief that it was entirely made in Shanghai between 1940 and 1941.

It had been recorded that the Japanese reception of the Chinese-made animated film was a *dai shokku* (big shock). They found it unbelievable that a wartorn and occupied China nearby (*o tonari no chūgoku*) could complete such a dedicated film project. Among the animation filmmakers and those working in the industry, many regarded it as the "earliest Eastern-made feature animated film," *tōyō de hatsu no daichōhen manga* (Yamaguchi and Watanabe, 1977: 40). There were rave reviews and enthusiastic response that praised the luxurious representation of animated images.

Although *Princess Iron Fan* was an entertaining and delightful film and was praised before for its originality, aesthetic invention, fantasy, humor, and lyrical qualities, thus providing an Eastern alternative response to the animated works from America, Bendazzi (1994: 183) is right in saying that the "narration often drags, the drawings and the animation of the characters are flawed, and the fusion between American techniques and Chinese artistic traditions is not in sync." In contrast, the *Momotarō* film series, particularly the 1945 sequel, showed a better grasp of animated techniques and its flaws were less visible. The film as a whole did not present obvious signs of jerkiness, nor did it display incongruent placements of the characters in an out-of-sync background. In overall aesthetic evaluation, the *Momotarō* film series was largely governed by the ulterior motive of military glorification, the triumph of wartime ideology, and the forward might of the Nippon Army at the time. Firstly, the animating story of *Momotarō no umiwashi* was modeled after the Japanese attack of Pearl Harbor in 1941, with clear directives given from the military, especially in appraising the naval division's victorious actions (Yamaguchi and Watanabe, 1977: 38). Subsequently, *Momotarō umi no shinpei* was based on a military directive that aimed to educate the public the aims and intentions of the Japanese Army in colonizing and developing the acquired territories, including particularly those that were in the South (the Southeast Asia region). Classified as a *nanpō eiga kōsaku*, which was part of the governing policy stipulated by the military, the animated story of *Momotarō umi no shinpei* was to project a grandiose vision of the expanded Japanese colonial empire and the realization of the Greater East Asia Co-prosperity Sphere. The Greater East Asia Co-prosperity Sphere was another outgrowth of the Asianism ideology. It emphasized Japan as "the bearer of modernity to the rest of Asia" (Moris-Suzuki, 1998: 100) in the areas of science, spirituality, freedom, and so on. In the context of *Momotarō umi no shinpei*, the film epitomized Japan's fantastic imagination of its colonial adventures in the Asia-Pacific region. McCormack (2001: 166) describes the above ideology as "a grotesque parody" of the imperialist European order. Therefore, it is shown again that the medium of animation did not assume a lesser role even toward the end of the Second World War. Together with live-action films, documentaries, news films, and the like, *manga eiga* remained a prominent medium throughout the intense militarization of Japan from the early 1930s, and it definitely maintained its progressive position during the Taishō and early Shōwa periods.

Here we see a Japan on a full-blown march to fulfill its potential and its self-identity in the early half of the twentieth century. Referring to Nishida Kitarō's philosophical writing which was also in circulation during this volatile period of Japanese history, there were indeed correlating nationalistic efforts to realize "a certain Self" — a "Self" that was not only technically proficient and artistically creative but was also intelligently aware of its empirical surroundings. In translating Nishida's 1923 work *Geijutsu to dōtōku* (Art and Morality), David A. Dilworth sees the philosopher's career reflecting the "modernization" of Japan as a whole even though it has the "perspective of academic philosophy in microcosm" (1973, xi). The point is, while Nishida labored on his *microcosmic* world of philosophy, his fellow-men in reality, whether engaged in expressing philosophy or not, or in other pursuits, were also productively living that "historical period" in acts of doing and making. For example, the activity of making animated films was valued as a form of creative subjectivity to be reckoned with and utilized. It would, ultimately, accomplish greater objective goals.

While *Princess Iron Fan* was a wake-up call for all Chinese to protect and act selflessly for their homeland and an aesthetic endeavor to memorialize the cultural heritage of a civilization, the *Momotarō* film series continually carried militarization messages with illusionary dream-like effects. Although Momotarō and his team of animal-friends were realistically "framed" and animated for depicting their "good-hearted" military activities, the film series paradoxically portrayed a wartime mascot "not in sync" with the changing foreign political developments and atrocities that its Imperial Army had committed abroad.[31] It only egoistically portrayed a military government that was immensely self-obsessed with image-creating and propagating unrealistic ideological messages to the nation. In one of the recent papers written on the *Momotaro* film series, specialist manga-writer Akita Takahiro (2004: 255–267) questions the anthropomorphic functions found in Japanese wartime cartoons. For example, he notices that in the film *Momotarō umi no shinpei*, Momotarō is illustrated as a human character in the second half of the film; he is singularly presented as a young man with a human face and body and he is the only one who speaks with a clear definitive tone among his anthropomorphic comrades. The others, including the island natives, are all illustrated as animal-like characters and orangutans and monkeys are presented as the native chief representatives. However, toward the end of the film, when the Western colonists are captured, they are illustrated as comic human figures. What is subtly disturbing in my observation is the robot-like, inhuman gaze of the central figure, Momotarō. He may be the symbolic leader of the Imperial Army but in fact he can be perceived to be the Japanese emperor himself because of his bestowed *kamisama* status; his field of vision is tilted at an optical angle as if it is inappropriate to have direct eye contact with his comrades and subjects and even with the spectators who are watching the film. In this way, director Seo unconsciously revealed the relationship between the Japanese emperor and his subjects during the imperialistic period. Moreover, the "gaze" of Momotarō's eyes lacks distinct human warmth. What is depicted is a plain cold steel-like determination. However, the assemblage of animal-creatures, together with the clownish-looking Anglo-American military men who surrender, features a mixture of lively and humanly imperfect behaviors which ironically manage to arouse a sense of empathy from the spectators.

Quintessentially, the film *animatedly* reveals the deep-seated grand narrative that has already been discussed in the preceding chapters. At the end of the film, Momotarō does manage to sit face to face with the Western colonists, and demands the acquisition of land and authority. His "challenging requests" are finally granted. However, that momentary meeting of "superpowers" does not feature any "monkeys" and "orangutans." Neither are other native-islander residents like the "elephants, "rhinoceroses," and "tigers" present. This arrangement tells, indirectly and disturbingly, the expansionistic intentions of the savior Momotarō.[32] In addition, the climax of the film occurs in an earlier sequence which contains animated frames that feature the ambush, capture and brutal killings of the enemy, the Anglo-American military forces. Toward the end of the film, there are also flashbacks featuring Momotarō reminiscing about his "childhood" days when life was familiarly cozy, village-like, carefree, and playful. Intrinsically, it demonstrates a reflective self who is subconsciously aware of his "loss of innocence" in the midst of imperialistic expansion. More importantly, the film symbolizes the arduous imaginary quest of a younger Eastern counterpart (as opposed to India or China, for example) in its lonesome battle to face the Western colonial powers triumphantly. Indeed, the character of Momotarō best befits the national consciousness of Japan at that time. He is a youthful hearty healthy boy while the Western colonists are represented by ruffled and half-bald characters and set-ways. Illustratively, the Momotarō film series does not hide the elevated status of the Japanese race as an incoming "protector and liberator" of Southern Asia. What it does hide or, rather, does not pay heed to and therefore does not express animatedly, are the widespread violence and rampage Japan had committed in those Southern lands and the occupied lands in Eastern and Northern Asia.

It is not known for sure whether the film series director and his team staff members were given the opportunity to see the highly acclaimed Disney production, *Snow White and the Seven Dwarfs* (1937), as many foreign films were banned in Japan as the war progressed. It is also not known whether the ambitious direction of the production staff and the sponsors had been influenced after watching the Disney films.[33] However, judging from the design background and the general flow of the animated frames, the films prevalently yield to the Disney standards of animating, and are rather different from its Eastern counterpart, the Chinese-made *Princess Iron Fan*. By that, I refer to the characters' fluid animated movements and the scenic design background that incline toward a Western-realist illustrative approach.

According to Sano's research, America's imminent involvement in the Pacific warfront doubly intensified Japanese animators' interest in the Disney model, besides their already established regard for its economic status. The film community was aware of the narrow artistic path that the country was treading. One film critic wrote in 1942 and described the American influences of animation as a form of "Yankee-ism" (Sano, 2006: 120). In other words, the animation industry faced a critical polemic dilemma in response to the dialectical East-West animation worlds as demonstrated by China on the one hand, and the United States on the other. Wherein and whereabouts then can we find *nihon shikō* ("Japan aspired") animation? (This topic will be directly cross-examined in Chapter 7, but the chapters that follow will show the future métier of Japanese animation after the war.)

Here I reserve overly critical judgment of director Seo for embarking on such an animation project. After the war, he became a target of criticism, either openly or otherwise, within the animation-making community. To put it in perspective, is it not arguably true that he was simply living up to the "historicity" of his lifetime? Could his subjective creation not be divorced from his country's political reality at the time? In Nishida's words, "that will is not merely a transcendent will, it must be a specific will that has content" (1973: 103). Hence, director Seo was merely fulfilling his expressive role in a complicated sweep of time when ultra-nationalism was at its height and when even the pictorial world of animation was deemed as nationalistically self-generating and self-fulfilling. The significant irony here is that Japan's quest to realize the Greater East Asia Co-Prosperity Sphere *visually* through the theatrical animating medium gradually became a defeated dream, because the lingering shadow of its mainland neighbor, *Shina* (as China was called at that time), managed to express this ideological Eastern Asiatic discourse more convincingly, both spiritually and aesthetically, through the animating language.

In summary, the *Momotarō* film series lacks a certain geo-political artistic statement that would credit the endeavor with a committed dynamic touch, one that heightens and contributes to the East-West dialogue and also evinces some higher human values. In other words, it gives the image of a corporate-like vanity project that both the sponsors and the makers created to fulfill some make-believe dreams — personal, nationalistic, or both. However, the *Momotarō* film series exerted a tremendous impact on one of Japan's most important popular culture creators in the later half of the twentieth century. He was the late manga artist, Tezuka Osamu, whom I shall discuss in the following chapter.

5

Postwar Japanese Animation Development and Toei Animation Studio[*]

> ... Japan's first color feature film, *Hakujaden,* received praise from all sectors, in addition to further making *Shōnen sarutobi sasuke, Saiyūki* ... etc., we are skillfully giving birth to American Disney-professional kind of excellent animation, ... 'Film is Toei' and Toei shall make every effort to produce various kinds of films and through 'films', we shall contribute to the happiness and national life of our people ...[1]
>
> Okawa Hiroshi
> President of Toei
> *Eiga nenkan,* 1960

> Animate (an'-i-mat). v.t. {L. animatus, past part. Of animare, fr. Anima breath, soul.} 1. To give natural life to; to make alive. 2. To give spirit or vigor to; to inspirit; also, to stimulate; rouse. 3. To impart an appearance of life to; as, to animate a cartoon. 4. To actuate; prompt.
>
> *Webster's New Collegiate Dictionary*

How did Japan emerge from a past that took lives of millions of young men who were called to serve on the front lines and many more of civilian children and women who either died or suffered in the atomic bombings at Hiroshima and Nagasaki? Compare the Japanese plight with the rest of Asia which had only just emerged from a multi-colonial past and had experienced another "liberator's" act of horrors and pseudo-promises. In what ways did Japan and other parts of Asia differ in building and shaping a new future? The large-scale economic reconstruction was obviously

---

[*] This chapter contains extracts of "The Animated Resurrection of the Legend of the White Snake in Japan" which has appeared in *Animation: An Interdisciplinary Journal*, Volume 2, No. 1, March 2007, published by Sage Publications.

an all-time important approach that Japan had taken; by the end of the 1970s, Japan was regarded as "number one," and was praised as a model country for other industrial nations to follow (Vogel, 1979).[2] But still, there existed an imaginative way which Japan alone took and did not forsake then (and now), and that is the *old* business of image-building and fantastic entertainment. This is not to suggest that other parts of Asia did not engage in building new images after the Second World War, which also historically marked the departure from the old colonial order. The reconstruction of cinema theaters and even the maintenance of mobile make-shift ones were just as vibrant in Japan as in other parts of Asia, as the newly appointed governments and cinema owners were quick to recognize the urgency, profitability, and competitiveness of the postwar era. However, Japan was again in an express-train mode. The country was "loading," creating, and embracing all kinds of images, and also learned to make selective "stops" as its postwar modernization journey gained momentum. In film-making, again the animation medium was not belittled or neglected, and with the development of the manga genre and the rise of television viewing as a popular form of entertainment, the animation medium assumed a unique role and became a distinctive stylistic representation in Japanese popular culture. This chapter primarily focuses on the post-Second World War industrial development of Japanese animation and theorizes in part on the medium's expressive symbolic role in postwar nation-building. After the war, the development of the medium was spearheaded not by a central hegemonic authority, but by the people themselves as individuals, consumers, creators, enterprise owners, and dream-builders.

SCAP and Animating a New "Dawn"

During the Allied Forces Occupation of Japan (1945–52), film-making activities did not come to a halt. Rather, the administration encouraged freedom of speech and repudiated the feudalistic way of thinking; instructions were handed down, demanding the film industry to get rid of its past militaristic inclinations. Thompson and Bordwell (1994: 462) recount that right from the beginning the new administration "took a keen interest in the film industry." To broaden the variety of film contents, opportunities to experiment with new film-making techniques were also offered. Many junior and younger film directors were given chances to make films. By the end of the Occupation, Japan already "accounted for about twenty percent of the world's total" in feature filmmaking (Thompson and Bordwell, 1994: 459). It was almost a quarter of the world's output while the Western world and the Soviet bloc contributed about 60 percent.

Led by the Americans and presided over by General Douglas MacArthur, the Occupation was also called as the Supreme Commander of the Allied Powers (SCAP). In the spring of 1946, over 200 film prints were burned by the SCAP due to the "feudalistic and/or anti-democratic content" as deemed by the SCAP officials. It was never really certain that all those prints earmarked for demolition, including the negatives and their theatrical release copies, were destroyed (Anderson and Richie, 1982: 161), or whether the SCAP had reviewed the large number of animated films made that were mainly of militaristic themes. Of one thing we are sure: the *Momotarō* feature film prints are still in existence in Japan today so are many of the animated shorts made during the war. Perhaps the SCAP did not find them serious enough to warrant any urgent attention, thanks to the "immateriality" of the narrative contents as compared to other live-action films in which real-life human characters and background were featured.[3]

Policies to consolidate the film industry personnel were carried out by the SCAP and at one point, a list of war criminals working in the industry was drawn up. It is not known whether any animator, animation director, or producer was ever named in the list, but for survival reasons, about 100 animators led by Yamanoto Sanae, Yasuji Murata, and Masaoka Kenzō made the critical decision to establish an organization called Shin Nihon Dōga Sha (in English, New Japan Animation Company) in late 1945 (the organization was later renamed as Nihon Manga Eiga Kabushiki Kaisha, or Japan Manga Film Corporation). Its formation was also probably due to the pressure from the SCAP as the animators anticipated that the SCAP might want to police their creative activities (Fan, 1997: 125).

One significant film made under this organization was *Sakura* (in English, "Cherry Blossom" or "Cherry Tree," also known as *Haru no gensō* ["Haru Fantasy" or "Haru Fantasia" meaning spring fantasy], 1946) directed by Masaoka Kenzō. Because of his experience in making war propaganda animated films, one might expect something similar to *Sakura*. However, *Sakura* shows no traces of any militaristic sentiments. Instead, it conveys the familiar image of spring in Japan: natural beams of sunshine rays, rhythmic raindrops, a girl clad in *kimono* (traditional Japanese attire) and *geta* (wooden clogs), the awakening of nature as depicted by lively butterflies, insects, beetles, and the like, and the overflowing presence of cherry blossoms. German romanticist composer Carl Maria von Weber's music (*Invitation to Waltz*) is played in the background. Eight minutes in length, the film is not so much propelled by the animated figures as by the rhythmic atmospheric changes. In keeping with the black and white presentation, there are no cluttered images or central narrative characters that call for attention. There are simply fragmentary frames of an early spring, and it seems that their aim is to pique any disgruntled soul not acknowledging the arrival of the delightful new season. However, records show that this poetical art-piece was considered out of place in a defeated Japan and was unwelcome generally by the distribution network because it lacked "commercial value" and was "buried" and seldom screened during those years (Tsugata, 2004: 116).

In the period immediately after the war, it was probably difficult and almost unimaginable for the average Japanese person to appreciate a new "dawn" era, much less to savor highly artistic work in the cinema. Food was scarce especially in the cities and the SCAP gave conflicting political directions. For example, overnationalistic and feudalistic practices were frowned upon, but extensive criticism of past militaristic activity and ideology was not encouraged as the Occupation was also wary of left-wing sentiment and its rising popular appeal, given the devastated state of the country (Thompson and Bordwell, 1994: 462). Thus, "democracy" was implemented the SCAP way, that is, the previous imperial system was to be kept with some convenient changes. It was hoped that by retaining the emperor as head of the state, the alien democratic path upon which Japan would embark would be stabilized. In other words, Emperor Hirohito's wartime responsibility and his presiding role in the entire militarization of Japan, including the Imperial Army's systematic inhumane militarist actions abroad, were never questioned thoroughly, examined, and tried by his own people.[4] His postwar symbolic head-of-state status and the historical ancestral sense of godly aura was more or less pristinely preserved and left intact, paradoxically by a democratic liberator who intended to engineer a less problematic and turbulent path in "modernizing" Japan.

Hence, the hybrid combinations of the "old" and the "new" were the essence of what postwar modern Japan was to become. What remained realistically viable and, in a survival sense, applicable was the mechanical drive to pursue economic growth for the country, to acquire personal material comfort and riches and, to relive an old familiar "Meiji dream," which was to further acquire technology and science. This time, however, was from a newer Pacific western land, the United States of America.[5] In an abstract sense, the animated film *Sakura* is an indication of a new dawn and a symbolic portrayal of a utopian postwar era. Quintessentially, the inner "soul" of Japan lives on since the cherry blossom is the national flower of the country and an aesthetic symbol of the Japanese culture. In animated terms, the *anima* still exists and the inspiriting nature proves it to be so.[6]

Despite the presence of light-hearted images in *Sakura* and a profuse sense of the feminine touch, some doubts about the film remain. It is precisely this collection of nature-based "harmless" images that arouses inquiry and further interpretation. A cat lazing in the sun, the momentary focus of a demure female face clad in traditional clothing, and lively fluttering butterflies, and so on, suggest a faintly familiar "floating world," that is, a world of sensuality, relaxation, and subtle eroticism. It is common knowledge that in the period immediately after the war, a number of Japanese women assumed the role of "comfort women"[7] for the GIs who arrived in great numbers, particularly in the city areas. The ruling authorities, including senior government officials and the police, were aware of such "romantic liaisons." The subtle policy of using the "feminine" to serve and stabilize the complicated situation has been discussed by Dower (1999) and Tanaka (2002). Thus, the animated film *Sakura* can be seen to fulfill a dual objective; *nationalistically*, the images of the spring season are representative of a newly dawned Japan, but *orientalistically*, such images are enticingly feminine, sensual, and innocent. Perhaps the dainty and delicate images were regarded as too close to home, making it controversial for the main sponsor Toho to publicly release the film in its commercial chain of cinemas. But its animator-director Masaoka knew better. In an interview which he gave years later, Masaoka revealed that after obtaining a print copy of the film from Toho, the film was pirated abroad under another title, *Haru no gensō*. When viewed today, the film is still appealing and entertaining, given the dreamlike oriental setting and the lingering mother-nature feminine feeling, even if one does not inquire about the historical context of its production.[8]

In comparison, the eleven-minute, black and white animated film called *Mahō no pen* ("Magic Pen") directed by Kumagawa Masao in 1946 is uncomfortably stark. Yet, its depiction of postwar Japan is subtle. The film was completed slightly after *Sakura* was made and by a close colleague of Masaoka Kenzō. It features an orphan boy and his dream-story (*yume monogatari*). The film begins with the orphan boy who picks up a Western-looking doll. Later at home, in the middle of his English language study, he falls asleep. He dreams that the doll gives him a pen to draw anything he likes, in return for his compassionate act of mending her broken body earlier.[9] Then, the following images appear: a tree, skyscrapers, apartment buildings, houses, a sports car, and expressways. Desolate parts of the city where the boy actually lives are also illustrated and are juxtaposed to these infrastructural luxurious images. The boy and the doll then spend some time together driving through the countryside of Japan while a song hailing a new Japan to be built is played in the background. The Western doll then says goodbye to the boy as she enters her chic convertible car. She gives the shy boy a handshake before they part. Later, the orphan boy wakes up and realizes that it is a dream.

In reality, the orphan boy's "dream" is not an illusion. It is a specific listing of national redevelopment items and material acquisitions, and a request for the help of a Western colonist. The content of the dream exudes an awkward and disquieting feeling because the Western doll is seen as a savior and life-giver, and although her generosity may seem comforting and consoling, it is also condescending in a manner that seems to suggest an Oriental lost child's search for a fairy godmother's blessing and fulfillment of wishes. In early 1946, the SCAP set up a unit within the Civil Information and Education Section whose central role was to view all completed films and approve them for theatrical release (Anderson and Richie, 1982: 162). It is very likely that *Mahō no pen* and *Sakura* passed the approval test. Moreover, explicit expressions of affection such as kissing and hugging as seen in *Mahō no pen* were in tune with the democratic guidelines stipulated by the SCAP.[10]

To summarize, nothing is more plain, open, and frank than the wishful montage of animated images that have been drawn by the orphan boy. In comparison with *Sakura*, *Mahō no pen* illustratively gathers the material realization of an anticipated new "dawn" and the animated narrative serves all the more to *actuate* and *prompt* a powerful master in providing the necessary assistance to fulfill the dream. Japan's subsequent national response was to "embrace defeat" with a thirst-like capitalistic mentality, concluding that

> What made America "great" was that it was so rich; and, for many,
> what made "democracy" appealing was that it apparently was the
> way to become prosperous. (Dower, 1999: 136)

In the above discussion, two animated films made immediately after the war are highlighted because they reflect the birth of an uneasy "dawn" as Japan emerged from a dark past, and interestingly, the frames of animation do not hide the realistic and dream-like expectations of another age, both in abstract and practical expressions.[11]

Founding of Toei Animation Studio

The animation medium was also kept alive in the period immediately after the war by a major sponsor Toho, which still owns a wide network of exhibiting facilities in present-day Japan. As mentioned in Chapter 4, in the mid-1930s Toho had already acquired two animation studios, P.C.L. and J.O. Company that worked on war-related film projects. In response to a need for new educational film productions in the postwar era, the Toho Kyōiku Eiga Sha was set up in 1948 (Tsugata, 2004: 119). At the same time, Masaoka and Yamamoto left Nihon Manga Eiga and established Nihon Dōga Sha to work on co-operative projects with Toho. However, the newly renamed Toho animation studio only lasted for a short period of time and, due to a lack of funding and possibly a lack of management interest from the parent company, it was later merged with Nihon Dōga and renamed as Nidō Eiga Kabushiki Kaisha. By then, a new film conglomerate had arrived on the film-making and distributing scene; it was Tokyo Motion Picture Distribution Company, in short, Toei.

All these mergers and regroupings might seem confusing and chaotic but, in reality, the animators and their newly-found sponsors simply adapted and renewed their enterprises according to the change of times. Although big film organizations such as Shochiku and Toho were prominent sponsors and producers of animated films and had powerful backing of the military during the war, both organizations receded into the background after the war. In the postwar era, it made sense to let a "new player" regroup and rejuvenate the industry so as to present a fresh image or, at least and at best, obscure the inglorious wartime propaganda film projects that had previously been taken on by the animators. One such player who had a resolute determination to take on this task and even accomplished more was Toei.

Toei was a relative latecomer in the film industry scene in Japan and other parts of Asia. The corporation was the result of a merger of Toyoko and Oizumi film production companies in 1951. In Chinese characters, Toei means "Eastern Film Company" (Hosogaya, 2000: 65). It had at its helm a newly appointed president, Okawa Hiroshi (1897–1971), who was also new to the film business. He was reassigned from the Toyoko Railway Company to manage the two medium-sized and debt-ridden film companies. A businessman and an accountant by training, Okawa was able to establish Toei as a formidable "brand name" in the East Asian film business by the second half the 1950s, as he was quick to cater to "those segments of the film audience not yet fully exploited: children, younger teenagers, the poorly educated and the farmers" (Anderson and Richie, 1982: 244) by building cinema theaters located at or near central urban and suburban railway stations, and by screening "double features at affordable prices." In other words, at Toei's cinemas, audiences were treated to two feature films per bill.[12] Among the other significant decisions that he made were to build a Disney-like animation studio with multitask facilities and to produce Asia's first color animated feature films.

Toei Animation Studio (officially known as Toei Animation Company) was founded in mid-1956. It was agreed that the management of Nidō led by Yamamoto Sanae would come under the administrative auspices of Toei. The success of the takeover was also due to the production of the film, *Ukare baiorin* (1955), contracted by Toei Kyōiku Eiga Bu (the educational film section of Toei).[13] Toei was pleased with the exquisite animated work produced by Nidō and knew that its staff members were some of the best and most experienced animators in the country. Toei was keen to invest in the "gem studio" for commercial development. Prior to its founding, a research committee had already been formed to investigate the market expansion opportunities of the animation industry. When Okawa became the founder-president of Toei Animation Studio, there were visionary plans to produce not only long and short feature animated films but also television commercials and other graphic works (*Eiga nenkan*, 1957: 180).

The Making of the *Legend of the White Snake* and Its Animated Version

Odd as it might seem, the postwar industrial development of Japanese animation began with the animated production of a legendary Chinese tale, *Legend of the White Snake* (also known as *White Snake Tale*, in Japanese, *Hakujaden*, 1958).[14] To this day, this epochal animated film ranks considerably low in the country's remembrance of all "anime masterpieces" ever made. Neither do many members of the Chinese communities in mainland China, Hong Kong, Taiwan, and Southeast Asia recall distinctly its existence at all. Yet, in the West, the animated film once attracted the attention of commercial producers and affirmed the resources that the Japanese animation industry could offer. The film also collected several awards abroad.

This section of the chapter traces the production background of *Hakujaden* and examines the circumstances of its making, especially in light of a post-Second World War era and Japan's conviction to rebuild a new image of itself. The analysis also utilizes the "concept of performativity" in discussing the "collective stagy operations" of the newly founded Toei Animation Studio which promoted itself as "Asia's largest animation studio" (a self-promoting description of the Studio found in Toei's early marketing literature). The course of my discussion maintains that the selection of a popular Chinese narrative and its subsequent animated production was not a random choice. It speaks of a period during which East Asia and Southeast Asia emerged from a colonial past, and carried with them memories of an "imperialist liberator" (Japan) and the horrors it had committed in the Second World War.

The theoretical approach in this section is also inspired by the recent work of film historian Donald Crafton who wrote the award-winning book *Before Mickey: The Animated Film 1898–1928* (1982). In a keynote address in 2002, Crafton reflected that if he could revise the book's contents, he would apply the critical framework of new Performance Studies theory.[15] The expanding academic perspective of Performance Studies has, on the whole, incorporated the terrain of language, semiotics, psychoanalysis, politics and culture, gender, and socio-historical materialism studies. For example, the work of Marvin Carlson and Richard Schechner has generated new far-reaching concepts of "performativity" and offers more possibilities in theorizing the extensive dynamics of performance. Carlson (2004: 4) acknowledges that the concept of performance can be applied to all human activity, including the perspective that all activity is "carried out with a consciousness of itself," whereas Schechner (2002: 24) stresses the interrelatedness of performance, as in "actions, interactions, and relationships."

Indeed, a number of early animated films depicted the artist-animator at work within the film itself as he "sketched," "drew," "painted" or "modeled" the image. One example is *Gertie the Dinosaur* (1914) in which the director and animator Winsor McCay (1867–1934) included himself as an actor in the film, overtly showing to the audience his "animated act" and key participation in the making of the animated frames. The "hand of the artist" self-figuration motif is an important component in animated performance, not unrelated to the discussion of performance, play, ritualistic repetition, and assembly. In this sense, the activity of animation is part of the act "showing doing," where Schechner defines this kind of performance as "pointing to, underlining, and displaying doing" (2002: 22–44). In acknowledging Schechner's cultural anthropological basis in explaining the activities of performance, Crafton foregrounds Schechner's encompassing definition that

> The underlying notion is that any action that is framed, presented, highlighted, or displayed is a performance. (2002: 2)

In doing so, Crafton argues that "at the heart of all classic animation … several kinds of performance converge … " One is "performance *in* animation" and the other, "performance *of* animation." While Schechner highlights key phrases like "what is to perform," "what is a performance," "functions of performance" and so on, Crafton narrows it down to two essential prepositional properties of classic animation, distinguishing "performance *in* animation" as "performances represented by artist animators," and "performance *of* animation" as "the practice of creating animated film."

My analysis of the animated production of *Legend of the White Snake* rests theoretically on these two performance categories as proposed by Crafton. However, the "nationalistic collective component" will be emphasized, as the overall animated performance is interpreted as an epitomization of a corporate cultural stance which should not be overlooked. It concerns more than just "large-scale institutional behavior" (Crafton, 2003: 11) and investigates the existence of a collective yet personal unconscious performative attempt in redeeming a lost innocence and a darker past. Disappointingly, somewhere along the performative process — the animated tale lost its intended original source of audienceship (that is, the Chinese-speaking communities) and became a means to an end to serve other corporate and geo-political purposes. The analysis therefore locates the animated folktale in the transactional crossroads of a juncture in time. It also acknowledges the producer, Toei Animation Studio, and its determined investment of talent, finances, and the like, in the business of "dream-building," regardless of the obstacles or the contending odds that might arise in the process.

What is Legend of the White Snake*?*

Legend of the White Snake is a popular vernacular Chinese folktale which dates back to the Tang dynasty. Originally, it was a moral story about a man's adulterous affair with a white snake disguised in human form and his subsequent death when he was reduced to liquid and bones upon returning home. The narrative content of the folktale had undergone changes through the ages. The Song dynasty was in sympathy with the innocent sexual desire of the male protagonist; during the Ming dynasty, both Madam White Snake and her human male partner were depicted as adversaries to the normal social order and accepted code of behavior, and the tale also included the growing support roles of Qing Qing, the snake's companion fish-sister, and the powerful didactic Buddhist monk, Fahai, who finally locked up the two creatures in the monastery's pagoda. By the Qing dynasty, this vernacular tale "humanized" Madam White Snake further and recounted her abilities to give birth to a son and to serve her husband and her community. In 1956, the communist-governed People's Republic of China published a new version of the tale in which the author Zhao Qingge emphasized its feudalistic elements, including the weak role of the male protagonist Xu Xian and his final transformation into a strong and unwavering protagonist in face of challenges and struggles (Huss, 1997).

The Japanese animated portrayal of *Hakujaden* is a mixture of the Ming, Qing and PRC versions of the tale and, interestingly, the Japanese producers' own interpretation of the tale. Especially pertaining to the latter, the conclusion of the tale shows that Madam White Snake and Xu Xian are able to gain the understanding and sympathy of the Buddhist monk Fahai as they decide to forge a new future together. In the Chinese case, as shown in the live-action films made in Hong Kong (1962, 1993) and Taiwan (1978), the conclusion is unavoidably tragic: there is always separation and death may occur. Historically, *Hakujaden* was already made known to the Japanese during the Edo period and was classified as a *yomihon* tale in which "Japanese images, texts and history" were woven into the Chinese original narrative (see Shirane, 2002: 565–567 and 583–598). However, the twentieth-century animated version was not adapted from the Japanese *yomihon* tale. None of the images in the animated version bears signs of a Japanese setting.[16] Rather, it encompasses the full-color world of a far-away land and its distinctive representations including the names of the characters featured. Why is it so?

Approaching an "appropriate" investor

The background of the founding of Toei Animation Studio (officially known as Toei Animation Company) in 1956 can be explained partly by the tremendous rise of film production activity in Hong Kong in the 1950s. For example, it was reported that in that decade alone, Hong Kong produced over 2,175 films (*Overseas Chinese Figures in Cinema*, 1992: 24) and in 1962 in Hong Kong alone, over 250 films were made, "more than that of US and Britain combined" (Thompson and Bordwell, 1994: 462).

Reports showed that Toei was in need of an investor and subsequently approached a Hong Kong producer, Zhang Guoli, for the sponsorship of the animation project. Throughout the 1950s and 1960s, well-established film studios such as Shochiku, Toho, and Daiei also co-operated with Hong Kong film companies because they had close connections with cinema-operators in Asia, thus making available the vast hinterland of Asian audiences. Several joint expensive film projects on epic Chinese historical tales were produced and on the Japanese side, the enthusiasm had even spilled over into live-theatrical productions as represented by Takarazuka productions.[17]

Among the live-action joint films made was *Madame White Snake* (in Japanese, *Byaku fujin no yōren*) produced by Toho and Shaw Brothers in 1956. The cast and crew members were all Japanese, including the lead actress Yamaguchi Yoshiko

(1920–). She also had a Chinese name Li Xianglan, and was a familiar star among the Chinese-speaking communities in East Asia and Southeast Asia. The film credits the Shaw Brothers with consultant supervision of the project but it is likely that the Hong Kong producers provided supervision in relation to the script-narrative development and parts of the interior shooting (Yau, 2000: 106) and left the other parts of the production work to the prerogative of the Japanese production crew.[18] However, distinctive representations are found in the animated version of *Legend of the White Snake* produced by Toei, and they demonstrate the cultural differences of the two countries, including their differing historical-psychological mindsets and the producers' conflicting perspectives on the medium of animation. Hong Kong's co-participation in the project was never realized and, according to one Japanese veteran animator, the partnership came to a halt due to arguments over the target audience and the narrative content of the story.[19]

Is animation a storytelling medium in which "everyone lives happily ever after"?

As mentioned earlier, *Legend of the White Snake* is not a literary piece of work penned by a specific author. It is a *chuanqi* and its Chinese title is *Bashechuan*, meaning the "legendary folktale of the White Snake." In other words, the story has been continuously passed on from generation to generation and has an oratorical element that tells the extraordinary. By the early Qing dynasty (1644–1911), the story had become a popular theme in opera and in *tanci*, which is a form of storytelling accompanied by stringed instruments. Like opera, *tanci* was often performed in public teahouses and other social gatherings at the time.

Since the Tang dynasty and in every dynastic period that followed, the tale turned progressively critical of the roles of the Daoist priest and the Buddhist monk Fahai, who paradoxically became a treacherous figure and the most disliked religious character featured in the story. In 1956, the full story appeared in book form. Although the author Zhao Qingge concluded the tale with a reunion of Madam White Snake and her loved ones, the menacing existence of Fahai still loomed behind. In the 1990s, the tale was retold by Hong Kong writer Li Bihua, who gave a bigger role to the Green Fish Qing Qing. In a subsequent live-action film adaptation, director Tsui Hark upheld the unending feud-relationship that Madam White Snake and Qing Qing had with Fahai. Hence, Fahai has never been portrayed as a benevolent father figure capable of remorse, compassion, and redemption. He remains a corrupt, self-righteous, hypocritical and authoritarian figure, who imposes his demands and views on those whose actions he deems immoral and wrong.

In the animated version of *Legend of the White Snake*, the Japanese producers literally brought the age-old vernacular tale to a close by portraying Fahai as a "re-born" Buddhist monk. In this version, he shows compassion and remorse for his past actions and judgmental behavior and even in the end, helps the suffering couple to overcome the ordeal which he has created in the first place. In the late twentieth-century Chinese versions of *Legend of the White Snake*, the male protagonist Xu Xian was portrayed as a cowardly character in terms of his physical abilities and weak mental make-up. Time and again, because of his indecision, suspicion, and selfishness, he betrayed the love of Madam White Snake and the sacrifices she made. Although in 1956 author Zhao Qingge portrayed him as a stronger character as the tale progressed toward the end, his foolish moves were often fortunately saved by the timely interventions of his female companions, namely Madam White Snake, Qing Qing, and even his sister-in-law. Hence, *Legend of the White Snake* is not a typical romance in which the male gender is portrayed as heroic, gallant, and chivalrous. On the contrary, the gender as represented by Xu Xian possesses the opposite characteristics, as he is effeminately weak and materialistically poor. In short, he is an average ordinary male despite his good looks.[20] He may have lust, which explains his attraction to the beautiful Bai Niang or Pai-nyan (Madam White Snake in Chinese and Japanese), but he is also dependent on her in charting his career and achieving a healthy meaningful family life.

In the Japanese-made animated film, Xu Xian, like the Buddhist monk Fahai, acquires a completely different set of qualities as the tale draws to a close. Toward the end of the film, as the narrative reaches a climax, Xu Xian becomes a strong swimmer and savior; he races to rescue the drowning Pai-nyan as she has lost her special powers.[21] Thus, he becomes a heroic male protagonist not unlike a Disneyesque Prince Charming animated character who arrives dramatically to save his beloved damsel in distress. The animated tale concludes with the couple sailing away in calm waters as they begin a new life together. It is a classic conclusion, dutifully affirming the "… and they lived happily after" ending.

Herein lies the ideological questions about the animation medium. Must it ultimately portray a wholesome, "all is well" world in keeping with the childlike innocent illustrative world of creation? Or should it leave the "uncanny" open, as the medium itself also carries with it a sense of the fantastic and the magical? How much consideration should the production team pay to its intended ethnically-based audience, taking into account the illustrative make-believe world of animating? Is there a set of formulaic representations and actions to follow and "to create" when making a piece of cel-based commercial animated feature film? The examination of the context of the animated production of *Legend of the White Snake* points to a calculative desired course of creation, which had already been tested and manifested by a much admired distant party, most notably the institution of Disney-made films. Moreover, between 1948 and 1954, many previously banned foreign-made films were screened in Japanese cinemas and there was also a revived popular interest in

Disney-made animated films. Thus, films like *Snow White and the Seven Dwarfs* (1937), *Bambi* (1942), *Pinocchio* (1940), *Dumbo* (1941), and *Cinderella* (1950) were finally shown to Japanese audiences. In the summer of 1950, Shochiku also put together a program of outstanding American animated films (*Amerika kessaku manga matsuri*) for cinema audiences who craved for old American animated works (Yamaguchi and Watanabe, 1977: 59–60).

Performing to "impress," to "heal," and to "become"

It is plausible that the above questions drove some of the underlying creative considerations as the joint sponsors and producers pondered the narrative development of the proposed animated tale. In regard to the business role of the Hong Kong film producer and the Chinese partners whom he sought to raise money and to agree on distribution prospects, we may speculate that at that time (by the early 1950s) the Japanese film producers were in urgent need of regional and international markets. In her paper "Hong Kong and Japan: Not One Less" (2000: 106), Yau gives the impression that the Hong Kong producers, particularly the Shaw Brothers, were actively involved in promoting joint co-operative works by Japan and Hong Kong. From a Hong Kong perspective, she is correct in pointing out that "the co-productions offered a good chance to learn about Japanese technology and to open up the Japanese market." However, the growing and multinational size of Shaw Brothers' film distribution network in Asia and that of other Chinese film companies should not be underestimated; the Japanese film industry intrinsically recognized the wide distribution networks that were available.

Regarding the history of the Japanese film industry, Anderson and Richie (1982: 248) note that the Japanese film producers, in trying to sell their products abroad in the 1950s, promoted the idea of co-production work. Apart from approaching American and European film producers and directors,[22] Hong Kong producers were also contacted and proposals were made. Perhaps a more effective tool in understanding the resurrection of the *White Snake Tale* in Japan and its presentation in its animated form can be found in the archives of the *Eiga nenkan* (Motion Picture Almanac) compiled by the Japanese Film Producers Association.[23] Another research source is Taiwanese film critic Lu Feng's paper (1980) which describes the post-Second World War exhibition network of Asian films. Lu (1980: 197) states that Japanese film producers led by Daiei's president Nagata Masaichi, apart from wanting to promote Japan-made films in Asia, had also wanted to correct the past negative militaristic image of Japan by means of culture and arts. Thus in 1953, the Southeast Asia Motion Pictures Producers' Association was established under the leadership of Japanese film producers with the co-support of Hong Kong film producers which included, notably, the Shaw Brothers. In 1954, the first Southeast

Asia Film Festival (later known as the Asian Film Festival) was held in Tokyo and during the event the first participating members of Japan, Taiwan, the Philippines, Hong Kong, Thailand, and Malaya (including Singapore) exhibited their respective domestic-made films. The *Eiga nenkan* dutifully reported on such gala film events and joint film projects. However, when the animated version of the *White Snake Tale* was completed, its title failed to appear on any of this regional film festival's program lists; neither the *Eiga nenkan* nor Lu Feng's paper mentions the exhibition of the animated film in the region's much publicized film festival.

As discussed earlier, the disagreement of the Hong Kong producer with the script was one factor; another might be the existence of the view that animation was considered a medium of lower status. When examining the history of the Asian Film Festival, for example, from 1954 to 1970, one will find that participating countries except Japan hardly submitted any, although time and again the Japanese submitted animated films in the competitive categories of the film festival. The Shaw Brothers Film Company, one of the most influential participating members, did not produce any animated films. However, on the Japanese side, right from the inception of the planned joint-film project (Otsuka, 2001: 30) which dated around mid-1956, the production process of the *White Snake Tale* had been widely reported in the local media. Perceptively, the Japanese producers recognized the strategic performative power of animation in the aftermath of a world war.

In the 1958 yearbook of the *Eiga nenkan*, a portion was devoted to the examination of films as an important leisure activity for children and young people in Japan. With the establishment of the *seishōnen eiga shingikai*, a discussion group formulating the film industry's responsibilities in providing entertainment for the young, it was decided that for young people between the ages of 15 and 18 (those who were attending upper secondary to pre-university studies), films should be made specifically for their *seinenmuki* (towards the direction of adolescents) category, while for children attending primary and lower secondary schools, they should be watching films made for the *shōnenmuki* (towards the direction of children and younger adolescents) category. Especially for the *seinenmuki* category, the following film production aims were formulated:

> to cultivate the appreciation of aesthetics and heighten the awareness of noble and positive emotions,
>
> to promote concern for and discussion of society's development,
>
> to promote right knowledge and cultivate deep understanding of ethics,
>
> to educate the love for humanity,
>
> to make bright entertainment films for positive reactions.[24]

Toei, in marketing itself as a newly established postwar film company, also tried to create a "brand niche" in the production of educational, cultural, children's and animated films. In the period of 1956–58, while the *White Snake Tale* was in production, the parent company promoted its plan to set up a three-storey high animation studio that would house the latest state-of-the-art technology, complete with air-conditioned facilities in certain sections of a concrete building complex. In the words of the studio's founder Okawa Hiroshi, "… we shall progressively produce and give birth to American-Disney's professional standard of animated films …" (*Eiga nenkan*, 1960: 332).

Thus, in 1958 when *Hakujaden* was completed and screened in Toei's chain of commercial cinemas in Japan, it attracted the attention of many talented high school and university graduates. Produced in Eastman color (rather than Japan's own Fuji color), this 78-minute color animated feature was Asia's first, comprising over 200,000 cel-drawings and other exquisite artwork that attracted job-seeking graduates from prestigious universities in Japan. Majoring in such diverse subjects as French literature, economics, accountancy, business administration, film studies, and Japanese and Western art, the graduates competed for jobs offered by the studio. Among them were Miyazaki Hayao and Takahata Isao, who were to make historical contributions to the development of Japanese animation in the later part of the twentieth century. In other words, the *sakuhin* (the performed work), together with the corporate image that the parent company promoted, had the power to "impress" and attract talents that the ambitious animation studio needed. By "exhibiting" the studio's capability to produce work at Disney's level, the studio also hoped to attract recruits who were drawn toward the senior training staff and the skills of experienced animators that the management had employed earlier.[25]

Animation scholar Maureen Furniss (1998: 17) writes that cel-based animation has an assembly-line application that resembles the Taylor form of scientific management, which ensures standardized processes in mechanization and labor-intensiveness.[26] When the Toei Animation Studio was established, the adoption of such management economics and animation production methodology fitted the postwar nation-building picture of Japan. From the management's perspective, the "dream-studio" provided jobs and created products for rebuilding a "happy national life" (*Eiga nenkan*, 1960: 333). However, dwelling at a deeper level of many Japanese minds were memories, regrets, disappointments, and unresolved issues of the large-scale prolonged war fought in the first-half of the twentieth century.[27] Therefore, many of the administrative and production staff members saw the studio as a place of "rebirth" in which they could "perform" a contributory role in rebuilding a new future for the current generation of children. Many of Toei's new recruits who joined at the end of the 1950s experienced the devastations of the war when they were children. Some were too young to serve in the military and some were called up to serve towards the end of the war. Collectively, the performative component of the studio served several dimensions and they were interwoven with intense personal self-healing feelings. In its workers' attempts to recover a lost innocence or childhood, and by participating in the childlike world that they had lost (many were under the spell of imperialistic ideology), the studio was regarded as a communal place to realize goals of modernization. This observation is based on my interviews with a number of retired and veteran Toei staff members in Tokyo from September 1998 to March 2000 and from August 2003 to July 2004.

Where the animated narrative of *White Snake Tale* is concerned, it may be too hasty to propound the idea that the "lived happily ever after" ending is a deliberate pro-Disney choice. However, a case can be made for this viewpoint, as I will elaborate in my conclusion. For now, I simply want to advance the notion that the positive ending of the animated tale, particularly the compassion, remorse, and the changed behavior of the Buddhist monk Fahai, could be explained as a kind of Jungian psychoanalytical act that indirectly symbolizes the nationalistic desire to be forgiven and the quest for a chance to reform and to recognize its past erroneous actions. Culturally, it could also be argued that the Japanese have a different perspective of a monk's lifestyle. In contrast to Indian and Chinese Buddhism, a Japanese Buddhist monk is allowed to have a family life if he so chooses and, like his fellow Shintō priests, his religious duties and responsibilities can be hereditary. In the Japanese case, Fahai's final ability to understand the man-woman relationship of Xu Xian and Pai-nyan was not a far-stretched development.[28] Therefore, although Yabushita Taiji was the director and scriptwriter of *Hakujaden*, the narrative contents of the animated story were a collective work. Furthermore, certain prominent animated segments of the film were supervised by the late Mori Yasuji (1925–92) who is remembered for the symbolic "happy animal communities" which he often designed and animated (see *Ukare baiorin*, 1955). For example, in *Hakujaden*, Panda and his group of animal-friends and their illustrated good deeds and friendship were created and chiefly designed by him. Applying psychoanalytic theory to Mori's early post-Second World War illustrated works, Yokota Masao (2004) argues that Mori chose the artistic path of animation in his search for salvation, peace, and happiness. (He was originally a trained architect.) Mori Yasuji was a much-respected senior training staff member in Toei during the foundational period. In interviews that I conducted for this research, many retired Toei members considered him the "best animation teacher," who had touched their lives in many ways — through his animated work, his kind and respectful demeanor, his dislike for authoritarian behavior, and his unselfish willingness to impart animation skills to others.[29]

Otsuka Yasuo (1931–), who was a younger staff member at Toei and had regarded Mori Yasuji as his senior, describes the new postwar animation era as *atarashii jidai* ("new age"):

> A time when all animators concerned, regarded the animated film "as a gift to children."

> Many of us had that dream ... as we made we saw ourselves as adult audiences not able to obtain something, as adults our communal feeling to achieve something, in live-action film which we do not get to see an egalitarian society emerging before us ... (Matsunomoto and Otsuka eds., 2004: 58)[30]

In other words, the making of commercial animation was viewed as a collective effort although it was recognized as a form of venture-enterprise in the first place. It was precisely this *shūdan*, "collective body" that Miyazaki Hayao writes about in his book, *Shuppatsuten* (1996) when describing his early animating experience at Toei Animation Studio.

The Chinese communities in East Asia and Southeast Asia were hardly aware of the Japanese-made animated version of the *White Snake Tale* until recently, although several live-action films made on the subject were widely known. According to the present senior managing director of the studio Yoshioka Osamu, the film was said to be shown in Southeast Asia during the time of its international release.[31] However, Yamaguchi and Watanabe (1977: 66) write that there was a report stating that Okawa Hiroshi contacted a Hong Kong film distributor for possible screening opportunities in the region and that versions dubbed with several Chinese dialects would be made. However, it is unclear whether the film was shown in that part of the world because Japanese-made films were banned in Korea and Taiwan in the decades that followed. In other parts of Southeast Asia, unless the films were internationally acclaimed (such as *Rashōmon* [1950] and *Seven Samurai* [1954] directed by Kurosawa Akira, and the *Tokyo Story* [1953] directed by Ozu Yasujiro) or were marketed as successful joint-projects (for example, with the Shaw Brothers Film Company), the region at the time was suspicious of films made in Japan due to its past militaristic actions.[32] In *Eiga nekan*, there were also occasional reports documenting the fear of the Japanese contingent when the film festival was held in one of the cities in Southeast Asia. The participating Japanese members were sensitive about the issue and were concerned with the *warui kuni* ("bad country") image that Japan had acquired from the last world war.

North America and Europe, however, were devoid of direct experiences of Japanese imperialism and had less painful memories of Japanese invasion. The reception of the animated tale therefore seemed more open and less complicated. Thus, it was precisely the color-animated *White Snake Tale* that launched the Toei Animation Studio to the world. The studio effectively promoted this flagship film in international film festivals in Europe and several film awards were given to the film.[33] Strategically, Toei was sharp in recognizing the exotic appeal of the tale, especially to Western viewers. For example, at the Berlin Film Festival in 1956, the live-action film version received a special award for its photographic color effects (*Eiga nenkan*, 1957: 149). Specifically, it can be inferred that from Toei management's long-term vision, a rather covert courtship was directed at the American market. The *Eiga nenkan* accounted that Toei executives visited the United States on several occasions to solicit joint co-operation and other possible contractual work. Through a local American agency called "Hits Incorporated,"[34] Toei even contacted Warner Brothers for possible engagement work. All these international marketing activities, especially those aimed at Western industrialized countries, implied that at a higher corporate level, the heavily invested animation studio was in search of wealthy partners for co-production and other contractual projects.[35]

The events recorded in *Eiga nenkan* also revealed that Toei's management producers were consistently patient and persistent in courting American investors. For example, when Hits Incorporated was not able to raise money for a joint project and wanted to abandon the planned partnership, Toei was willing to wait for a better opportunity and even took the initiative to keep the communication going. In contrast, a joint project with a Hong Kong producer came to a halt at a certain point and its final status was hardly reported or followed up at all.[36] The determination with which the studio had courted Western partners shows an underlying continuous trait in Japan's modernization history. While the country had failed miserably in the display of military and moral might towards the end of the Second World War, in aesthetic enticement and economic prowess, Japan continued (and still continues) to forge a long and lasting dialectical impression on the West. Toei's semi-nationalistic perseverance at last paid off, because in the mid-1960s a segment of the studio's workforce were devoted to American animated contract work. Among the earliest joint productions included *King Kong*, *Tom Thumb* (1967) and *Rats on the Mayflower* (1968). Both had been shown on the ABC television network in the United States (Toei, 1989: 55).

In summary, although *Hakujaden* succeeded in proving to the Japanese public the high standards of production which the studio could offer, there were mixed feelings towards the production direction of the animated tale. A newspaper reporter questioned critically the overall narrative treatment of the tale, particularly the "un-Chineseness" and the "un-Japaneseness" that resulted, and that the studio had neglected the deeper sensitive meaning of the tale by simplifying the conclusion.[37] Other film reviewers understood the "export-oriented" intentions of the animated tale, but dismissed it as an unnationalistic venture because the producers chose to work on a non-Japanese classic tale. As this analysis has so far demonstrated, the new patron-narrator of *Legend of the White Snake* had set its goals in a long-term economic perspective and was only mindful of its ethnic origin to a certain extent. What mattered was commercial entertainment which eventually unfolded a phenomenon of competitive growth in the animation medium in Japan, especially with the arrival of television as a screening medium later.

Specifically, in "exhibiting" its ability to animate a non-Japanese tale, the studio went a long way in proving to the Western world the working qualities of a group of Eastern people in telling stories and expressing art in peaceful times. In a collective corporate sense, the resurrection of *Legend of the White Snake* on Japanese soil was an advantageous performative venture because the end in sight was not only to attract subsequent international business contracts to its enterprise, but also to seek opportunities for animating Western-based children stories so that — ideologically, economically, and aesthetically — the East–West communication link with Japan would prevail. In analyzing the global economic success of Japan in the late twentieth century, Dower (1999: 557) describes "the genie had come out of the bottle again, only this time in a business suit rather than in khaki." In actuality, it need not necessarily be as material as a business suit, for the "uncanny and fantastic" is just as effectively representative and in fact more subtle and indirectly sensual. Madam White Snake became nationally displaced and borrowed by another; in illustrating her animatedly, her powers were equally dynamic and far-reaching, she was renarrated to reach out to the Occidental world.

God of Comics: Tezuka Osamu

Becoming the Disney of the Orient

The late manga artist Tezuka Osamu (1928–89) came from a well-educated background. Although a medical doctor by training, he chose to tread the paths of manga and animation and his phenomenal rise in the 1960s was one of the contributing factors to Japan's further expansion in animation production. In his memoirs, written at a time when he was already a highly celebrated manga artist in Japan, Tezuka remembered fondly the lyrical aspects of wartime animation film, *Momotarō umi no shinpei*. He was attracted especially to the "emotion" and "dream-like" elements and vowed to become a professional animator. Incidentally, those aesthetic sequences were animated by Masaoka Kenzō (NHK documentary series on "History of Japanese Animation," November 1998). Tezuka paid tribute to the *Momotarō* film (1945) which he saw in a theater despite the dangerous air raids. He described how he became tearful when watching the film and vowed that he would like to make similar animation in the future (*The Animation Filmography of Osamu Tezuka*, 1991: 8). The memoirs first appeared in a Tokyo newspaper in the mid-1960s. Tezuka's glowing tribute to the film has been questioned by some contemporary animation and manga critics, producers, and animators in Japan who are puzzled by his "silence" toward the obviously racist overtones and violent war elements found in the film.[38] A Kansai resident, Tezuka once traveled to Tokyo and approached an animation company for an apprentice job. His work was rejected due to its manga-like approach and was instead praised for its print publishing potential. Disheartened and disappointed, Tezuka returned to Osaka. Years later, he had already become a medical doctor after graduating from the Osaka University College of Medicine when the screening of Toei's *Hakujuden* rekindled his innermost interest in animation.

However, Tezuka's aspirations had grown into a bigger Walt Disney-like dream; like Toei Animation Studio, he also harbored covert ambitions. Tezuka was known to have watched every pre-war Disney-made production and was described as a "fanatical fan" (Schodt, 1983: 160).[39] Following in the footsteps of Disney who owned a kingdom of well-loved cartoon characters, Tezuka had by the late 1950s created his own pool of characters based on his successful manga stories.

After he was rejected as an animator apprentice, Tezuka did take up the publishing challenge and in 1947 his manga stories began to appear in publications for children and youths. Throughout his undergraduate years he continued his manga pursuits, and by the time he graduated in 1951, his works were a common sight in dailies and periodicals and were dramatized in radio programs as well. His best-known manga works include *New Treasure Island, Jungle Taitei* (also known as *Kimba, the White Lion*), and *Tetsuwan Atomu* (or internationally known as *Astro Boy*). Unofficial records report that his *New Treasure Island* sold "between 400,000 and 800,000" copies and the comic book itself carries 200 pages (Schodt, 1983: 62).

By the mid-1950s, Tezuka was reported to be the richest commercial artist in the Kansai region. Because of his popularity, Toei decided to collaborate with him in 1958. The project was based on his comic work *Saiyūki*, which Tezuka wrote in 1952. The story was based on a legendary Chinese folktale known as *Journey to the West*. The collaboration marked his entry into the world of animation production and he quickly learned the techniques. *Saiyūki* (1960), Tezuka's first animated work with Toei, had a hybrid touch that was in sync with the export-oriented objectives of Toei's management. Like the narrative direction of *Hakujaden*, Tezuka's version of *Saiyūki* did not adhere to an ordinary Chinese understanding of the tale. For example, the main male protagonist, the Monkey God, had a lover throughout the film, and intermingled within the film were motifs of Greek gods and modern telecommunication equipment. It was noted that for the conceptual development of *Saiyūki*, Tezuka and his key staff members had reread the original Chinese tale and rewatched the Chinese animated production of *Princess Iron Fan* and many other old Disney animated works (Yamaguchi and Watanabe, 1977: 72).[40] *Saiyūki* was marketed to the West with such English titles as *Enchanted Monkey* and *Alakazam the Great*, and the film received several film awards in Europe. Later, Toei even made a film segment which copied Walt Disney's way of introducing his cartoon characters from his executive office. While Walt Disney had Mickey Mouse posing side by side "live" with him, Toei's president Okawa Hiroshi selected the cartoon character of Monkey God to do the same.

In 1961, Tezuka established his own animation production studio, which was later known as Mushi Productions. With the arrival of television as a popular tool of mass communication in the early 1960s, Tezuka's manga works were to influence the development of Japanese animation, leading to the birth of a new genre called *anime*, now, a significant entertainment medium-genre in the world of animation.

New comic style: Gekiga

Tezuka's manga style revolutionizes the rigid frame-by-frame presentation of comic narrative. Firstly, the page layout becomes more fluid and creative. There is a strong presence of sound effects and he also "experimented with close-ups and different angles" (Schodt, 1983: 63) in order to emphasize action and the mental states of the characters. His illustrations largely incorporate filmic-like effects with strong emphasis on shadows and shades. As his contributions to the artistic and industrial development of the Japanese comic industry are qualitative, quantitative, and even spiritual in the minds of millions of Japanese readers, he has been given the title "God of Comics" (in Japanese, *manga no kamisama*) within his lifetime, and still holds the title today.[41]

However, Tezuka was not alone in elevating the manga medium to new heights. His cinematic "drama picture" or *gekiga* was also used by other manga artists including Shirato Sanpei, Saitō Takao, Satō Masaaki, and Tatsumi Yoshihiro (Yaguchi et al., 1998).[42] Ideologically, the generic title of this new comic art form speaks of its fresh revolutionary stance. The Chinese character *geki* means "theater" and "drama" while *ga* means "picture." In other words, this "theatrical picture" comic art form aims to bring more realism into comic reading. Themes of suspense and mystery are focal points of the work of the artists mentioned above and are expressed through execution, story development, and psychological disposition of the characters. This is a deliberately rebellious diversion from the comic medium's seemingly innocent outlook. The intensity of *gekiga* expressions is stretched further with the adoption of photo-realist illustrations. For example, Miyaya Kazuhiko's manga, *Tokyo tomin ereji-* (1973, translated as "Tokyo Manslaughter Elegy") was among the first to portray Tokyo in all its facets and shapes. Intentionally drawn at a detailed photo-realist level, the complexities, the mazes, and the dirt of downtown Tokyo are given in "full glory" for the reading eyes of the beholder (Natsume, 1995: 228–233).

We may consider *gekiga* a twentieth-century development and variant of the earlier *ukiyo-e* and *gentō* illustrative media. Especially during the late Edo period, *ukiyo-e* paintings became more life-like because of the influence of photography. On the subject of character portrayal, the mesmerizing angle pose, the deliberate placement of the body figure from the waist upwards, the detailed rendering of the attire, and the additional "sparkle" of the eyes ("catchlight" or *shiroi ten*)[43] were all newfound features in *ukiyo-e* in the later part of the Edo period. During that period, as in a large portion of manga-anime work produced from the 1960s onward, popular cultural characters were portrayed as "heroes." While *ukiyo-e* and *gentō* featured samurai heroes such as the *Forty-seven rōnin* and other Meiji military heroes and statesmen that came after, a substantial amount of manga-anime present heroic characters in robotic outfits. These include, for example, the highly successful *Gundam* series (since 1979) created by Tomino Yoshiyuki,[44] the *Macross* series (since 1982),[45] the *Evangelion* series (1995) directed by Anno Hideaki, and even female robot characters as exemplified by director Oshii Mamoru's animated films, *Ghost in the Shell* (1995) and *Ghost in the Shell 2: Innocence* (2004).

The growing appeal of manga in Japan since after the war is also due to the medium's ability to expand its readership base. It is able to cater to different age groups in terms of style and selection of story contents. The evolution of *gekiga* in response to the changing social circumstances has been reflected in not only innovation and style but also ideology. High school and university students and working adults have become the target audience. The increasingly realistic portrayal of subject matter in postwar Japan was in part due to the changing social circumstances and mounting dissatisfaction with superficial directions the society was taking (Yaguchi et al., 1998).[46] From a larger socio-political perspective, postwar Japan (especially from the early 1960s to the 1970s) had acquired an international reputation for being an "economic animal" because of its relentless capitalistic industrial drive. Internally, there were also new pressures in addition to unsolved issues and legacies.

The ultimate marriage of the two media, manga and animation, reflected Japan's rapid industrial and economic growth from the 1960s onward. The combination of the two genres was to become an essential part of postwar Japanese popular culture, which would influence the trends of Japanese animation development. Tezuka Osamu played a primary role in the gestation of anime, but it would be short-sighted to attribute to him sole responsibility for this new phenomenal development. His creative ventures only demonstrate the old and evolving cultural developments of the country, which include the continuing search for a geo-political identity and the best means to express graphically and emotionally in non-verbal and non-rationalistic settings.

Defining Anime and the Reception of Anime

Tezuka's first television animated series, *Astro Boy*, was aired on Fuji Television in January 1963.[47] Although the series had a major sponsor (the Meiji Sweets Company), Tezuka's subsequent lack of experience in managing both the business and technical aspects of animation production left an indelible mark on the postwar development of Japanese animation. (See Chapter 7 where I discuss the bankruptcy of Mushi Productions in 1973 and the low salaries of contemporary Japanese animators.)

On the other hand, from a cultural-creative perspective, Tezuka's enthusiasm in transforming his manga into television animated works contributed a new development in postwar Japanese animation. Under his supervision, animated movements and frames found in the *Astro Boy* series were limited and static. The reasons behind this "creative" consequence were multifold. From a critical perspective, it could be argued that Tezuka's haste in converting his manga work into television animation had neglected the artistic and technical requirements of the animation medium. Moreover, the production schedule for a 30-minute weekly episode was demanding and Tezuka lacked experienced animators who could assist him.[48] It was inevitable that the resulting production work was regarded as "out of the ordinary." In mainstream commercial full animation, especially if one aspires to the Disney feature film standard, as many as 24 drawn animated frames per second could be expected. In other words, full animation requires a maximum possible number of drawings (Noake, 1988: 105). In Tezuka's *Astro Boy* animated series, there were fewer drawn animated frames; sometimes as few as two frames per second were present.

However, Tezuka was already a successful well-known manga artist. His comic stories by now bore his permanent auteurish mark. So when television audiences viewed his transformed comic story in a different medium, his original manga narrative, his collection of established characters, and pre-existing drawn cinematic panel pictures were reflected in their minds. Therefore, by sheer fame and a firm belief in his manga genius, Tezuka was confident in the size of audiences he could amass for his newly directed animated television series, and he was right in trusting his auteurish appeal. The "limited animation" of *Astro Boy* gradually gained a stable ground of audiences, so much so that rival television networks and subsequent converted manga-animated works adopted this formulaic form of animation production.[49]

Tezuka's form of limited animation has been criticized for its self-centeredness, which is a self-glorification commercial enterprise that celebrates the inward-looking world of creative work (see Miyazaki, 1996; Takahata, 1991; Otsuka, 2001). In reality, the appeal of this form of animation cannot be originated from the creator alone. As Noake (1988: 105) has cautioned,

> … there is a danger in confusing full animation with good animation. At its best it can be excellent. But if full animation is used as the norm by which all other animation is judged, this can promote a crude and narrow attitude. It is best to judge the different categories of animation on their own terms, rather than imposing a single set of criteria onto a very wide spectrum of work.

In the case of the Japanese form of limited animation and its pro-manga and pro-television origins, the reception aspects of the medium-genre have to be examined.

How viewers accept and respond to a "new" genre involves experiences of the past, which include the pre-existing array of literary forms and art forms that are available and active in cultural memory and practice. Astro Boy's limited and so-called "stiff" movements in animated television frames, in a way, are similar to the slow acting pace of a *nō* actor. The external spectacle may be resting in an inert pose and mode, but what matters most is the innate psychological state of the character that is being portrayed. Although anime may harness modern technology to perform, how the audience makes sense of the performance is another important consideration.

Moreover, anime has a modern predecessor. Dating back to the early Shōwa period, picture-card storytelling was a form of open-air theater in which children listened to stories as picture cards were displayed. These picture-card storytellers, in Japanese *kamishibai*, traveled from village to village with their mobile stalls of picture-cards and sweets *(okashi)*. A *kamishibai* usually set up his stall at an alley corner of the village and children would swarm toward his makeshift open-air theater with their hand-carried stools. The storytelling hours would pass leisurely as the *kamishibai* displayed his picture cards with animated elocution. The set of especially prepared picture-cards were individually created as many *kamishibai* were artists by training (Tsurumi, 1987: 33). The subtle draw of the show was the *okashi* which the *kamishibai* distributed at the beginning of his performance in exchange for the entertainment fare he charged. Like *kamishibai*, anime plays an important storytelling role, except that it can be viewed more conveniently in the comfort of a living room and at designated times every week.

I have met many Japanese in their thirties and forties, who informed me that anime literally "baby-sat" them as they grew up in the 1960s and 1970s. Prime-time television began in the late afternoon or early evening (6 p.m.) every day and continued for about two hours. During this period, several manga-turned-animated works were screened. The target audiences came from different age groups, ranging from kindergarten and primary school children to junior and senior high school youths. Manga-anime television series were therefore lined up in the order according to the age groups to which their target audiences belonged. Competing television stations all followed this format and each station was a patron to several popular manga-anime.[50]

In writing about the influence of manga especially on those who were born after the Second World War, performance studies scholar Fukushima Yoshiko (2003: 8)[51] notes the pervasive pattern: "It is common today to see these children, now working adults, reading *manga* on commuter trains." She further points out the language function of manga: "*Manga* images appear everywhere in advertisements and public service announcements, helping to soften a complicated social and written system by adding a playful tone." Interestingly, Tezuka did not consider his manga drawings as pictures

> I think of them as a type of hieroglyphics ... In reality, I'm not drawing. I am writing a story with a unique type of symbol. (Schodt, 1983: 25)

The above refers to the language inquiry that is posed in the first chapter of this book. Isn't anime part of the extension of a "visual language" that the Japanese have pursued and valued apart from the daily use of a language that has been constructed through the ages? Or, isn't this "visual language" an amalgamation of cultural art forms and ideas, including the embodiment of socio-historical changes that the country has undergone so far? In Japan alone, the medium of animation has been given different names. They include *anime-shon, manga-eiga, dōga, anime manga, komikku eiga, manga fuirumu, bideo ge-mu anime*, and so on. Furthermore, an average Japanese also addresses the medium of animation as *anime*, be it Turkish anime, Russian anime, or French anime. He or she is not generally aware that, globally, the term *anime* possesses specific generic meanings that pertain to Japan alone. Manga critic, Yonezawa Yoshihiro (2005: 160–161), sums up the kind of popular animation that has emerged from Japan since the 1960s this way: whether it is a feature-length *manga eiga, terebi manga,* or *terebi anime*, in actuality, one is watching *ugoku manga* (meaning "moving manga") as the "pictures come alive" before a screen. Yonezawa also puts forward the view that contemporary animation director Miyazaki Hayao's works have been highly popular among Japanese viewers because he is able to conglomerate three seemingly different visual genres — the traditional *e monogatari* (picture narrative or tale), *manga* (comic story), and *anime* (animation) — into one visual presentation.[52]

As mentioned in Chapter 4, Yamaguchi and Watanabe (1977: 12–13) designate the term *senga eiga* ("line drawing film") as the earliest title given to animation in Japan. Since the picture carried "moving lines," as seen from the early imported Western cartoons, *senga eiga* was considered a specific film genre. Later, *manga* was used to categorize comics with a focus on current affairs; the term was first used toward the end of the nineteenth century by comic artist Kitazawa Rakuten (1876–1955), who wanted to differentiate his works from the run-of-the-mill, slapstick-like comic works. *Manga* became a popular term for denoting comic with a storyline. *Manga eiga* ("manga film") gradually came to be regarded as a story-based form of animation whereas *senga eiga* was appreciated for its graphical presentation of "machines, plants, and animals," especially the inner sketches, designs, and networks. Other early name terms of animation that had already been used before the end of the war include *byōga eiga* ("drawing film"), *kongō eiga* ("mixed film"), and *dōga* ("moving picture").

It is interesting to note that the term *manga eiga* was once regarded as an American-influenced type of animation comprising "slapstick humor" and "gags." This was the time when animators and film critics in Japan analyzed the Chinese-made animated film, *Princess Iron Fan* (1941, see Chapter 4). That film was acclaimed as an "art film" (*kaiga eiga*) because of its "complex" narrative contents (see Takakiba, 1942 and *Eiga Gijutsu*, 1942).

Yamaguchi and Watanabe also recount that the term *dōga* was a relative latecomer in Japanese animation vocabulary because it was only introduced in 1937 when animation master Masaoka Kenzō set up the Nihon Dōga Kyōkai ("Japan Animation Association") in Kyoto.[53] Etymologically, the Japanese were the first to coin the term *manga* (in Chinese *manhua*) and some dictionaries in Japan attribute the origin of the term to *ukiyo-e* artist, Katsushika Hokusai (1760–1849), who published a collection of drawings and caricatures entitled *Hokusai manga* in 1814.[54] The word *man* means casual, free, and careless; it can also mean boundless and overflowing. *Ga* means picture or drawing. When combined, the two characters convey a free imaginative world in which rules and regulations retreat to the background. What surfaces and permeates is another visual cosmic space that can give rein to all kinds of expressions and communicative yearnings.[55] After the war, *anime-shon* (written in the *katakana* script) became a commonly used term in the film industry and also in Japanese lingua franca, largely due to the heightened process of Westernization during the Allied Forces Occupation when many Anglo-Saxon vocabulary terms were adopted into the Japanese language. Veteran animator Otsuka Yasuo (2001: 29), when writing on the history of Toei Animation Studio, notes that during that time, animators preferred the term *anime-shon*, as it depicted more possibilities of the medium, particularly its technical expressiveness as compared to the older, pre-war linguistic term, *manga eiga*. It is not sure when exactly the term *anime* became entrenched in Japanese vocabulary. Browsing through the literature printed in the 1970s, including promotional leaflets and film magazines, the term *anime* often appears. However, it is possible to presume that the abbreviated term already existed in the 1960s, during which *anime-shon* or *anime* was fast becoming a popular new genre or visual form in Japanese popular culture. Yamaguchi and Watanabe (1977: 91) note that it was in the early months of 1960 that Japanese newsreaders began to use the terms *anime-shon* and *anime-ta* in their broadcasts although the term *manga eiga* continued to be used as well.

It is possible that the term *anime-shon* was abbreviated to *anime* at the same time when manga-based stories became important sources for animated works. Indefinite, variegated, and diversified as they may seem, the multilingual terms of animation available in the Japanese language serve to testify to the fluid perspective from which the society views the medium. Moreover, the potentialities and limits of this thriving "visual language" need a variety of audiences to support it, not to mention the equally important participating institutions and business corporations.

In short, anime is part of this visual bond or nexus of Japanese cultural history. Its growth has been organic and voluntary as seen especially from the second industrial development of Japanese animation shortly after the Second World War.

6

Miyazaki and Takahata Anime Cinema

> It is well-known that Japan is an economic superpower — the world's greatest asset country — with the biggest per capita GNP, the biggest aid budgets, the biggest banks, and many of the biggest corporations in the world, and the center of the most dynamic sector of the world-trading system. But can it be assumed that, because Japan is economically resoundingly successful as a nation, its people are correspondingly happy, wealthy and enjoying the fruits of that success?
>
> McCormack (2001: 78)

This chapter continues to trace the postwar development of Japanese animation from the 1970s onward. In particular, the rise of master animator Miyazaki Hayao and his colleague, animation director Takahata Isao, will be discussed in detail. In examining the eminence of Japan's animation industry, the close working relationship of Miyazaki and Takahata in the past cannot be overlooked. It is important to examine the common elements found in their works. They founded Studio Ghibli in 1985, which almost equaled the status of Toei Dōga. The establishment of such a Toei-like animation studio was aimed primarily to produce animated feature films. Since the mid-1980s, Studio Ghibli's films have become well-known in Japan and abroad. The colorful and meandering maze of Japanese animation in the late twentieth and early twenty-first centuries is explored in this chapter. In the process, I cross-examine the animated works of Miyazaki and Takahata and others in the wider socio-economic development of contemporary Japan. Given the prominent directorial narrating worlds of Miyazaki and Takahata, the "auteur model" is applied in analyzing their animated works. My analysis attempts to show how they have utilized the expressive medium of animation in responding to the changing socio-cultural environment of later post-Second World War Japan.

The Continual Growth of Other Forms of Animation

Despite the large-scale commercialization of Japanese animation since the 1960s, which has led to the birth of the new medium-genre *manga-anime*, there are animators who have remained independent and are working from their home studios and small offices. Others have formed small-group enterprise studios serving the needs and interests of the non-commercial sector. Most of these independent animators are specialist artists, who are often from non-cel animation fields and prefer to animate with clay, puppets, and so on. Among the earliest is artist-animator Kuri Yoji (1928–) who, together with two friends, designer Yanagihara Ryōhei (1931–) and illustrator Manabe Hiroshi (1932–2000), founded in 1960 an animation exhibition group called *Anime-shon sannin no kai*. The group focused on the experimentation and innovation of Japanese animation. From the onset, they were more interested in producing short animated films for exhibition purposes and introduced other forms of animation from overseas. Their efforts led to international recognition of their work. In particular, Kuri's creations were highly regarded because his independent animated films once again renewed the country's tradition of artistic contributions to world animation. A manga artist at heart, Kuri's work is known for its surrealistic and satirical content that comments on the ills of an industrial society.

This three-member animation group started an important trend in exhibiting independent animation. In 1964, they founded what was to become a prominent annual screening event called Animation Festival in an urban hall in Tokyo. The event was later extended to Osaka, Nagoya, Kyoto, Fukuoka, and other cities. In addition, the trio was able to attract the attention of television stations, which began to air their works. Ideologically, the trio wanted to show the many possibilities and potentialities of animation and to express the view that the medium should not be limited to the Disney kind of animation. Another objective that the group wanted to achieve was to liberalize and lobby for more exhibiting space for independent animated works (Yamaguchi and Watanabe, 1977: 93).

Other independent artists who achieved artistic excellence and international recognition include the late Okamoto Tadanari (1932–90) whose ingenious use of textile thread material in creating animated characters and movements won the hearts of both children and adults; and master puppet animator, the late Mochinaga Tadahito (1919–99), was known not only for his animated work but the time and effort he spent in nurturing young animators both in Japan and in China. Kawamoto Kihachiro (1924–), one of Mochinaga's students, became a familiar name in international animation as he adapted some of the techniques and narrative styles of Czech puppet master animator, Jiri Trnka (1912–), with whom he understudied for a period of time. Kawamoto's animated works also incorporate the *nō* storytelling method skillfully by using delicate filming angles and traditional Japanese music soundtracks to evoke a classical Japanese theatrical atmosphere.

The above-mentioned animator-artists were some of the notable founders of Japan Animation Film Association (JAFA) in 1971 whose aim was "to promote animation culture in Japan." That period also saw the creation of two independent 16 mm films, *History of Japanese Animation Part I and II* (directed by Yabushita Taiji, 1970, 1972), charting the rise of Japanese animation from the early twentieth century. JAFA was renamed Japan Animation Association (JAA) in 1978 and has since held annual or bi-annual film festivals which provide exhibiting space for independent animations. The association currently has about 130 members with job descriptions ranging from animators to film researchers, producers, screenwriters, and educators. As it is a non-profit organization, most of its members volunteer to raise funds for the organization's events.

The mid-1970s saw the formation of an avant-garde group under the auspices of the prestigious Image Forum in central Tokyo. Linked to this group were students and amateur animators looking for a platform to produce and screen their works. The inauguration of Hiroshima International Animation Festival in 1985 created an exciting trend that encourages members of JAA, Image Forum, and even commercial animators to produce and submit high-quality independent works for international competition.

While the film industry has annually submitted animation films to regional and international film competitions and festivals since the mid-1950s (see Chapter 5), the country's animation industry per se has its own way of recognizing outstanding animated works. Named after animator Ofugi Noburo who passed away in 1961, a film award called the *Ofugi Noburo Prize* was established soon after his death with the assistance of Nihon University, Mainichi Shimbun and other associated film institutions. This prestigious and much coveted animation film award has since honored works by Tezuka Osamu, Miyazaki Hayao, Takahata Isao, Sugii Gisaburo, Kawamoto Kihachiro, Katsuhiro Ōtomo, and others.

Today, Japan's independent animation artists belong broadly to two groups: one relies on short-term commercial projects in areas of advertising, MTV, and educational projects to survive, and the other relies mainly on non-profit organizations such as academic institutions and ad hoc artistic projects to support their more experimental and avant-garde creations. Generally, both groups tend to avoid commercial manga-anime studio work. They prefer to work on their independent productions. For example, according to independent animator Yamamura Kōji (1964–), his artistic independence is fortunately "insured" by the use of computer, which enables him to meet production demands of manageable projects. Otherwise, he would be quite ready to return to anime studio work if independent projects became scarce.[1] Yamamura has since made an indelible mark in Japanese independent animation. His short animated work *Atama yama* (2002) earned an Academy Award nomination in 2003. It catapulted him to national fame that almost equalled Miyazaki's. Incidentally, Miyazaki's directed commercial animated film, *Sen to chihiro no kamikakushi* (*Spirited Away*, 2001) won an Oscar for Best Animated Feature Film in 2003.

Lately, a number of independent animators who have acquired strong 3-D animating skills have also begun making better known manga-anime film projects. For example, some of the sequences in the films *Ghost in the Shell 2 Innocence* (2003) and *Doraemon* (2004) were animated by the husband and wife team, IKIF (Ishida Kifune Image Factory), with the assistance of students from Tokyo Zokei University.[2]

When outlining the steady but not as prominent growth of independent animation in Japan, NHK (the country's public broadcasting network) deserves to be mentioned. It continues to play a significant role in sustaining non-commercial animation. For example, it supported the pioneer trio's (Kuri and his two partners) animated work in the 1960s by sponsoring special television projects and series. For various puppetry works of Okamoto and Kawamoto and others, as well as many non-manga-based short-term and medium-term animation series, NHK has been an important broadcasting space. Both veteran and up-and-coming independent animators compete for airtime on the network. Its long-running animated musical series for children, *Minna no uta* ("Everyone's Songs," since 1961), is a delightful audio-visual program to watch; each new song is introduced in an animated form that pushes creativity and community education to new heights. Other television stations such as TBS have also produced memorable animated series like the popular *Nihon mukashi banashi* ("Once Upon a Time in Japan"). It is an educational project based on a collection of Japanese children's folktales. A total of 39 series were made from 1975 to 1994 (see http://www.tbs.co.jp/program/mukashibanashi.html and also Yamaguchi and Watanabe, 1977: 343).[3]

Miyazaki and Takahata's Early Partnership Years

At Toei Dōga (1963–71)

Although Toei was a nurturing ground for many fine artists, producers, and animators, a number of the staff eventually left to pursue their own careers. The most notable *nakama* pair who later made a name for themselves in the late twentieth century was perhaps Miyazaki Hayao and Isao Takahata. Their partnership began in 1963–64. According to Takahata, "there were countless things we wanted to do" (*Kinema Junpō*, July 16, 1995). For example, both wanted to produce films as good as Walt Disney's animated films and other influential European works such as the award-winning Russian animated film, *The Snow Queen* (1957)[4] and the French animated film, *La Bergère et le Ramoneur* ("The Curious Adventures of Mr Wonderbird," 1953).[5]

During that time, Takahata was already an up-and-coming young director while Miyazaki worked as an in-between artist in the feature film, *The Doggie March* (*Wan Wan Chūshingura*, 1963). Because of his drawing abilities and enthusiasm for storyboarding and story development, Miyazaki's talent began to attract the attention of directors in the studio and one of them was Takahata.[6] It is known within the industry that Miyazaki's rise was due to Takahata's appreciation of his animating skills. Takahata was confident in expanding his younger colleague's work portfolio from a low-in-between animator-artist to a key animator and scenic set designer. In an interview which Takahata gave some thirty years later, he attributed Miyazaki's talent to his "power of perseverance" and described him as "an energetic young man with a huge talent" (*Kinema Junpō*, 1995: 16–25). Their *nakama* relationship at Toei was also a driving force behind their partnership. *Nakama* is a Japanese term which means a "friend, a partner, a comrade, or a confidante." According to Takahata, there were many *nakama* relationships at Toei during their time and it was partly due to the intense and hectic schedule of their labor-intensive work. He also paid tribute to his other *nakama* relationship with Otsuka Yasuo, his senior/*senpai* who was more experienced and a key supervising animator of *Taiyo no ōji horusu no daibōken* (*Prince of the Sun: The Great Adventures of Hols*, 1968).[7] The film occupies an important and historic place in Japanese animation cinema. By 1964, Takahata, Miyazaki, and Otsuka were actively involved in Toei Dōga Labor Union activities. Miyazaki was then the union's secretary-general while Takahata was the vice-chairman. Miyazaki began to work closely with Isao Takahata on a television series *Hustle Punch* (*Hassuru Punch*). He was a key animator. Later, it was the animated feature film *Hols* that tested their ability to work together successfully.

In the mid-1960s, Toei also faced stiff competition from rival studios that produced lucrative television animation series. During that period, television had become a popular medium of entertainment and communication in Japan, and Toei's management also decided to focus on producing animated television series. Eventually, there was a shortage of staff to work on the production of *Hols*. As a result, the film was made during a period that was shrouded with heated management arguments, threats, and labor disputes. In terms of artistic achievement, the animated story appealed both visually and narratively to university students and high school graduates (Fan, 1997: 141). Surprisingly, the film was only shown for ten days in the theater and Toei was disappointed with the "kind" of audience attending the film; the management was most concerned that the film did not seem to attract younger viewers, especially children. *Hols* became the lowest earning animation film in Toei Dōga's box office returns and consequently, Takahata was demoted to assistant director.

As a result of their trade union activities and "die-hard" attitude toward the making of *Hols*, the period in which Miyazaki and Takahata worked at Toei Dōga has often been regarded by critics and industry sources as a revolutionary part of their partnership. Contemporary animator Mamoru Oshii regards the "militant tendencies" of this *nakama* pair as a mixture of Marxist and animation fervor (*Kinema Junpō*, July 16, 1995). Indeed, embedded ideological meanings are found in the narrative content of the film itself and are reflective of the ongoing labor disputes at Toei Dōga and the popular citizen movements in Japan during the 1960s.[8] The film *Hols* might have become a sacrificial lamb, as was Takahata's film career at Toei, but the film marked a new chapter in Japanese animation cinema especially in its thematic appeal of young people's idealism. Fan (1997: 141) describes *Hols* as a historic "li zhi de qin chun dong hua" meaning the film focused on values like youthful determination and perseverance. In other words, a new category of animation was born which became characteristic of future animated works of Miyazaki and Takahata and especially that of Studio Ghibli later on.

Going independent (from 1971–early 1980s)

> Our aim was to produce work that we liked and there were challenges
> as Toei was no longer able to provide that.[9]

Soon after senior colleague Otsuka Yasuo resigned from Toei in 1971, Takahata, Miyazaki, and a close colleague Kotabe Yōichi decided to follow suit. As television animation became more popular and a growing number of manga stories were adapted and animated as television series, these ex-Toei colleagues also accepted work assignments that were commissioned for the television screen. Such works included the increasingly popular *Lupin III*, which was based on a manga series by Monkey Punch.[10] Takahata and Miyazaki partially or fully directed 23 episodes. Their senior colleague Otsuka Yasuo was also involved in animating some episodes. In 1972, the team made a 33-minute animation film called *Panda kopanda* ("Panda and Child"). Takahata was the director while Miyazaki, Otsuka, Kotabe, and a new staff artist Kondō Yoshifumi (1950–98) were responsible for the animation. Miyazaki was the chief character designer and it was said that the panda figure was the prototype of Totoro which Miyazaki produced some 15 years later. The idea was based on the normalization of bilateral ties with China in 1972, a historic episode in Japan's post-Second World War history. China commemorated the event by giving two pandas to Japan. In 1973, a film sequel entitled *Panda kopanda amefurisa-kasu no maki* ("Panda Child: Rainy Day Circus") was also made. It was a 38-minute short feature film. Miyazaki again took the lead in animation and design while Takahata directed the film.

In between making those films, the group was also animating and directing television series on an ad hoc basis. From 1974 onward, they were involved in the creation of several highly popular television series and each of them made an indelible mark on the history of Japanese television animation. They included *Arupusu no shōjo haiji* (*Heidi: Girl of the Alps/Alpine Girl, Heidi,* 1974), *Haha wo tazunete sanzenri* (*Three Thousand Miles in Search of Mother,* 1976) and *Akage no an* (*Anne of Green Gables,* 1979). Each series consists of 50 episodes or so; because of its audio-visual appeal (art design, music and story development), these television series were able to draw the emotional attachment of viewers from one episode to the next, week after week. These works were produced by Nippon Animation, Tokyo Movie Shinsha, and Zuyō Eizō, either jointly or separately. They became known as part of the *Sekai meisaku gekijō* ("World Masterpiece Theater").[11]

Miyazaki, on the other hand, also began to develop his own television series in 1977. In 1978, *Mirai shonen conan* (*Future Boy Conan*) was launched. The popular series was aired in an early evening prime time slot on NHK every Sunday. It carried 26 episodes and was widely regarded as the prototype for his later films, *Nausicaä of the Valley of the Wind* (1984) and *Laputa: The Castle in the Sky* (1986). *Future Boy Conan* was also hailed as the first manga-like anime television series ever to be commissioned by a public television station.[12] Finally, in 1979, Miyazaki was invited to direct a special feature animated film, *Lupin III: Castle of Cagliostro* (in Japanese, *Rupan sansei: Kariosutoro no shiro*). Assisted by the experienced Otsuka, Miyazaki was the co-writer and storyboard designer of this 100-minute film. It was his first animation film in which he fully directed, and it marked a new beginning in his animation career.

Takahata, on the other hand, directed *Jarinko Chie* (1981), which was based on a popular manga story by Haruki Etsumi. The success of the animated feature film led to the production of an animated television series, *Jarinko Chie*. In the same year, he also directed an independent animated film, *Serohiki no gō-shu* (*Gōshu: The Cellist*), which was based on a short story by a well-known Meiji writer, Miyazawa Kenji (1896–1933). Like *Castle of Cagliostro*, this film was awarded the prestigious Ofuji Noburo Prize. Thus by the turn of the decade, Takahata and Miyazaki and their colleagues had become a formidable force in the animation industry. Their work and the rest of the animation workforce in Japan were also capturing the attention of international producers. Miyazaki and Takahata were invited to develop and participate in overseas animation projects, some of which materialized on screen while others were abandoned at various stages.[13] Their enthusiasm in animation-making was boundless; while Miyazaki continued his creative expansion in manga and picture-book publication, Takahata was keen on participating in discussion seminars and writing books related to animation.

In 1981, publishing conglomerate Tokuma Shoten Co. Ltd. launched an animation magazine called *Animage*, which focuses news and special reports on new television animation series, animated feature films, and manga stories. It also became the "art patron" of Miyazaki and his teammates' animation ambitions. In 1982, Miyazaki's manga, *Kaze no tani no nausicaä* (*Nausicaä of the Valley of the*

Wind), was serialized in *Animage* magazine. By 1983 animation production work on the manga story had begun. In November 1984, the 116-minute feature film was screened in Japan and Miyazaki was the chief director and took charge of its screenplay, storyboard, and direction. Ex-colleagues and friends also helped in the administration or creation of the film. For example, Hara Toru from Topcraft Studio was in charge of production management and his studio also provided 60 core production staff to help with the making of the film. Takahata was the executive producer and focused on promotion and publicity. It was known within the industry at the time that "a Disney in Japan was in the making" and those involved were excited to see that Miyazaki's dream materialized.

In retrospect, the founding of Studio Ghibli was also the direct result of Miyazaki's initial endeavor in manga publishing. Up until today in contemporary Japan, animators have fewer opportunities to work on independent animation films as compared to manga-based projects which are often welcomed by publishers and potential investors. Miyazaki's career growth proved to be no exception. Miyazaki's venture into manga production eventually attracted the attention of investors and led to a higher recognition of his animating talents. He has not returned to manga work since then.[14]

Auteur Model and Its Application

Authorship and the auteur model

The auteur model has been a polemic element in Hollywood live-action cinema discussion. Generally, it is not applied to animation cinema studies because animation feature films have almost always involved large-scale studio production work that requires more than 100 people. As a result of this, defining the main contributions of an auteur-director seems impossible. Moreover, animation is popularly perceived as a genre for children. It would seem incongruent and odd that an auteur-artist would want to express his or her personal and aesthetic visions through a secondary form of cinematic entertainment.

The origins of cinema are embedded in such apparati as magic lantern, plaxinoscope and zoetrope, and humankind's desire to see images in illusory motion dates back to prehistoric times. It is, however, live-action films and *not* animation films that have dominated contemporary popular cinema entertainment. Interestingly though, animation continues to enjoy an important status in Japan's media industry, especially after the Second World War. As mentioned in the preceding discussion, manga has become the driving force behind the launch of every television anime, animated feature film, and line of merchandising products since the 1960s. In Japan's publishing industry alone, manga significantly occupies a premier status.[15]

In reality, "manga" is said to be "a god" as it brings revenue to the original producers as well as the cinema owners and live-action filmmakers. The spin-off profits in turn provide funding for non-anime film projects. For example, in 1999, the highly popular manga-anime television series *GTO-Great Teacher Onizuka* (authored by manga-artist Toru Fujisawa) was adapted into an eagerly-awaited live-action film which starred popular television actors and actresses. In other words, manga-anime audiences are courted enthusiastically to support locally-produced live-action films and the medium-genre also provides jobs for those working in live-action filming. This shows that the generic medium is not considered "a foe" but "a friend."[16] On the outer periphery, the high-tech video-game industry also benefits from the medium-genre by including value-added elements in their products, e.g. dazzling graphic designs and functions that enable interactions between consumers and the animated characters. The three leading companies, Sony Computer Entertainment, Sega Enterprises, and Nintendo Co., are always on the look-out for lucrative manga story characters and will try to weave them into a video-game that would help to boost sales and turn the game into a bestseller. But so far, animated works produced by Studio Ghibli have no such "high-tech profitable links" and it is probably due to the exclusive artistic auteurist image with which they project their works.[17]

In general, auteur animators tend to work independently and prefer to share their creations with a small handful of trusted co-workers. One reason is that animators enjoy freedom of expression and have full artistic control of their work in an independent environment. In the case of film directors Miyazaki and Takahata, their commercial studio production work is both labor and capital-intensive. In addition, they are serious auteur-artists who strive to express their vision in a structured studio environment. Using the auteur model and at the same time recognizing its limitations, this chapter seeks to provide a theoretical framework for analyzing the anime cinema of Miyazaki and Takahata. Since an animation feature film is a product of a large co-operative workforce and in Japan, the medium of anime is also very much embedded in the social, economic, and cultural environment of the country, my approach to the auteur model involves "an acknowledgement of forces conditioning the individual artist" (Buscombe, 1981: 27). It takes into account the complex combination of circumstances which led to the creation of animated works par excellence.

The auteur model appeared during the 1950s–1960s period when a group of French critics and filmmakers promoted "the auteur" as a unique individual who tried to produce personal films within commercial filmmaking constraints. It evolved out of the influential film journal *Cahiers du Cinema*, in which a group of filmmakers and critics including Eric Rohmer, Jean-Luc Godard, Francois Truffant, and Andre Bazin wrote essays to theorize Hollywood cinema. In a series of essays, they paid tribute to American studio film directors such as John Ford, Alfred Hitchcock, Orson Welles, Howard Hawks, and others, and propounded the belief that it was valuable to study American cinema in depth (Wollen, 1972).

Their critical writings were also a kind of self-reflexive reaction toward the form of art cinema which was prevalent in Europe at that time. Contrary to a Hollywood film director, a typical European film director was regarded as one who could openly express his or her artistic aspirations and exercise full control over films. As such, the auteur model sought to elevate film directors, who hitherto had been dismissed as second-rate and salaried film workers operating within the commercial filmmaking machinery. The model recognized that a Hollywood film director had to work hard to balance two opposing forces. The first was entertainment which existed in the world of capitalism and popular culture and the second was his or her own personal vision of film art which belonged to the realm of his or her unique stylistic expression.

Given the dynamic environment of Japanese animation, particularly the influence of manga and the volatile popular cultural scene in urban Tokyo, the positions of auteur-animation directors such as Miyazaki and Takahata are unique and are open to intriguing observations. From a historical perspective, it is worthwhile to trace the lineage of past master film directors in Japan's live-action cinema and locate the ever-growing pristine status of anime cinema, especially in view of the later dismal developments of Japan's live-action cinema and its eventual decline to mediocrity.

Auteurs and Japan's post-Second World War live action cinema

Film scholars and critics tend to apply the auteur model in the analysis of Japan's postwar cinema. One reason is the impressive line-up of auteurs that had appeared after the war. Leading this list is the late film director Kurosawa Akira whose *Rashomon* attracted international attention to Japanese films. Thereafter, film directors like Ozu Yasujiro, Mizoguchi Kenji, Naruse Mikio, and Kinoshita Keisuke began to receive global acclaim as international film analysts sought to study their auteurist visions.

Like their counterparts in Hollywood cinema, these filmmakers worked with established film companies and studios. Among the pioneer writers who helped to introduce Japanese postwar auteur cinema to the English-speaking world are Joseph I. Anderson and Donald Richie. Working on this maxim, "each of those men has created a world of his own, one governed by the laws of this personality. Each is, in his own way, the best that Japan has produced" (1982: 350), these two authors pay tribute to the auteurs who are said to be the covert forces that led to the Second Golden Age of Japanese cinema from the mid-1940s to 1950s.

Researching in the 1980s, film scholar David Desser also applied the auteur model in his study of Japanese New Wave Cinema in the 1960s. That decade saw Japan in its full-blown march towards postwar industrialization, and it was also a turbulent period in the country's history; there were various sporadic labor, student, and citizen movements. In light of the historical-cultural epoch of the 1960s, Desser aimed to "show how certain Japanese filmmakers used cinema as a tool, a weapon in a cultural struggle" (1988: 3). He focused on the films of a few directors including Oshima Nagisa, Shinoda Mashiro, Yoshida Yoshihige, and Imamura Shohei, and analyzed their artistic contributions to the cinema in the wider context of Japanese society during that time.

There are three significant eras in Japan's mainstream cinema. The first is the Golden Age of the 1930s when the *shomin-geki* genre was highly popular because of its emphasis on the plight of the lower class. The Second Golden Age began immediately after the world and spanned from the mid-1940s to the 1950s. This period is also known as the "master-directors era." Then came the 1960s; the decade is designated as the New Wave Period when younger film directors representing the baby-boomer generation expressed their alienated feelings and social concerns through the cinema medium. In Japan, they are also known as the "social film directors." The New Wave Period ended in the early 1970s, Desser designates this period as "the last 'golden age' of the Japanese cinema" and according to him, "no subsequent cinematic movements have risen in Japan" (1988: 12).

By that, Desser indirectly implies that the master-auteur lineage had come to an end because it was difficult to find another *unique group* of film directors from the 1970s onward who exhibited unified nationality styles and points of vision. Broadly speaking, a quick mental sketch of Japanese cinema from the mid-1960s onward usually consists of images of *yakuza*, soft pornography ("pink"),[18] and manga-anime films. One may also notice that film genres have become an important yardstick formula for contemporary Japanese film production.[19]

On closer examination, there are, however, individual film directors whose works stand out from the rest. Most notable is Yamada Yōji (1931–) and his popular series of *Tora-san* which is about a wandering character in the urban landscape of Japan. A total of 49 episodes, the series is an understatement of Japan's postwar industrialization. Then there are other independent film directors like the late Itami Jūzō (1933–97). His first film, *The Funeral* (1984), is a sensitive satire of contemporary Tokyo citizens. Directors from the New Wave Period such as Imamura Shōhei (1926–2006) continued their thematic form of cinema by making isolated films between periods of long rest. Imamura revived international attention to Japanese live-action cinema with his award-winning production, *The Ballad of Narayama* (1983), which portrays Japan in its primitive past with a thematic focus on spiritual maternal strength and the essence of Japanese identity. The film was awarded the Palme d'Or at the 1983 Cannes Film Festival. More than a decade later, in the late 1990s, comedian and variety show host Beat Takeshi (Kitano Takeshi) also rekindled international attention to Japan's live-action cinema with his philosophical-essay film, *Hana-Bi*.

From the above, we can see that the rise of the auteur-animation directors such as Miyazaki and Takahata is contingent upon the country's postwar entertainment developments. The gradual growth of their fame is stimulated by the change of time as well as their inborn talents. The fragmented live-action cinema scene of Japan from the 1970s onward is also due to the fact that many creative talents have been absorbed into the *manga-anime* industries. As the late eminent film director, Kurosawa Akira (1910–98) lamented,

> Though *My Neighbor, Totoro* (1988) is an *anime* film, I am very touched by it. The cat-bus has such an immensely lively feeling ... I am also very moved by the film, *Kiki's Delivery Service*. Really, if only such talents would work in the live-action cinema sector ... young people will be attracted to come forward and express their creativity in filmmaking.[20]

Auteur model and the anime cinema of Miyazaki and Takahata

Since its inception in the 1960s, when a number of *Cahiers du Cinema* writings were translated into English by film critics including Peter Woollen and Andrew Sarris, the auteur model has become an attractive theory for analyzing classic cinema. The model is particularly attractive because of its impressive list of pre-selected distinguished auteurs. However, it has been heavily criticized for its romanticism and its celebration of the "auteur" as the criterion of value.

Feminist film critics in the 1970s further denounced the theory as being male-oriented and claimed that it adulated the male film director as the "romantic hero faced with a post-industrial world" (Kuhn and Radstone, 1990: 31). Another criticism is that "the star" is noticeably neglected and that a typical successful Hollywood film is unimaginable without the individualistic and appealing forces of a leading actor or actress. Moreover, the model has neglected and misrepresented a number of film workers who have also contributed actively to commercial film productions. In short, the auteur model is inadequate in presenting any one national cinema because it narrowly focuses and pays tribute to a group of pre-selected directors.

In popular cultural arts in Japan, the "status of an auteur-artist" has only been bestowed upon the late Tezuka Osamu, who still holds the prestigious "god of manga" title, whereas animation film directors Miyazaki and Takahata have yet to reach the *kamisama* or god-like status. Although Miyazaki has been unofficially named the "new Disney of Japan," the majority of the population and of the professional animation community tend to perceive his works as commercial theatrical projects which could not be produced by one man alone.[21] To date, specifically among retired Toei staff and the peers of Miyazaki and Takahata, the late animator Mori Yasuji was regarded as the "god of animation." This title, *anime-shon no kamisama*, appears in a title article in *Nihon manga eiga no zenbō* (Matsunomoto and Otsuka, 2004: 47–55). The book mainly charts the history of commercial animated films in Japan.

In the history of Japanese feature film animation, it is the brand name of "Miyazaki-Takahata," or better known as "Studio Ghibli films," that accorded their theatrical works with special status. In the case of Miyazaki, his theatrical releases enjoy record-breaking box office success, which local film distributors have come to expect. The point is that both directors are not simply "la politique des auteurs," because their status and fame are also tinted by the myth-generating machinery of a media conglomerate and the country's overall capitalistic economy. Although Miyazaki and Takahata would loathe to think of themselves as agents and bondservants of the capitalistic media industry, they are also "self-conscious auteurs" who have the luxury and freedom to promote their auteur-artist image.

One of the serious challenges of the auteur model in contemporary film analysis and, in particular, in the case of Miyazaki and Takahata, is that at the "producers" and the "creators" end, they also, consciously or subconsciously, apply the model in their marketing and self-promotion strategies. Thus, although my approach to the auteur model incorporates analysis and description of their production techniques, it also critically examines their "auteur status" in light of the macro-cultural and socio-economic environment in which their animated works are produced.

Style and techniques of production

Studio style production

Dick Wong, a Hong Kong veteran animator, once pointed out that in order to embark on an animation feature film, "three basic ingredients are needed from the beginning: talent, money, and story contents."[22] When Tokuma Shoten agreed to finance Miyazaki's first 35 mm feature film, *Nausicaä of the Valley of the Wind*, the three basic ingredients were present. However, it was not the end of the story. Tokuma was merely a publishing company and it did not have the facilities and equipment to complete such an ambitious project.

Luck was on the side of Miyazaki because his ex-Toei producer-colleague Hara Toru was running a successful animation film studio, Topcraft. Established in 1972, the studio specialized in making animation feature film on behalf of its American partner, Rankin/Bass Productions. Almost all of the animation projects at Topcraft were 35 mm feature films which included works such as *It Was the Night before Christmas* (1974), *Frosty's Winter Wonderland* (1976), *The Stingiest Man in Town* (1978), and *The Last Unicorn* (1981).

The studio already had an impressive list of animated film releases when Miyazaki approached Hara for his assistance in 1983. Hara was also the producer of the much-underrated Toei animated film *Prince of the Sun: The Great Adventures of Hols* (1968) when Takahata was the director and Miyazaki was the key animator. Here, once again, the previous web of professional relationships was resurrected as Topcraft was contracted to produce *Nausicaä of the Valley of Wind*. The studio was located at Asagaya in western Tokyo back then, and the entire staff of over 60 members provided assistance from the start.

Miyazaki's choice of Topcraft was unavoidable because, apart from Toei, Topcraft was said to be one of the very few animation studios in Tokyo which had the infrastructure and experience to make a full animated feature during that period.[23] Because of their specialized experience in making animated feature films for the American market, the studio did not often produce limited animation such as the *manga-anime* type in Japan. Among Topcraft's fully-equipped facilities included sound recording and editing studios and the 35 mm multi-plane camera. It was not easy to house the camera, as most buildings in downtown Tokyo had low ceilings. When given a higher budget from the US, Topcraft was able to produce high-quality animation. For example, *The Last Unicorn* had more than 75,000 cel drawings with Disney-like quality background art.[24] Incidentally, it was also the equivalent of early Studio Ghibli's films.

Thus, the beginnings of Studio Ghibli were rooted in a classic style of animation. The techniques are Disney-like and are solely of the drawn animation discipline with emphasis on quality production. The studio is organized according to the flow of production work and the work process is broken into separate activities and departments. This ensures efficient and consistent output and quality. In any Disney-style studio, a high-budget production is often anticipated and therefore, meeting a deadline is extremely important. Studio Ghibli is no exception. The staff at Studio Ghibli are known to work for days without sleep as the film project advances, and the most uniting factor is that the staff believes in the auteur magic of the anime cinema of Miyazaki and Takahata, no matter what the outcome will be.

Studio Ghibli is probably the only classic animation studio in the world today. In addition, the studio has only two auteur-directors, Miyazaki and Takahata, and each works in his own style. Miyazaki draws, animates, directs, and works during the day. Takahata mainly directs and works at night; he also tends to leave the working processes to his staff. They have different personalities and are known to have fought for talented assistants during the early days of Studio Ghibli.[25] In the West, Disney-style studios have lost their dominance since the advent of computer technology. It is also partly due to the passing of master-animators (Noake, 1988: 106). In Japan, Miyazaki and Takahata have revived the tradition of studio-style production and demonstrated their ability to reach new potentiality. However, these are achieved through their efforts in maintaining a large studio together.

Mise-en-scene and the realism/reality approach

In animation studies, the mise-en-scene of an animated work has been described as aspects of "images, color and line, movement and kinetics" (Furniss, 1998: 62). In general, it is referred to as "the staging" or "everything that is put in front of the camera in preparation for filming" (Kasdan et al., 1993: 49). What distinguishes the works of Miyazaki and Takahata from other run-of-the-mill *manga-anime* in Japan and Disney-like animation feature films is their approach and emphasis on realism. It is realism that has become a major, if not primordial, ideological backbone of their animation aspirations. The constant desire and struggle to portray reality, often at all costs, are reflected in their storytelling process, especially in the thematic contents and technical expressions. The principle has motivated their careers and is both a common characteristic and a theme in their works.

The visual components of the mise-en-scene of any Miyazaki and Takahata feature film (except *My Neighbors the Yamadas* [2000]) are often photo-realist, and are fluid and natural in movements. The former is achieved by real-time location hunting, photo-taking, video-filming, and superior art directorship. For example, the authentic backdrop of *Pom Poko* (also known as *The Raccoon War* or in Japanese, *Heisei Tanuki Gassen Pon Poko*, 1994) is based on the hilly and yet fast developing parts of Tama City, which is located in the western countryside outside Tokyo. Oga Kazuo, the art director of the film, said that regardless of the weather, his team took photographs of the construction sites that were amidst the idyllic natural habitats nearby. Based on directorial instructions from Takahata, he had to create scenarios that did not only portray the natural homes of the raccoons but also created the effect that when the audience saw the place, they would feel sorry for the raccoons for having had to live in such an environment (Haraguchi, 1997, Vol. 5: 13).

Intrinsic in any animated mise-en-scene is the treatment of color. Both Miyazaki and Takahata are known to have spent a considerable amount of time discussing with their chief colorists so that they could find the best colors. For example, in the making of *Omohide Poro Poro* (*Only Yesterday* [1991]), in order to achieve reality, 450 different colors were used. As the scenery of the film is based on a farm community in Yamagata Prefecture, it was reported that the color department took a year to find the right shade of "red" that looked like the bright flowers blooming during the summer time. Color design supervisor Yasuda Michiyo recalled that the main female character's experience on the overnight train and the morning scenery she encountered when the train was moving in Yamagata were what the production crew also experienced during location filming (Shibaguchi, 1997: 192–193). In other words, there is the constant "hands-on experience" to help recreate the realistic event and atmosphere.

The realistic imagery of Miyazaki and Takahata's cinema is also achieved through the unique skills of its "special effects" staff. Their work is sometimes credited as *ha-moni-shori,* which means harmony management. They give the final magic touch to Miyazaki and Takahata's cinema, and create the magical realist world in which there are subtle hues, shades, shadows, sense of depth and space, and the like. Because of such careful attention to finer details, the overall result is astounding when these refined images are projected on a theater screen.[26] As film has finer resolution than television, such realist components add that extra "X" factor to their animated works.

Takahata once wrote that Miyazaki has lived up to his name, *Hayao,* which was given by his father (Miyazaki, 1998: 571). *Hayao* means quick in action and the *kanji* character even has a "horse" radical sign. Miyazaki certainly has not disappointed his father, because he is quick in finishing his animation work and once told his friends that he could animate faster than a computer.[27] During a press event at the Venice Film Festival in August 2008, Miyazaki said that he would continue to use pencils as long as he can.[28] At Studio Ghibli, drawn animation is the first and foremost, and it is almost the only animation technique used. Led by Miyazaki himself, the animators can draw quickly and accurately; in the early period, some were veteran staff who had worked with Miyazaki and Takahata in the 1970s. Their "oldest" staff member is chief color supervisor Yasuda, who has worked with them since the Toei days.

Both Miyazaki and Takahata had their first animation training at Toei which has always concentrated on hand-drawn animation. Hara, with his previous experience as producer at Toei, later joined them from Topcraft. He became the chief executive officer of Studio Ghibli and helped to implement the key drawing method, which is an efficient administrative process in managing and processing full animation film projects. The key drawing method is also known as the "pose-to-pose" method; the experienced chief animators create the first and last positions of each movement and assistant animators draw the developments in-between. It is known in the industry that Miyazaki often oversteps his work boundaries as he is a skillful "in-betweener" as well.

Depending on the contents of the film, there are usually 12 movement drawings per second in a typical Studio Ghibli animated film. Recycled movements are unheard of, given the one-off theatrical release of each completed work. Metamorphosis or "the changing of object or position into action" (Taylor, 1996: 34) is also commonly used in the anime of Miyazaki and Takahata, including *My Neighbor Totoro*, *Pom Poko* and *Princess Mononoke*. In *Princess Mononoke*, computer techniques were used for the first time at Studio Ghibli but the process was not treated as an end to itself; the techniques were only applied to enhance the storytelling. The studio has been praised for its ability to combine 3-D and 2-D graphics without the audience's apparent notice.[29]

Apart from the movements, there are also the transcendental effects of combining sensible camera filming and lighting adjustments. Guided by the realism principle, for example in *My Neighbor Totoro*, Miyazaki took pains to express and animate the exemplary summer moods of Japan and he said in several interviews that he was exalted by the results and spoke at length about the aesthetic efforts of filming (Miyazaki, 1998)

Another noticeable feature is the subtle use of limited animation techniques to achieve a certain goal. For example, there are silent moments in their animated works where there is no action; they are simply quiet images with the panning camera moving over still or almost motionless drawings. However, the audience is mesmerized by the details of the mise-en-scene without realizing the limited movement. In short, it is the authorial intention of Miyazaki and Takahata, wanting to make the audience linger on the aesthetic feeling visually, auditorily, and in memory recollection. Technically, these shots are filmed vertically and the background artwork is usually multilayered to create spatial distance and depth; special lighting effects, camera techniques, and a considerable amount of experimental time are also required to achieve the desired results.

Sound, editing and narrative structure

The realism principle also governs the non-visual aspects of Miyazaki and Takahata's anime cinema. Believing in the cinematic appeal of their works, sensible attention is paid to soundtracks so as to realize their aesthetic goals and thematic messages. Director Takahata is known for his musical sensibilities and is knowledgeable about music. Miyazaki is said to have learned from him the finer details of sound synchronization, an inseparable element in any successful feature film.[30]

In the area of dialogue and voice-over, both directors hire live-action film and television stars to play the character roles. They look for voice talents who are most suited to execute the dialogue lines. For *My Neighbor Totoro*, Miyazaki even approached a copywriter/journalist to play the part of the father character as he thought his voice best matched the character's personality. Indeed, one of the main differences between the anime of Miyazaki and Takahata and the manga-anime type is the use of real-voice acting. Miyazaki and Takahata do not use stylized, cute or funny voices. As a result, the viewer's sense of reality is drawn out by the real voice soundtrack, which enables the viewer to feel empathy for and identify with the character's image and movement.

Realistic sound effects are extensively present in Miyazaki and Takahata's films. Due to the abundant action-packed movements in Miyazaki's animation, including his fetish for machines, the sound effects are sometimes noisy and loud with a fast and staccato tempo. Overall, these sound effects contribute to the energetic and challenging atmosphere of his work. The animated works of Takahata, on the other hand, are more documentary-like and melodramatic; hence, the sound effects include live recordings from such places as busy train stations, construction site, *matsuri* summer festivals, and urban streets.

Musical scores play an important and inspirational role in the cinema of Miyazaki and Takahata, as they underscore the major themes of their works and aim particularly to invoke desired emotional responses from the audience. Since *Nausicäa of the Valley of the Wind*, Miyazaki has engaged the help of composer Joe Higashi who has provided most of the background music for his works. As "mid-air space" and "flying experience" are recurrent visual images in Miyazaki's anime, a certain symphonic music is present in all his films and it creates a euphoric mood related to the story's period setting. Takahata's films, on the other hand, do not have recurrent visual images; thus the music found in each of his films is of a different genre and it is composed to meet the dramatic needs of the story. He often commissions original music scores and at times uses copyrighted music to cue the audience to make certain associations.

The editing process in the films of Miyazaki and Takahata begins early in the preparation stage. As the medium involves lip sync and images are hand-drawn, detailed time sheets and bar charts are designed to ensure that the film footage, image frames, and the soundtracks are in good order. Editing is a continual process which carries over into the post-production stage; in between, there are line tests of key drawings, layouts, color adjustments, and so on. The entire editing process is reviewed periodically with the director. Staff working in Studio Ghibli learn to adjust to the different editing styles of Miyazaki and Takahata and their diverse personalities.[31]

The narrative structure of Miyazaki and Takahata's animated films are usually based on a classic storytelling format which includes a beginning, a mid-way stage of the storytelling and an ending. The audience is absorbed into the storytelling process in a linear way where actions and events are unfolded in a timely pattern and progress from conflicts to climaxes and resolutions. Miyazaki and Takahata have also adopted powerful techniques of storytelling from live-action cinema. They have brought into the medium new ways of articulating space, time, and themes. For example, they have incorporated a great deal of off-camera dialogue in the narrative, thus saving numerous lip-sync shots. Master-animator Miyazaki can then devote more time to other fully animated narrative images. Takahata frequently uses off-camera dialogue to create subtle moods and developments and by doing so, he ensures smooth narrative continuity. The off-camera dialogue approach frees the audience from the artificial lip sync moments of a cartoon character's speech. Narrative information or emotion is conveyed by other omniscient camera shots. This preserves a wholesome realism world where points of view are believable, despite its non live-action setting.

Miyazaki's later epic films, *Princess Mononoke* and *Spirited Away*, break new ground as the ending of each film is deliberately left open despite a series of events, twists, and resolutions. The audience is confronted with a deliberate authorial choice. The traditional Disney ending in which the female protagonist rests happily in the hero's arms and the couple "lives happily after," is refuted. The astounding box-office returns in Japan also show that Japanese audiences and fans of Miyazaki's anime are open to these unconventional and inconclusive narratives.[32] Takahata, on the other hand, raises the medium to new heights as he experiments with a regressive mode of storytelling. In *Only Yesterday*, he juxtaposes two contrasting periods and characters in single frames so as to create psychological memories and remembrances. As a result, he injects a sense of poetry and lyricism into conventional linear narration, and proves that animation cinema is more than a medium of physical moments, gags, and slapstick sequences.

Common auteur themes

A special inter-auteur relationship

The Miyazaki-Takahata professional relationship has evolved over many years. Their collaboration began in the so-called rebellious and idealistic era at Toei during the 1960s. Then, the team moved on to their bread-and-butter days in the 1970s when making television anime was literally the business of the day. Miyazaki came to be known as a major manga-artist in the 1980s while senior colleague Takahata commended his debut in the world of anime film directorship. Eventually, their bi-auteur yet singular directorial productions have been made under the auspices of Studio Ghibli from the 1990s onward.

Age-wise, neither director belongs to the baby-boomer generation. Both have strong memories of the Second World War years which they experienced as children. Both later studied at prestigious universities and, like many university students during that time, they participated in the *Anpo* protest movement. Ultimately, what distinguishes them from other animation industry personnel is their constant self-regard of themselves as "social and cultural filmmakers." Their films are not only for entertainment, but also carry personal, artistic and social-political messages.

This sub-section serves to provide further insightful background information about this auteur-pair. It attempts to reveal the mutual competition and tension between the two auteurs. I also try to show that the concept of studying Miyazaki as the source and center of the film text, or Takahata for that matter, would be incomplete if one did not cross-reference their works as a play of forces, exchanges, and discourses. The intriguing observation is that each director's dossier of works determines the reading of the other. Since the last decade, they have agreed not to cross "turf" and focus on their own creative projects. Yet, due to commercial considerations, both names are included in the credits when they are promoting for the launch and release of their new films. Psychology studies scholar Yokota Masao, who has written a series of papers on the animation films of Miyazaki and

Takahata, sums up candidly that this unusual director-pair "has somehow outlived their [marriage], though [divorced] now, their work continues to share certain hallmarks and contributions that one cannot discount from Japanese animation developments."[33]

Their decades-old liaison is admired by their own peers and contemporaries[34] who are familiar with their individual personalities, strengths, and weaknesses. Each auteur is said to have a stubborn streak and is known to be very protective and defensive of their creative integrity. One of their senior ex-Toei colleagues has said, "how they sustain their relationship till today is not easy but it is admirable, because as artists we are prone to explosive moods and at times, peculiar demeanor."[35] One television program also documents their past "fights" during the filming of *Only Yesterday* when Miyazaki was said to have complained fervently about Takahata's failure to meet production deadlines.[36] Takahata also wrote about their stormy relationship during that period and how they eventually made up.[37]

In a television interview for the promotion of *My Neighbors the Yamadas*, Miyazaki gave an account of their professional relationship in the past: "… it was like we spent more time with each other than with our wives."[38] By that he was referring to the first two or three decades of their partnership. In my subsequent interview with Takahata, he cited an example that when they had to meet the tight schedule of weekly television anime production in the 1970s, most of the production staff including Miyazaki and himself often returned home only once a week.[39]

> My meeting with Pak-san has been an important and decisive one.
> His influence on me has been big. The two of us have a lot in common
> … Our relationship has been close … When he faces obstacles with
> his work, I know … When the skills of studio staff do not match the
> director's requirements for his thoughts and images, it is frustrating
> and the goals become unreachable …[40]

> Oh, Miyazaki influenced me too. Who influenced each other more,
> that I cannot tell. There is too much and it is also too difficult to be
> exact. Initially, he was among the animation staff I worked with …
> As he is now a co-owner of Studio Ghibli, he has other management
> concerns too whereas for me, I mainly work from project to project
> only … but we are still friends and are aware of each other's
> presence.[41]

In view of their family, educational and occupational backgrounds, inborn talents, creative inclinations, and personal social concerns, it is not surprising that their auteur works are inherently similar and yet controversially different at the same time. To begin with, both are individual artists who regard animation as more than a medium for children or a commercial form of entertainment. Unarguably, both believe that cinema is a platform for expressing their personal and artistic visions.

As the main tenor of this chapter has suggested, they have deftly used the cinematic medium to express social and even political concerns.

They may no longer be regarded as "a consummate pair" any more (this is a question which only the two auteurs can answer themselves).[42] Structurally, there are common thematic features which make their works immediately recognizable and which audiences have come to consciously and subconsciously anticipate. On the creativity level, these themes also situate some of the motivational impulses of the auteurs which, in my opinion, form the "obsessed" commitments of their cinematic projects. Placing Miyazaki and Takahata's anime cinema within the specific history of postwar Japan, the following identified common themes also function as a proposed strategy in reading and compartmentalizing the patterns of work on their rare and historic auteur partnership.

Ecology and community living

The first two major themes tend to come hand in hand in Miyazaki and Takahata's anime cinema. They are also closely linked to the sub-themes of nostalgia and memory recollection. The group of related themes form the core of their fictional world. As the above themes suggest, they are more than personal singular statements and visions. In fact, they mirror an urban society at which the pair aim their anime and reflect their ceaseless search for a spiritual home.

In his attempt to further theorize and broaden the application of the auteur model, Peter Wollen argues that a film auteur is not simply a matter of "a creative source" but rather

> … the presence of a structure in the text can often be connected with the presence of a director on the set, but the situation in the cinema, where the director's primary task is often one of co-ordination and rationalization, is very different from that in other arts, where there is much more direct relationship between artist and work. It is in this sense that is possible to speak of a film *auteur* as an unconscious catalyst. (1972: 168)

My approach is not so much the idea of the auteur as an unconscious catalyst.[43] Rather, I am of the view that directors Miyazaki and Takahata were "conscious" of their agency roles; moreover, the medium in which they chose to work was grounded with mass audience. Theirs is a case of a specifically localized context in which there is a tradition of using art forms as a subtle yet expansive platform for expressing social, cultural and political concerns. As I have suggested in the preceding chapters, there is also an indigenous appreciation of the aesthetics of the anime language. As far as the anime of Miyazaki and Takahata is concerned, their works share a coherent set of recurrent themes which is contingent upon the historic-social milieu of Japan.

Firstly, their primary creative worldview is that in making anime they hope to entertain and educate the public at the same time. In their combined curriculum vitae, the binary themes of ecology and community living have stretched across four decades. The themes first appeared in *Prince of the Sun: The Great Adventures of Hols* (1968) and finally re-emerged in Miyazaki's film, *Princess Mononoke* (1997). In between, these themes were also featured prominently in Miyazaki's works such as the *Future Boy Conan* (1978), *Nausicaä of the Valley of the Wind* (1984), and *My Neighbor Totoro* (1988), and Takahata's works such as *Heidi: Girl of the Alps* (1974), *Yanakawa horiwari monogatari* (1987), *Only Yesterday* (1991), and *Pom Poko* (1994).

While other anime or Western productions have focused on such themes as ecology and nature preservation, what makes the anime of Miyazaki and Takahata unique is that such clichéd themes are presented in the dialectical motif of realism and fantasy and are targeted at localized audiences.[44] (Yet, these themes are universal and have a global dimension.) One major reason is that, from the onset, the films are intended for homegrown audiences only. This helps minimize the drawbacks of global aggrandizement and patronization of which such popular themes are capable.

Saving the earth, fighting off alien forces, and defending a neo-postmodern Tokyo from natural disasters are some of the typical stories that can be found in manga-anime as well. By comparison, the cinema of Miyazaki and Takahata draws upon a rustic environment in which simplicity and artlessness still take hold, despite the underlying serious message that the film seeks to communicate. In addition, the distinct difference is that anthropomorphized creatures/objects such as stylized cute animals and shining robots are not used to present the story. The subject, notwithstanding the human inhabited worlds, is the question of human beings' relationship to nature and the social and cultural aspects of community living.

In *Future Boy Conan* and *Nausicaä of the Valley of the Wind*, both stories begin in the aftermath of a devastating, apocalyptic-like nuclear war. The survivors either have to live on the remnants of a material past, or restart from a pre-modern stage where technology is basic, plain, and almost primitive. The surviving community portrayed in both productions is one that has become self-sustaining and has acquired an undominating attitude toward its physical environment. In the former, youths like Conan and his orphaned friend Jimsy survive on their own wits; they value friendship and independence and harbor no guile in their innocent world.

In *My Neighbor Totoro* and *Only Yesterday*, positive messages about country life are projected subtly through the holiday experiences of the characters. In *Pom Poko*, *Princess Mononoke* and *My Neighbor Totoro*, both auteurs return to *shintō* beliefs and make them the alluring point of their ecological messages. The word *shintō*, meaning "the way of the gods," could also be defined as "nature's administrative laws" or "gods' way of functions and operations." As discussed in Chapter 3, unlike imported religious doctrines such as Buddhism, Confucianism, and Christianity, Shintoism is native-based and is essentially a form of nature-worship. It has survived until today in one of the world's most advanced industrialized nations.

The late historian, George Sansom (1963, Vol.1: 25) pointed out succinctly that Shintoism was "an expression of the intimate and vital sentiments of the Japanese people ... based upon a feeling that all things are animate and in their degree partake of sentiment existence." He also pointed out that

> Objects of popular devotion were not those somewhat political abstractions that figure as the ancestral deities of the ruling class. They were the humbler but none the less powerful influences that determine the fortunes of men in an agricultural society, of the cultivator and his family no less than the territorial lord. They were the forces of nature in their divine embodiments as gods of mountain and valley, field and stream, fire and water, rain and wind. (1963, Vol.1: 25)

In short, they also include other manifestations of nature, however minute or gigantic, be it a stone, a cave, or a forest. Embedded within nature is the general belief of an existent *kami* who has a certain power to heal and also to destruct.

My Neighbor Totoro is set in the pre-television era of the 1950s in Japan. Indirect ecological messages are communicated in the film in which children find solace in agricultural countryside precincts and also meet Totoro, a cat or rabbit-like creature who resides in woods, trees, and dark places, and other bug-like creatures who dwell in the dark and airy spaces of a traditional Japanese house. In contrast to *Nausicaä of the Valley of the Wind,* which is based on the director's epic-manga, *My Neighbor Totoro* has none of the science-fiction aura and the stereotypical portrayal of a holocaust-damaged earth. In its place is a tranquil Japan in an eternal summertime where it is full of breezes, sunshine, and rain. At the same time, nature's other living creatures bask in peace and contentment.

From the perspective of the children, Totoro is a fantasy figure and a kind of superman who can fly them to the sky and across vast lands, and make their wildest dreams come true. He can protect one from dangers and difficult situations. Totoro is like Doraemon except that he is not a robotic cat and only resides in places where one would usually be afraid to venture alone. Moreover, he is not necessarily a physical being and can also manifest in different sizes; he is everywhere and yet nowhere to be seen.

Behind this innocent façade storyline, there is, however, a nostalgic imagery that appeals to the adult audience. For example, the house into which the sisters and their father move is a fine architectural example of many traditional, yet eclectic, Japanese family homes where spaces are interchangeable. There are wide sliding doors and glass window panes that open into the garden. The idyllic and plain setting of a rural environment is a contrast to the crammed city lifestyle in Tokyo.[45] Shots of a roadside *shintō* shrine and the presence of a grandmother who tells centuries-old folktales are reminiscent of Japan's traditional past and her close association to nature.

The storyline of Takahata's *Only Yesterday* is entirely different from *My Neighbor Totoro*, and the setting of the film is based on Yamagata Prefecture. However, the film once again demonstrates Studio Ghibli's trademark artistic presentation of Japan's agrarian side. Adapted from a manga story with the same title, the anime film is about an office lady, Taeko, who enjoys spending her vacations with a farming family and relives her childhood yearnings for a vacation home in the countryside. The original manga story by author Okamoto Hotaru (and drawn by Tone Yūko) is a semi-autobiographical account of the author's primary school years. In the screenplay, Takahata introduces 27-year-old Taeko, now a college graduate and an office lady who also faces pressure to get married. Although the English title of the film is *Only Yesterday*, its translated meaning is "shedding of tears in remembrance." The Japanese title, *Omoide Poro Poro,* is filled with emotional sentiments of locked-up memories. It also carries the weight of beholding and the expressive act of releasing.

To make the anime in tune with social developments and contemporary events, the countryside family is portrayed as a progressive entity who are engaged in organic farming. In addition, a *sarari-man*-turned-farmer, Toshio, is introduced as Taeko's potential husband as the film unfolds. Story-wise, the contents are not unbelievable. After the Second World War, families and young people left their hometowns in search for better lives and secure jobs in the cities, and people continue to do so to this day. In Taeko's case, during her childhood years she was saddened that her grandparents had given up their ancestral home when they moved to Tokyo, while some of her classmates were able to spend their vacations with relatives who lived in the countryside. The character of Toshio is a representation of a "born-again farmer".[46] Since the mid-1980s, there have been state-sponsored programs encouraging city dwellers to move into rural communities.

In *Pom Poko*, raccoons and foxes are featured as endangered animals. At the beginning of the anime film, foxes are featured as "more practical and intelligent" as they are able to adapt better to the changing suburban landscape. Raccoons, on other hand, as the title *Pom Poko* implies, are by nature fun-loving. They have bulgy stomachs and a group-based mentality. Alluding the audience with old Japanese folktales about raccoons and foxes and the animals' ability to change forms and disturb the peace of households, *Pom Poko* spins an allusive satire in which the raccoons subsequently live up to their folkloric potential when they find that their habitats have been gradually destroyed by deforestation and land development.

As the film progresses, the solidarity of the raccoons is emphasized despite internal strife and disagreements among the members. In order not to overanthropomorphize the raccoons, they assume human identities only when their causes require, and none appears more humanized than the others. As the film progresses, the raccoons' war against humans assumes a satirical attitude; it is almost like a parody of the eleventh-century *Animals at Play* picture scroll. This time, politicians and land developers are singled out portraying their powerful relationships in a late twentieth-century Japan.[47]

Japan has its own share of ecological disasters due to scandalous human mistakes and negligence. The process of industrialization has introduced strange diseases and new kinds of pollution. Miyazaki's *Nausicaä of the Valley of the Wind*, *Princess Mononoke* and, to a certain extent, *Spirited Away,* feature a revengeful nature. They remind the audience of events such as the Minamata Incident (1950s). Victims residing in Kumamoto Prefecture suffered from a strange disease which was later known to be linked to the polluted bay contaminated with industrial waste. The Minamata Incident initiated various residents' movements against pollution and environmental violations committed by irresponsible industrialists and the state government.

The merging of themes becomes more complex in *Hols* and *Princess Mononoke*; the former was directed by Takahata and the latter by Miyazaki. Made over a period of three years in a decade in which political rebellions, youthful protests, and movements of various interest groups were on the rise in many parts of the world including Japan, *Hols* is a film which expresses the idealism and anxiety of that period in a country that was rocked by such mass events. The fictional film represents indirectly an exceptional Japan which was mindful of world events and was also critical of political and social developments at home. In my interviews with various members of the production team, the Vietnam War was singled out as the propelling factor in the making of the film.

As most of the production members were former college students and were supporters of the *Anpo* protest movement at the turn of 1960, the outbreak of the Vietnam War encapsulated their anger, fear, and disappointment in their supposedly peace-loving constitution,[48] and the sovereignty and identity of Japan. Basically, *Hols* is about a fishing village being attacked by a despotic, cold-blooded prince. As the film progresses, the main plot of the story is interwoven with a composite of sub-plots and the featured characters and imagery become more complex; they are actually metaphorical representations of contemporary political issues. In my interview with Takahata, he candidly disclosed the symbolic identities of the characters and images: Grunwald is the personification of the United States and imperialism as a whole, his double-personality sister, Hilda is the American soldier/pawn (or his secret weapon), and *mura*, the village, personifies Vietnam. However, there are also two variants of the village imagery. In domestic politics, the Nordic-like fishing village is in fact a symbol of Hokkaido's Ainu minority group whose livelihood is closely connected with their aquatic environment and fishing culture.[49]

Yet, another undercurrent mental discourse is the issue of Okinawa, the southernmost island-state which has become a colony for American military activities in the Far East after the Second World War.

Nostalgia and memory recollection

The sub-themes of nostalgia and memory recollection are rooted in the Japanese aesthetic concept of *mono no aware*. As discussed in Chapter 3, it means sensitivity to things and the language of feeling the incommunicable, as words are limited in expressing the intuitive undertaking. It is precisely this self-indulgent concept that has the power to ignite shared feelings common to the Japanese cultural psyche. The above dual sub-themes, as compared to the two major themes that I have discussed, are even more subjectively ingrained in the anime cinema of Miyazaki and Takahata. In fact, they exert a confidential, centripetal force that arouses nationalistic sentiments of the spectators, in particular, remembrance of their country's historic experiences and its ironic deviation from a peaceful womb-like world, or their *furusato*.

No matter how universal and humanistic the binary themes of ecology and community living are, the anime of Miyazaki and Takahata is also founded on a patriotic search for a lost utopia which seems to have been abducted from recent memory. The cinematic screen thus becomes a space to relive and find the past; in creating anime, it becomes a platform for presenting that idealistic microcosm through performative artistic human endeavors, that is, the hands-on dedication of the lost sons and daughters and their united search to recall and recollect "what is the real Japanese village and community."

The Chinese characters of *furusato* mean "native village," that is, a homeland in which one has lived before, so have one's parents, grandparents, and ancestors. *Sato* refers to "a village," or "a community of people" who have settled and become connected to the natural environment. *Furu* carries meanings of the past. It also means the origin/reason of something, or "once upon." Foreign Japanese studies scholars in their research on Japanese nationalism and modern thought have referred to *furusato* as a continuous nationalist project in the Japanese cultural psyche. Irwin Scheiner calls it "imagined communities" as

> Over the past several decades Japanese have shown a vast capacity to create an idealized past. Even more apparent has been their effort to establish this past as an ideological basis for present conceptions of the Japanese state and people . . . ideas about ethos of the Japanese, echoing ideas of the prewar *kokutai*, have appeared in the works of government-sponsored academics and newly founded institutes for the study of Japanese culture and history. But nothing has perhaps touched the Japanese more deeply than the evocation of *furusato*, the old town or community. (1998: 67)

Auteurs Miyazaki and Takahata are supporters of this nostalgic project of yearning a certain native past and an estranged native community. It is also what Jennifer Robertson refers to as the activity of "native place-making" (1998: 110–129). In my interview with Takahata, he explained that the themes of ecology and community living were major concerns of his anime work but they were not about fantasizing or searching for utopia. To him, the concept of "utopia" evoked the idea of a futuristic place somewhere. He cited the Chinese proverb *onkochishin* as the visionary guidance of his career. For him, only in understanding the past could we learn to face the future; absorbing new knowledge and living in the present and the future could only be meaningful if we took the past in perspective. He also stressed nostalgic sentiments, and implied that *real utopia* had existed in Japan's past, and refuted my suggestion that his work might idealize a utopian future.[50]

In a television program, Miyazaki also spoke about the importance of *kokyō*, which is an equivalent term for *furusato*. In the program, he brought up several key concepts that were central to his creative work and Studio Ghibli's recruitment of production staff; these include memories (*kioku*), scenery (*fūkei*), one's experiences with hometown (*kokyō*), one's identity and understanding of local customs and environmental conditions (*fūdosei*), and one's original experiences with sunset (*yūyake*). Although he also spoke about one's knowledge of foreign materials (*kaigai chishiki*) and how it could affect one's childhood, it is clear that his emphasis was on one's birthplace and identity and how it affected a person's feeling of art (*bijutsu*) and talent (*sainō*).[51]

Certain sequences in *Princess Mononoke* trigger a *déjà vu* feeling and reminds one of an earlier film, *Hols*. For example, Ashitaka's village is a close parallel of the fishing village in *Hols*. The male protagonist Ashitaka is also as heroic as *Hols* in coping with circumstances beyond his control. Both stories are set in a distant past when the idyllic world began to crumble due to an advancing menace. Indeed, permutations of images and ideas in the works of Miyazaki and Takahata are not surprising, given my explanation above and analysis of their long-time co-operation.

With regards to the *déjà vu* factor in *Princess Mononoke*, Miyazaki extended it further by probing deeper into the cultural psyche and the historical knowledge of the spectators. Choosing a *jidaigeki* ("period film genre") is in itself selective, as the genre synthesizes elements of an old, familiar samurai world that the spectators would anticipate. There are some expectedly dramatic and violent scenes in *Princess Mononoke*. However, no samurai characters are prominently featured in the film although the period drama is set in the Muromachi period when the shogunate system was already in place. Rather, the main stars are the common folk, animals, and forest spirits. Animals that can talk directly to humankind (namely, the wolf god Moro and boar god Overload), and others like *kodama* (doll-like wood spirits that live on trees), are again manifestations of the common elements of Miyazaki and Takahata's anime and its reference to *shintō* beliefs.

Another striking and fragmentary feature in *Princess Mononoke* is the allusion to mythical literature, namely the *Kojiki* and *Nihon shoki*.[52] In the sequence when the injured Ashitaka encounters Shishi, the god of the forest (who is a deer-like spirit creature who has the dialectical powers to destroy and heal), various images are presented. These include shots of the tranquil forest, healing spring water in which Ashitaka has rested, mysterious movements of Shishi, and the subsiding pain of his infected and cursed hand. All these remind one of the heroic feats and attributes of Yamato Takeru — the legendary hero of Yamato (the mythical birthplace of Japan) in national folk studies.

In summary, "green" messages such as "save the earth" and "conserve natural resources" mean more in the Japanese context. It is not so much about protesting against the sales of fur coats or the illegal hunting of whales and elephants. Satisfying the visual appetite for *kawaii*[53] animals and developing empathy for their plight is one Japanese aesthetic sensibility; more profound is the subtle nationalistic sensibility intermingled with child-like and altruistic themes.

> … I see Japan and her scenery and by that I feel and realize what I saw when I was a child. Various short films I could make, how lucky indeed … (Miyazaki, 1998: 486)

> … the mountain backdrop makes one feels sentimental … Has my age caught up with me? Why that nostalgic flavor? Have I been thinking of lost things I've cherished and missed … ? (Takahata, 1999: 62)[54]

Ambition and indigenous drive

In the animation scene of Japan, there are other artists who have contributed artistically and selflessly to the growth of the medium worldwide. For example, the late veteran animator Mochinaga Tadahito and his wife Mochinaga Ayako had gone to China many times after the Second World War to help train young animators. They also helped re-establish friendship with China's master animators such as the Wan brothers. His generous act (I suspect) had affected the quantity of his own creative output but had also eventually earned him an honorary listing in China's Cinema Encyclopedia under his Chinese name, Fan Ming.[55] The relatively younger Kinoshita Renzo (1936–97), with his quiet manner and fluent English, was also one of the earliest Japanese animators who reached out to foreign animators. He and his wife Sayoko started by organizing mini film festivals in Tokyo, and introduced many foreign animators and their works to Japanese spectators. His subsequent founding and extended support of the biennial Hiroshima International Animation Festival also affected his independent output of creative work.[56] By comparison, Miyazaki and Takahata took a different path to reach out to the animation world. They have been trying to communicate to the outside world by making a united effort in their production. In this sense, their mission sets a separate agenda and there is a polemical side to it. This section primarily examines the impetus of their "obsessed commitments" and their industrious attempt to "revolutionize" the medium.

In retrospect, one may argue that the immaterialized television animated series, *Pippi Longstocking*, was one of the catalysts of their missionary zeal for animation in the later days. Miyazaki, Takahata, and Kotabe had left Toei in the hope that the *Pippi Longstocking* project would be a successful start for their collaboration. However, the project were later snubbed by Swedish author Astrid Lindgren (1907–2002), who refused to entrust her children's story to a production team whose nationality recalled memories of Second World War atrocities. The rejection was a major blow to their ambition.[57] This failure might have become a source of creative strength in their effort to prove their committed selves. However, it inadvertently sparked off an innate Japanese drive to match, if not surpass, the superiority of Western animation.

Their subsequent works, including the interviews they gave and their published writings, also exude that inextinguishable Meiji-era spirit, that is, the determination "to catch up with the West" and the die-hard, neo-samurai mentality to equal the "wealth and strength" of the powerfully advanced nations. The battle this time is not about acquiring materialistic elements needed for industrialization. Rather, it is concerned with the expression of cultural intangibles and the collective recognition of the animation medium. The *World Masterpiece Theater* series showed visible results of this unexorcized competitiveness in the 1970s. This collection gradually became naturalized anime classics in Japan and surprised audiences around the world that, although the stories originated from the West, the creative and artistic production was from a Japanese ensemble.[58] (One cannot help but notice the exclusivity of the selected titles because there is a stark absence of *the other* children stories, in particular, the stories that are outside of the strong and mighty Western world.) Internationally, the *World Masterpiece Theater* series attracted attention to Japan's ability to dramatize foreign children's stories for television. Some Swiss and Italian audiences today still remember the realist and sublime depictions of their countries and the meticulous emphasis on characterization, particularly the emotional and psychological portrayal. The martial spirit of their endeavors indeed sets them apart from classic auteurs and poses a fresh challenge to the auteur model. The adoption of the traditional auteurist analysis of an artist's vision proves to be insufficient in understanding this idiosyncrasy of Miyazaki and Takahata's anime cinema. For intermingled within that "vision" are also indigenous *bushidō* values of honor, loyalty, male chivalry, responsibility, and selfless service to collectiveness.[59] The title of Antonio Levi's pioneering book on Japanese anime, *Samurai from Outer Space* (1997), is perhaps connotative of this association.

It is interesting to note that fellow animator-director Oshii Mamoru once candidly described both Miyazaki and Takahata as "communist chiefs" and Studio

Ghibli was akin to the Kremlin. Oshii was critical of their social justification in making a film, remarking candidly that their ideological approach to animation could bleed fascism.[60] Although anecdotal, his candid remarks are reasonable to a certain extent. From an outsider's point of view, it is without doubt that the anime stories of Miyazaki and Takahata are able to evoke empathy from foreign viewers. However, at times, certain animated or silent angle shots, whether prolonged or tracked, show deliberate attempts to arouse the memory of scenic Japan. For example, the colors, the hues, the typography and even the *shintō* symbols in the illustrations of paddy fields in *My Neighbor Totoro* demonstrate an auteurship struck by pedagogic interests that are retraceable to pre-Meiji painters such as Shiba Kōkan. Shiba advocated that art should serve practical purposes, that is, paintings should serve as "an instrument in the service of the nation" (Keene, 1969: 66). Moreover, the onus is on the auteur who directs and orchestrates the execution of an essentially two-dimensional art.

The auteur-pair's influence on their staff members is overwhelming. Apart from their talents, which have exerted much influence on the staff and instilled in them a team spirit, the medium in which they thrive and work also requires a collective effort that coincidentally aligns with the Japanese ideals of group responsibility, hierarchy, and steadfast achievement of goals. In Chapter 2, I discuss at length the role of traditional arts in Japan's past. Similarly, in post-Second World War Japan, cultural workers have found a medium that blends modernization and tradition and have included it in their struggle for a collective good. Miyazaki and Takahata are exemplary; in their lifelong careers, they have been producing cel animation in their studio, and have been committed to making one social film after another. Many of their contemporaries have diversified their artistic talents or moved on to other goals or careers.

Tsuchida Isamu, who was recruited by Toei in 1963 (the same year in which Miyazaki was recruited to work in Toei and was one of the art directors involved in making *Hols*), recalled that the film was their chance to express solidarity through a medium which had bound them together. The film marked a turning point in their careers at Toei as the founding and more experienced generation of Toei staff decided to take a less active role in production. However, he added that it was also the first and last memorable film project in the nurturing period of Toei. Internal strikes, pressure from the management, and other external issues later took a toll on their energies. Despite the physical and emotional exhaustion in making *Hols,* Tsuchida called it a once-in-a-lifetime working experience which drew out the best of his artistic capabilities. He remembered that during the making of the film, the staff competed internally in an open environment and shared their creative ideas with director Takahata, who would communicate back to them his narrative demands and the imagery storyboard he desired.[61] Otsuka Yasuo also talked about the Toei years when the auteur-pair discovered their common world views and artistic sensibilities during the political events of the 1960s, and also through their joint labor union activities and long debates of politics, society, and rights (*Kinema Junpō* 1995: 32–38).

The point is that animation has become an extension of their artistic selves and an expansion of their socialist and indigenous ideas in practice and in idealization. Thus, the classic concept of the romantic-alienated auteur is less applicable here, given their ambitions and, more precisely, their indigenous crusade. Moreover, the drive of their work is also "archetypal" and peculiar to the collective consciousness of the Japanese and the country's modernization experience. Studio Ghibli's *Pom Poko* was nominated to compete for the Best Foreign Language Film category at the 1995 American Academy Awards. The film was the highest-earning domestic motion picture in Japan that year, and the fact that it was selected by Japan's professional film critics to represent the country proved that the community had paid much attention to the auteur-pair's project.

It also shows that their fellow countrymen working in the film industry do not regard the animation medium as inferior and they are united in establishing the medium as a national art form in the global arena. Needless to say, Miyazaki's Oscar-winning *Spirited Away* brought much glory and pride to the country. In a NHK New Year news report in 2004, it was announced cheerfully that (the report seemed to have been included to help brighten up the gloomy economy in the midst of a festive season) Oshii Mamoru's animated feature film, *Ghost in the Shell 2 Innocence* (2003), was nominated for the Palme d'Or at the Cannes Film Festival in 2004. This is the highly elevated view with which the country beholds anime and the graphic language of animation.[62]

Anime in Asia: A Case of Cultural Imperialism?

Thailand is banking on the success of the movie,[1] which is released in Asian cinemas this month, as it prepares its challenge to longtime powerhouses Japan and South Korea as the capital of Asian animation.

Report dated August 25, 2006 in Sawfnews.com

Highly skilled but cheap laborers enabled South Korea to become a paradise for foreign animation production companies looking for good OEM. Due to this, South Korea became a country with many production companies, but without its own original works. In other words, "even with its 40-year history, it was like a malformed child with a hypertrophic body but no head."

Lee Yong-Bae[2]

This concluding chapter analyzes the development of the animation medium in various parts of Asia. It discusses not only the influence of anime per se but also that of Western animation to a certain extent, particularly American-made animation. It asks fundamentally why animated works (including film and television projects) made in South Korea, Taiwan, the Philippines, Malaysia, Thailand, Hong Kong, India, China, and so on, do not seem to create a lasting impression. Nor do they gain high popularity among international audiences. What are the underlying factors that cause certain recurrent problems and issues and affect the growth of animation in Asia, apart from those that are specifically Japanese-made? This chapter also queries whether such factors are embedded within an industrial "anime frame" and whether a survey of Asian animation would suffice if no attention was paid to the looming presence of Japanese animation worldwide, not to mention the American-made animation.

As mentioned in the introduction of this book, by isolating a particular animated frame or a series of frames, our awareness of the presented images is heightened, whether it is our sensitivity to the quality of the images and the background of their display, or the circumstances under which the images are produced. In recent years, there has been a surge of interest in developing animation in various parts of Asia. However, many of the reasons given for this enthusiastic surge are not adequately helpful and persuasive in explaining why the medium has been suddenly elevated to the "centre-stage." In applying the macro-perspective view of the development of animation in Asia, one should also examine what then "entrapped" or "framed" the producers in their endeavors to create animated works that compete with Japanese anime, the increasingly popular American-made CG animation (computer graphics animation), and the classic Disney- type of animation. Given the presumably scarce resources in some of the above-mentioned Asian countries (especially the availability of monetary funds and other necessary capital) and the presence of other socio-political and infrastructural issues that need utmost attention (such as eradicating poverty, providing equal education opportunities to youths, building and maintaining decent medical facilities, and guarding basic human rights including freedom of speech), the idea of advancing the animation medium seems prestigiously inviting, but it is not one of the real "needs" and "wants" of the nation. Furthermore, does the make-up of any culture possess the necessary backbone to support the animation medium spiritedly and materially as seen in the Japanese case? In expressing a narrative, is animation, or specifically the anime kind, the most effective?

This chapter explores the current "quest" by Asia to develop the animation medium, probes into the politics of the phenomenon, and argues that the factors affecting the growth of animation in Asia are multidimensional. It is not simply a case of cultural imperialism. My final analysis also reiterates the buried, cultural layers of anime as discussed in the preceding chapters and cautions that imitating the manga-like narratives and applying the formulaic methods of anime-making would only result in more anime-like galore in the world and contribute to the existence of already predominant images.

Cheap Labor and the Dominance of Manga

The Japanese animation industry has been seen as exploitative of cheap offshore labor from various Asian production studios such as those in South Korea, Thailand, the Philippines, India, Taiwan, and China. The cost-cutting formula enables large-scale productions of anime which fill not only Japanese television but also that of overseas countries. However, Japan is not alone in tapping cheap labor and talent from its Asian neighbors. Western animation studios like Hanna Barbera and others also adopt this cost-cutting strategy (Lent, 1998). As discussed in the previous chapter, Japan's visual appetite literally expanded by leaps and bounds after the Second World War. A large number of manga stories have been adapted into animated images. Moreover, in terms of subcontractual work, Japan (beginning with Toei and later other local animation studios) also took the lead in soliciting the interest of Western countries in its qualitative, yet less expensive, animated labor.

In Japan alone, the volume of anime and overseas Western animated productions expanded rapidly and by the early 1970s, the subcontractual work began to radiate first from the larger studios in Tokyo to the smaller production companies in and outside Tokyo. The studios finally enlisted the help of other Asian artists and animators.[3] Labor strikes had already occurred in the country in the mid-1960s led by staff working at Toei. Because of the tripartite relationship among the sponsors, namely the television station, manga publisher, and commercial sponsor(s), the animation studio contracted to produce the moving manga images became a less significant participant in the business arrangement (see Chapter 5, section on Tezuka Osamu). This also happened to the creative aspects of making animated images.[4] Animation staff found themselves working "un-creatively" to meet already set production guidelines; there was the over-presence of pre-drawn manga images and pre-created story. While neighboring countries such as South Korea and Taiwan seek to develop their manga publishing industries by recognizing the inherent potential in each successful manga story, there ironically exists in Japan a discourse that criticizes the influence of manga on the animated medium. This discourse is led by ex-Toei staff members including Otsuka Yasuo, Takahata Isao, and Miyazaki Hayao. In their published memoirs, interviews, and other published works, a sense of disappointment and dejection is expressed when they talk about the development of animation in their country and the earlier rebellious activities they led in the labor strikes at Toei.

Protesting against long working hours and meager salaries was one matter but at a spiritual level, leading animators and directors experienced a loss of the *shūdan sagyō*, or "collective work" spirit (Miyazaki, 1996: 46), because of the imposed monotonous work of merely animating pre-established images and narratives. In other words, they regarded animation as a form of "collective labor." According to senior animator Otsuka, although initially there was a division of labor in animation production and the roles of teachers, seniors, and juniors were clearly defined and hierarchized, it was within *minshu* ("a democratic-work" environment) that they worked together. He further describes Toei's form of animation work as *eiri jigyō*, a commercial enterprise as opposed to *sakka shūdan* (referring to manga-adapted anime which is often evolved from work created by one author-artist) which is a self-glorifiying, auteurish inward-looking world of creative work (2001: 101). Takahata is also critical of the "superhero" image as portrayed in many manga-adapted animation stories in which, despite much violence and destruction, the main protagonist still lives from one episode to another, and from one series to another (1991: 128). In the 1960s, Otsuka, Takahata, and Miyazaki were close associates and labour union members in the leading Toei animation studio and, ideologically, they considered animation as a fulfillment practice of their socialist ideals, a means to build a new Japan devoid of pre-war imperialist values, and a medium that embodied fresh youthful stories as Japan rebuilt herself by learning from her dismal war experiences.

As mentioned in Chapter 5, the development of the animation studio at Toei also coincided with the rise of Japan's manga-artist star Tezuka Osamu, who eventually approached Toei to animate one of his manga stories, *Saiyūki*. In recent years, Toei Animation Company and Studio Ghibli have jointly held museum exhibitions which foreground their artistic contributions to the animation industry in Japan.[5] In these exhibitions, the animated feature films take precedence over the television animated series in terms of the exhibition space occupied, and the documented notes featuring Toei's earlier film and television animated productions were also highlighted as they were made in a period when manga-contractual work was scarce.

While various parts of Asia persist in valuing the Japanese way of producing anime, particularly formula for making attractive and lucrative manga adaptations, "silent" protests and strikes still exist among animation workers in Japan. A sizeable protest took place in the mid-1990s when protesters strolled through the wealthy and fashionable Ginza district in central Tokyo so as to attract public attention to their plight. Such protests first appeared when manga stories were conveniently and quickly adapted into animated productions in the early 1960s. When Tezuka Osamu's Mushi Productions declared bankruptcy in 1973, he lamented how television animation had taken shape in the country and felt sorry for the mistakes he had committed in underestimating the artistic and business issues of animation production (Yamaguchi and Watanabe, 1977: 173, see also Chapter 5). In fact, one of the objectives of the Association of Japanese Animation (AJA), which was only formed in 2002, is to encourage participating agencies (such as sponsors and television stations) to raise funds for animation studios (big or small), so that the animators can have higher salaries.[6] In particular, owners of small and medium-sized animation studios lament that television stations, publishing houses, and a few animation production companies monopolize the copyrights of animation characters and other related merchandise. The anime industry places their patrons and sponsors at the helm while a large number of animation artists are exploited as cheap labor despite their vital contributions to the growth and development of the industry (Yuasa, 2004).

It is also a known and accepted fact in the industry that the cost of a commercial animation project in Japan is low by Western standards. The amount of time and effort given by the production team is, however, greater. For example, Arisako Toshihiko, production director at Toei, has stated that while it might take an American production team a year to prepare a pilot television animation series from the preparation of the storyboards and script, to the airing of the first episode, it could be done in about four months in Japan.[7] In Taiwan and the Philippines, subcontractor studios reiterate that Japanese animation projects tend to demand more of their labor effort but pay less than the Americans.[8] However, anime subcontractual projects often come regularly due to the popularity of animation in Japan all year round. In Tokyo alone, an average animator who works for anime production (especially of the manga-adapted kind) is paid about ¥50,000 monthly, which is hardly sufficient for renting a one-room apartment. It is reported that even at Studio Ghibli, a junior animator starts at ¥160,000 a month (Yuasa, 2004). One can imagine that offshore animator-artists are being paid even less.

Following or Rejecting the Anime Path?

By "following the anime path," I refer to works with distinctive anime design characteristics. These include, for example, cute characters with large sparkling eyes and the presence of realistic and picturesque backgrounds. At times, scenes of violence may be aggrandized, and their graphic presentations are foregrounded in detail. There are also deliberate attempts to mimic certain storylines found in other anime productions. In terms of production quality, pattern of distribution, and market penetration, animation studios in Asia which are working on subcontractual projects or productions that aspire to anime-like quality have yet to attain the same level of economic success and stable industrial input which Japan and their sponsors enjoy, the above-mentioned characteristics are often promoted and stressed by the Asian studios in order to gain a flying start and grab public attention.

In Hong Kong, several animation ventures were made by following the anime path. A notable example is *A Chinese Ghost Story* (1997). It is an animation of the classic trilogy of live-action films, *A Chinese Ghost Story I, II III*. Deemed as a personal project of Tsui Hark, an eminent Hong Kong live-action film director and producer, the first "fatal" mistake he made was to design the male and female protagonists with anime characteristics. As a result, the trademark sparkling eyes of many anime characters were transferred to non-Japanese animated characters and the ethnic origins of the film story were muddled up.[9] Another incongruent element found in the film is the overuse of three-dimensional (3-D) computer effects to achieve animated movements which do not fit the creative flow of a typical anime film. The contrasting feature is in the use of computer techniques. Although these are employed in a Japanese-made anime film, they are not treated as an end but merely as a means to enhance the storytelling. From Miyazaki's *Princess Mononoke* (1997) to Ōtomo's *Steamboy* (2004), Japanese creators simply combine three-dimensional graphics and two-dimensional (2-D) graphics without affecting the audience's notice of their combination processes.[10] Animation director and teacher Richard Taylor (1996: 7) notes that coordinating animation techniques is an important responsibility of the director. Each technique contributes to the storytelling process.

In other words, the quality of the movements guides the viewer to understand and appreciate the narrative. Technique-wise, by comparison, the 3-D graphics found in animated *Chinese Ghost Story* appear to be foregrounded, especially when they do not merge effectively with the 2-D animation storyboard.

The animated film failed in the box office in Hong Kong and Southeast Asia, unlike its live-action versions which were also popular among non-Chinese audiences. Apart from the *kawaii*-ness of the main characters, as one Japanese film critic has commented,[11] the other featured characters are well-designed with quirky and eccentric characteristics. But the dividing line of what makes a romantic anime film successful is not necessarily based on a pretty character although it is one of the artistic hallmarks of the anime model. Native aesthetic concepts of "space," "pause," and other Buddhist-influenced and indigenous sentiments are often found in anime productions even when the subject matter denotes a scientific rational world (see Chapter 2). One may argue that the presence of such "inertia moments" is due to a limited budget (which is typical of many manga-turned-anime narratives), but it can also be said that the appeal of anime is cumulative of both technical and cultural modification so much so that, in the process, a distinctive nationalistic genre is born. Moreover, it is a self-generating genre in which its sponsor-producers constantly scout for pictorial and literary stories to extend its existence, and in addition, there is also a sizeable home audience that helps sustain the growth of the industry.

A Chinese Ghost Story in the end did not make the grade and the plans of further developing the pilot film into a television anime series were shelved. The interested sponsors from Japan and Southeast Asia disappeared too. It is also important to note that how the commercial formula for anime production in Japan works. First, there is often a successful adaptation of a manga for television, or OVA.[12] Various profit-generating merchandise and collectible items such as 3-D video games and toys will appear subsequently. After that, the animated feature film release will follow. In recent years, the formula has been applied to help prolong the "shelf life" of its original manga-anime. One strategy is to produce a live-action film version that hires popular television actors. The *GTO — Great Teacher Onizuka* (authored by manga artist Tooru Fujisawa in 1997) is one example. It was successfully adapted into a live-action film in 1999. In contrast, *A Chinese Ghost Story* followed an opposite path where the step-by-step, cumulative pattern was reversed. The overall animated version of the live-action film story was thus upset, especially in terms of its visual appeal. Consequently, the desire of the audience to see the story in animated form was much decreased.

Apart from Hong Kong, South Korea has also been producing her own brand of anime. Several Korean productions have received international awards,[13] but the storylines, aesthetic backgrounds, and even the affective aspects of these works carry a *déjà vu* feeling that reminds the audience of previously shown anime feature films.[14] Take *Hammerboy* (2003) as an example. From its character design to its storyline development, there is a strong sense of *déjà vu* in the film that reminds one of Miyazaki's *Future Boy Conan* and *Laputa*, because the Korean production also features a rustic science fiction world imbued with romance and adventure, and the main characters are young adolescents with heroic characteristics. *Hammerboy* is in fact based on a manga created by Korean author Hur Young-man. It becomes obvious that when encountering such Korean-made anime productions, the audience is also inadvertently led to recall the collection of animated works made by Japan's top-notch animation studio, Studio Ghibli. In other words, the *déjà vu* feeling is inevitable because the Korean producers aim to reach the standards set by Studio Ghibli. In *Oseam* (2003), the splendid cel-like picturesque background and the emotive story of the young orphan boy and his elder sister recall memories of Takahata's earlier animated film, *Grave of the Fireflies*, which is also filled with sentimental and realistic images apart from its theme on the fragility of life. In *My Beautiful Girl Mairi* (2001), some sequences of the magical tale remind the anime-savvy audience of Miyazaki's *Nausicaä of the Valley of the Wind*; these include especially the segments that depict the fantastical settings of sea-plants and water and how the pair of male and female protagonists develop their friendship and romance in such an out-of-the-world environment.

Apart from the above-mentioned Korean animations that aim to achieve the standards set by Studio Ghibli, there is also a mega production with a budget of US$13 million. Focusing on a high-tech science fiction world, part of the appeal of the film is its animation and display of violent graphic images. *Wonderful Days* (2003) has lived up to its promise of "state-of-the-art 3D and 2D animation" because excellent animated images are included in the film. However, as the film progresses, it becomes increasingly clear that the storyline is weak and the production direction seems more inclined and interested in incorporating anime images already seen in such well-known anime films as *Akira* and *Ghost in the Shell*. These two films are landmark anime productions known for their expressive and intense violent sequences, and their narrative is focused on an almost lawless world and its degenerated conditions. The two anime films are especially popular in the West[15] and, seen from this perspective, it is evident that the Korean producers of *Wonderful Days* might have trodden the same path given its proven popularity among audiences around the world who were interested in such animated stories.

In "rejecting" the anime path, some Asian-produced animated works follow the "other" path that imitates the popular forms of American animation. They include, for example, the South Korean production *Empress Chung* (2004), the mainland Chinese production *Lotus Lantern* (1999), and the Taiwan-China joint production *The Butterfly Lovers* (2004). Such works are produced in a Disney format and contain clear-cut good-versus-evil story elements, strong hand-drawn graphics, and fluid animated moments including a cast of supporting animal characters who often accompany the hero and heroine. It is ironic that Nelson Shin, director of

Empress Chung, promoted the animated story as "full of our Korean tradition" (Russell, 2005) because its overall appeal is rather American. For example, the undersea animated sequences are reminiscent of a Disney film, *The Little Mermaid* (1989).[16] In Thailand, the animated film *Khan Kluay* (2006) which features a heroic elephant takes a slightly different path by using CG animation. Not only does the 3-D animation in *Khan Kluay* resemble those of American Pixar and DreamWorks, the story is also rather Americanized and Disney-like. It reminds us of *Lion King* (1994) and *Land before Time* (1988); both films feature a young, lost, and orphaned animal character and the challenges that it faces as the film progresses.

Popular Culture and the Economic Appeal of Anime

In view of the above-mentioned animated works, both the pro-anime and the pro-American animation kinds and also taking into account the hefty sums of money already invested by the Asian government and non-government sponsors in the animation industry so far, one can envisage an increasingly repetitive storytelling world cluttered with circulative and accumulative look-alike images, graphic representations and even formulaic ways of storytelling. In terms of creativity, it is fair to argue that because of years of foreign subcontractual work, the animating skills and modes of thinking have become entrenched in certain directions. Therefore, animation production studios in Asia can only work with established "archetypes" with which they are familiar. Although working on subcontractual projects does help to introduce basic techniques of animation-making to aspiring animators and provide jobs in general, it can hinder creativity in the long run. Work-wise, especially those in the past, many of the overseas subcontractual projects consist of tasks such as cel drawing, coloring, inking, and basic camera work (Lent, 1998).

Given the proximity of Japan to its Asian neighbors, particularly in East and Southeast Asia, the impact of its popular cultural influences cannot be denied. From J-pop to sushi restaurants, karaoke to video games and Japanese television dramas, one could experience the ubiquitousness of their appeal in any major city in East Asia and Southeast Asia.[17] Needless to say, manga and anime are highly popular too, but the difference between consumption and production matters especially when it involves *active* appropriation and desirability. The popularity of manga and anime operates on an exceptional plane when it is compared to the leisure attractions of other popular cultural forms.

As stated above, anime is not made in Japan alone. Anime production often involves input from offshore collaborators and their contributions are often revealed in the production credits.[18] Cheap labor costs in Asia are one reason why Japan subcontracts their anime production to these countries. The appeal of anime-making to its subcontractual producers is understandable. For example, many artists in

Indonesia first gained their experience in animation when they worked for companies that collaborated with Japan on anime projects. As a result, the anime archetype is seen as a standard to be achieved; cel-based animation and technologically advanced looking 3-D video games featuring familiar anime characteristics and stories are particularly appealing to these budding animators.[19] In an interview, Hong Kong animation art director Frankie Chung said that he grew up watching television animation series from Japan and reading manga, thus "subconsciously I have been influenced by a foreign sub-culture." He was also forthright in stressing that his character design work had been self-measured by anime's design characteristics, about which he "need not be apologetic."[20]

On a larger, economic and industrial basis, the popularity of anime also attracts the attention of bureaucratic institutions and business organizations. While the popularity of Japanese songs and sushi have not led to the establishments of serious academic and research centers that are dedicated to the education and advancement of Japanese song composition and sushi-making , the consumption and production of anime have proven to be otherwise. In Asian countries such as South Korea, Taiwan, Singapore, and Indonesia, publicly and privately-funded educational institutions have introduced packaged courses on anime productions to their students. In some instances, the "Miyazaki brand" and the "corporate image of video game" have been used literally to persuade students and parents of the model's educational and economic value. For example, by associating the successful career of a Japanese animator with the aims and objectives of a newly launched course, it makes the students think that their time and money are well spent and justified. Likewise, the appeal of studying video games production denotes an exciting IT (information technology) world and inevitably, brand names such as Sega and Nintendo come to mind. It helps to map career aspirations of young students in the IT industry and may help them to obtain their parents' support for training in anime production.

"Manga mamas" and "Manga papas" (*The Straits Times*, April 20, 2003) are also in demand in Southeast Asia where young people are eager to attend training classes conducted by retired or visiting manga artists from Japan. Magazines published in the local language devoted to the practical aspects of manga drawing are also popular. The Economic Development Board in Singapore, a government-funded organization in charge of promoting trade and business, has in recent years offered scholarships periodically and established training schemes to youths who are interested in job attachments to Japanese video-game production companies and IT organizations that develop and design 3-D animation software. Overemphasis on commercial animation can further be seen from the international animation festivals and conferences organized in the region. Successful manga artists, anime directors, and producers are often invited to attend these events and to introduce Japan's commercially successful animated works to overseas countries. Such activities and events display a one-sided spectrum of Japanese animation that is detrimental to other forms of animation which the country produces.

The Nurturing and Development of Animation in the Local Context

On the surface, it seems convenient to apply the theory of cultural imperialism in explaining the dominance of anime in the media landscape of Asia. At the outset, it appears that a form of media culture is imposing or thwarting the development and progress of another. However, as I have described above, the appeal of anime is multifold in the Asian context. On one hand, its commodified status excites and attracts corporate party interests, especially in recognizing its economic strength and acknowledging its so-called IT amour, but on the other, the base of the appeal also lies with the receiving parties, notably the consumers and audiences.

Although it is impossible to list here each anime production that has been shown in Asia and relate the meanings they have generated with their specific recipients, it is essential to concede or to see that anime offers alternatives to other Western animated works and even locally-made ones. A more fundamental reason is that in most Asian countries, the promotion and development of animation have been less enthusiastic and progressive as compared to those in Japan (see Chapter 5). To probe further, why has the rest of Asia neglected the medium until recently? After all, the "Hollywoods" of Asia like India and Hong Kong have been able to sustain their local markets despite the apparent dominance of American films. Judging from the recent surge of interest in developing the medium in the region, both profit-oriented sponsors and government agencies have attempted either single-handedly or jointly to advance the growth of the medium.[21] The supported works produced so far, however, tend to be self-measured by the popular anime model or the American alternatives.

Implicit within the cultural imperialism theory is another belief that the "essence of cultural imperialism is dominated by one nation over another" (White, 2001: 3). In the past, it pointed to a situation in which less affluent Asian nations were engaged in co-production of media works that were mainly for the consumption of more industrially advanced nations. From a structural perspective, it could be argued that as the broadcasting industries in such countries were still being developed at that time, it is inevitable that the "developmental learning curve" was charted this way. On the other hand, at a local socio-cultural level, other factors are at play as well and they include the individual society's demands and desires of the animated medium, the relationship of the medium to other aspects of the native culture concerned, and government policies toward the availability and interest of animation technologies and methodologies. Therefore, blaming the exploitativeness of foreign contractual work does not explain the current "imitativeness" and "scarcity" of animated works produced in other parts of Asia.

In view of the fervor and importance which the Japanese have continued to place on animation and manga, Asian nations and interested sponsors from the region that are presently engaged in developing animation need to put greater effort in examining and evaluating the values of the medium in relation to local society and culture. Moreover, the Japanese inclination toward pictorial images of both the moving and non-moving kind is extraordinary and excessive. It has acquired a built-in cultural dimension as its own history progresses. Japan's virility in producing and consuming pictorial narratives is not simply a matter of advanced technology and pure capitalism, as I have demonstrated in the preceding chapters. This kingdom of anime and manga thrives in a dialectic world of fantasy and illusion in spite of its highly industrial and modernistic outlook. Yet, it somehow has the innate ability to transform this abstract realm into specific products for commercial markets. Other nations in Asia have to take into account this subtle imaginative trait in attempting to develop a homegrown animation industry.

This imaginative trait also gives rise to an expanding *otaku* market that further supports the anime and manga media. According to a research organization's report (*Asahi Shimbun*, August 24, 2004), the *otaku* market in Japan has over 2.8 million consumers and can be divided into four categories, namely anime, idol, comics, and game (the market is worth 260 billion yen). The comics and anime categories have higher proportions of *otaku* consumers, constituting "16 percent" and "13 percent" of the market respectively. The report cites the growing purchasing power of the *otaku* consumers, especially new electronic products such as DVD machines and digital cameras.[22] The question to ask is: Do the other parts of Asia have such sizeable influential *otaku* consumers in sustaining an anime-like animation industry?[23] Or will they be prepared to foster or encourage the growth of an *otaku* subculture in the long run? I do not intend to discuss at great length the characteristics of the *otaku* subculture in Japan here, but I am not taking a negative critical view of this subculture. It would not give justice to the subject by examining it in a chapter or two. However, it is important to pay attention to the fact that the anime industry in Japan is also buttressed by this unusual subculture specific to Japan alone. It has been commented elsewhere that the *otaku* subculture is transnational, especially with the availability of new media technologies (Lamarre, 2004/05: 183). There are isolated *otaku*-like consumers residing in other parts of world, but this does not override the fact that the core of the *otaku* subculture presides strongly in urban Japan. Moreover, the age range of the *otaku* in Japan stretches from mid-teens to middle age and above and the *otaku* community often includes married individuals and their families. More than half of the anime goods are reported to have been bought by adults who have experienced anime popular culture in their youths (*Imidas*, 2000: 1215). Statistical research has shown that, as an example, more than one-third of the audience who went to a Studio Ghibli animation film was in the 20–34 age group, while those from the 35–45 and 16–19 age groups constitute another one-third of the audience (G.B. et. al, 2002:17).

It should also be noted that while the term *otaku* is popularly equated as "fans of anime" in North America, this playful usage of the term does not exist in the

Japanese context. Lodged within the *otaku* phenomenon are issues and sites of fetish desires, erotic pleasures, taboos, and so on. Anthropologist Anne Allison's book, *Permitted and Prohibited Desires* (1996), may have touched the tip of the iceberg as she examines the subject of desire in postwar capitalist Japan.[24] The subject of *otaku* in Japan is covered multidimensionally in *Mōjōgenron efu kai*: "*Postmodern Otaku Sexuality*", a volume edited by Azuma Hiroki (2003). It addresses directly what is considered to be the "corporate body of the *otaku*" (2003: 7) and describes and discusses critically the common misconceptions and multifaceted complexities of the Japanese *otaku*. In examining the cultural and social demographics of the *otaku* market, Anzai Masayuki, a NHK senior producer, also points out that the intricate and composite nature of the *otaku* subculture in urban Japan is connected to an *asobi shiti* ("play city") culture and that the strong affinity for anime in Japan also pertains to self-identification and simulation of idol characters that include Lolita complex fetishes. (In Japan, the word *lolicon* has become a generic term for a form of manga or anime that depicts underaged or childlike female characters in an erotic manner.)[25] For example, the highly popular *Sailor Moon* television anime series does not necessarily appeal to young female adolescent viewers only. According to Anzai, while the "play city" allows rooms for "huge turnover" and presents new business opportunities, the complexities of the *otaku* subculture have presented "difficulties" for advertising agencies, including "big names" such as Dentsu and Hakuhodo, to delineate specific wants and desires of *otaku* consumers. Although Anzai singles out Akihabara (the electronics cavern in Tokyo which is regarded as one of the main shopping districts for *otaku*), he is apprehensive and cautious of this special group of subculture consumers.[26]

In reality, the *otaku* subculture is also supported by an expanding force of amateur manga producers who compete to exhibit their work at the biannual Comic Market or *Komiket*. Dating back to 1975, this decades-old event provides an exhibition space for amateur manga writers and subaltern manga artists to publicize and distribute their creations. Works exhibited are mostly of the underground kind and are accompanied by various paraphernalia, such as CDs, video tapes, posters, and character costume-dressing. This convention is known to have attracted hundreds of thousands of participants and attendants, and many have returned for repeat visits during the three-day event.[27] Armed with a yellow-pages-sized catalogue bought at the entrance, attendants are familiar with the guiding codes, the detailed small-font print found in the catalogue, and ways of finding their target buys and exhibitors.

A number of the manga works exhibited are actually parodies of existing manga stories. For example, a young female manga artist may display her own parodied version of Miyazaki's *Mononoke Hime* in print form, which focuses on the relationship between Princess Mononoke and the male protagonist Ashikaga. Indeed, this "expressive voice-vein activity" is representative of a reproductive trait which regenerates the manga-anime industry. For instance, *Kidou-keisatsu Patlabor*

(1988), which is known as *Mobile Police Patlabor* outside Japan,[28] was originally a parody of the *Gundam* series and other robotic anime stories. Resurrection of this robotic theme never seems to retire, and in the 1990s the *Evangelion* series was another addition that paid parodied homage and allusions to earlier robotic anime. Its creator Anno Hideaki (who was born in the 1960s) produced a story that reflected the pains and doubts of his generation. The contents of his manga-anime carry covert criticism of his country's stagnant socio-political conditions; these include the hopeless situations which the younger generations are facing, and the fears and the general lack of confidence to change the established order of things. Apart from parody, there are also a variety of erotic and sexually explicit mangas on display at the Comic Market, and these are usually snapped up within a day or two by *otaku* male patrons. Sharon Kinsella, in her study of manga in Japanese society from 1986 to 1995, explains this event as "a remarkably invisible subculture in Japanese society," and says that it is also part of an underground manga movement which caters to the "specialist requirements of amateur manga artists and fans" (1996: 169 and 172), and a place for established publishers to hunt for new talents. By the late 1990s, this so-called "subculture manga event" was no longer that "invisible," because it had become an important event for producers or sponsors to look out for new creative ventures. For example, NHK senior producer Anzai Masayuki admitted that the subcultural creations were perhaps for the "maniacs and fanatics," but the large group of amateur producers gathered at the event was a notable potential commercial force.

Returning to other Asian cities, one may wonder if there are shopping caverns that are like Akihabara, which is representative of a highly successful industrialized capitalistic nation and demonstrates the nation's electronic innovativeness and modernization goals. It is also apparent that animation in Japan means more than just entertainment (for children and young adults, as well as the whole family); anime and its *otaku* connections have shown us so.[29] Thus, it is an uphill task for the other Asian nations if they would like to establish a successful animation industry just like the one in Japan. It is almost akin to imparting a foreign culture, regardless of the origins and complexities of the industry.

Taiwan and Hong Kong host a Comic Market-like exhibition event for homegrown manga and anime fans annually, but these events largely serve as a venue for Japanese manga artists and anime directors to meet with their local fans and in the process the sales of manga-anime goods are further encouraged. It remains to be seen whether such events will help to build a competitive pool of local talents who are determined to promote their work to the public. These artists may be using the event as a platform for expressing their different creative interests and for proposing alternatives to mainstream manga-comic and adapted animation. However, the current practice is still guided by the goal to adopt manga-anime design characteristics. Its widespread influence was demonstrated at the "Asia in Comics

2004: Comics by Asian Women Forum" held in Tokyo on February 21, 2004. It was an eye-opening experience to see that most of the works from South Korea, Taiwan, Indonesia, and Singapore displayed features in character designs and visual styles that are similar to those of the archetype. These include female characters that have big and sparkling eyes with long tresses, and slim long legs and arms. Comics from the Philippines were the only exception; their contents reflected the indigenous mix of its readers and the country's colonial past.

In Taiwan, a new monthly comic magazine, *Tiao Zhang Zhe* (meaning "The Challenger), was launched in May 2004. According to the founding editor, Lin Elie, the objective was to publish comic stories contributed by readers. Lack of support from interested patrons is one reason that leads to the stagnating growth of local talent in Taiwan. She intends to fulfill the role of promoting comic writing, even to the extent of accepting works that show outright imitations of manga. "After all, we grew up reading manga and watching anime; starting from imitation is the only way to nurture future talent."[30] In Taiwan, the production of comics had been substantially controlled by the government until the mid-1990s and foreign comics and anime, especially those from Japan, were imported to fill the void. As a result, the population tends to associate comics and animation with those that come from Japan. The same can be said of South Korea where censorship on Japanese pop culture has eventually led to an underground demand for manga and anime. Thus, when promoting Korean-created comic stories, current publishers are inclined to bring in the manga kind of work at the initial stage as the comics industry hopes to "expand into the USA and reach international audiences."[31]

A Gem of the Past: The Chinese Alternative

> In Japan, the production path is like this: first, there is the output of the manga, then extracts of the manga are animated. Later, efforts are made to promote the animated work. This is a step-by-step, scientific, and realistic method. Regretfully, China does not have such a well-rounded animation industry; neither do we have a market like Japan that can flexibly adapt to changes. I believe that Chinese animation will eventually take on a market-oriented strategy for development. After all, an animated feature film needs to make money too. How can we make good progress if we are always dependent on government funding to foot the production costs? (Author's translation)
>
> A student at Beijing Film Academy
> October–November, 1993

> When comparing Japanese animation with Chinese animation, I would say that every piece of Chinese animated work has a nationalistic intention. For the Chinese, there is a strong sense of intention to

> express ethnic styles and traditions. Thus, when Japanese people see
> Chinese animation, there is a hindrance. In a way, it is a little shocking
> to realize that the Japanese local way of producing animation is
> inclined toward foreign viewership. (Author's translation)
>
> Otsuka Yasuo, 1991 (see Takahata, 1991: 148)

Prior to the international success of Studio Ghibli productions and when the industry in Japan was focusing on commercial animation, there existed a form of animation in Asia which was rare and exquisite in terms of its methods of expression, production, and exhibition. This old Chinese generic model has been a subject for discussion. It also drew covert admiration among animation practitioners in Japan. Although this model is considered a "gem of the past" as China no longer produces such an exquisite form of animation and the development of the medium is geared toward profit-making goals (especially in view of the capitalistic path which China's economy has undertaken), the animated works produced from this past model are still remembered fondly and highly regarded by contemporary animators and film critics in Japan. See, for example, the publication entitled, *Sekai to Nihon no anime-shon besito 150* ("Best 150 World and Japanese Animation Films Selected by Professionals") (Saitani, 2003). The only other Asian animation appraised in the publication apart from Japanese animation is mainland Chinese animation.[32]

Since the foundational period of Toei from the mid-1950s to the rapid expansion of the Japanese animation industry in the mid-1980s, Japanese animators who were searching for new paths of creation and expression saw renewed nationalistic elements embedded within Chinese animation. As mentioned in Chapter 6, a group of innovative animators and directors, including Takahata Isao, Miyazaki Hayao, and Otsuka Yasuo, were dissatisfied with the voluminous influence of manga on Japanese animation. Consequently, they were actively seeking new forms of animation that expressed different narrative styles and from which they might find inspiration and new perspectives in making animation. The subsequent publication of the book, *Anime no sekai* (Okada, "World Animation," 1988), which includes contributions from authors such as Takahata, attested to their worldwide survey of excellent animation. In the book, apart from Japanese animation, the only Asian animation that is mentioned and given due credit is Chinese animation produced by the Shanghai Animation Studio. Western animated works including those from Eastern Europe and the Soviet Union are also listed and appraised.

As discussed in the last chapters, the expanding operations of Toei concurred with the robust economic growth of Japan during the 1960s. While the management and staff saw the commercial and collective value of animation, there was also preference and admiration for animated works made in Europe, including especially those from the Soviet Union bloc.[33] One former Toei staff member, Yamaguchi Yasuo, explained in an interview that animated works from the Soviet Union were highly regarded because of their "artistic-ness" as opposed to Disney-like works from the USA. By that, he referred to the latter's overemphasis on the "commercial aspects."[34] Russian film theorist and historian Sergeevich Semen Ginzburg best captures the Japanese attraction to animation from the Soviet Union in the opening passage from his translated book, *Dōga eiga ron* (1960):

> ... may Japanese art be able to express the modern times, that it carries the special characteristics of its people, may Japan's art and craft in any century continue to progress with shining light and maintain that experience. About animation, it is the same. The animated works of my country's directors were influenced by Walt Disney's productions as well. It has also taken the imitative mode. But this is just a part. When we look into our multiracial pool of artistic skills, indeed, a great creative path could be found ...[35]

Similarly, the Japanese recognized and observed closely the nationalistic and ethnic efforts which the Chinese animators had shown in their creative productions.

When translating Ginzburg's work at the end of the 1950s, Kawagishi stressed that it was not coincidental that "both superpowers," *nidai kyōkoku*, referring to the USA and the Soviet Union, had a progressive outlook toward animation (1960: 293–294). While one was propelled by monetary impetus, the other was driven by *bunka katsudō* ("cultural activity"). Kawagishi wrote that there was much that Japan could learn from their experiences as the country considered plans for developing a *shikaku bunka* ("visual culture"). I would argue that the Japanese native culture has never forsaken the visual aspects of cultural communication, however majestic or humble (or imitative or innovative) they might have been. The urge and drive to modernize since the Meiji period had contributed substantially to the advancement of an existing visual arts culture. Therefore, when discovering that a once culturally-close foreign neighbor had attempted to recoup a traditional past (in particular its artistic heritage), the Japanese animation artists and producers went through a *re-educating* experience; they began to "rethink" and "retract" the development of animation in the country and acquired a different vision from a non-Western perspective (see quote at the beginning of this section from Otsuka above, cited in Takahata [1991: 148]). In China, animation film is also specifically referred to as *meishu dianying*, a rather high-brow generic term that categorizes "animation" as "art." Since its establishment in the 1950s, Shanghai Animation Studio has promoted itself as *Shanghai meishu dianying zhipian chang,* meaning "Shanghai Art Film Production Plant" (*chang* also means "factory" or "works").

In other words, at the intra-regional level, the anime model has a "significant other" to measure up to, and it is China, from which Japan had adopted its superior cultural distinctions until the late Tokugawa period. For China, despite its isolationist status after the Second World War, it has also produced some of the world's most astonishing animated work that inadvertently places the model, specifically the manga-anime genre, in a cheap and derogatory light. Created by artists including the Wan Brothers at the Shanghai Animation Studio and supported by the communist government, the cherished traditions of *shanshui hua* (meaning "mountain and water painting"; the term generically refers to ink and water-color paintings) became breathtaking artistic gems when transferred onto animated frames. Originally the notion of "profit" as a motivation was never considered in such productions as they were supported by the communist government funds. Ironically, the resultant artistic and highly exquisite nature of these works was later regarded as "bourgeois" and "feudal-like" by the government. Consequently, their creators were banished and the studio was closed (Enrlich, 1993). Chronologically, both the commercial anime model and the state-supported Chinese model appeared at almost the same time in the late 1950s. However their fates differed and so did that of their creators and production staff (see Appendix 2). For example, during the mid-1960s, Toei's investment in animation had expanded into television production and, concurrently, Tezuka's manga works were successfully adapted into film and for television. To this day, the growth of the medium remains unabated in Japan. By contrast, animation in China had been in limbo for more than a decade since 1965 and the industry only emerged in 1979 when the making of the animated film *Nezha Shakes the Sea* began.[36]

Japanese animation artists in the early 1980s recognized not only the self-contained microcosmic world of Chinese animation, like the attention given to minute details and the individual choice of a mundane natural world as shown in *Cowherd's Flute* (1963) and *Tadpoles in Search of Mummy* (1960), they also acknowledged the macrocosmic and dynamic aspects of Chinese culture. These include, in particular, the ethnically strong heroism and subtle historical ideology as expressed in *Nezha Shakes the Sea*, *Confusion in the Sky* (Part I and II, 1961, 1964), and *Princess Iron Fan* (1941) (see Takahata, 1991: 144–154). Introspectively, the Chinese form of animation and its ethnocentricity had prompted some animation artists and producers to ponder further the development of animation in Japan and the ethnic origins and orientations of Japanese animation (*nihon teki*, see Chapter 4). In fact, the contemporaries of Miyazaki and Takahata at Toei then were among the first to return to Japanese artistic origins when they were making *Taro, the Dragon Boy* (in Japanese, *Tatsunoko Tarō*) in 1979.[37] Adapted from an award-winning children's book of the same title written by Matsutani Miyoko, the animated tale expresses audio-visually the fantastical folk elements in the narrative. Set in a traditional Japanese ink and water-colored background, the 75-minute animated film came with dialogue and music that was resonant of the country's literary oral traditions. The film became a "rare rose among the thorns," in view of the fact that a great number of manga-influenced animated works were being produced at that time.

With regard to the *nakama* partnership of Miyazaki Hayao and Takahata Isao, the fervor with which they later directed their Studio Ghibli's animated works and the subtle yet confident kind of self-addressing nationalism indirectly expressed in their productions resonate faintly and responsively with their covert appreciation of Chinese animation and its blazonry of national culture and history. It is uncertain whether the characterization of the heroine Nausicaä in *Nausicaä of the Valley of the Wind* and its subsequent animation was subtly influenced by Miyazaki's critical appreciation of Nezha's heroic characteristics as expressed in *Nezha Shakes the Sea* (Takahata, 1991: 144–149), although the publication and serialization of his manga began in around 1982. Nor is it known whether the growing attention with which the Japanese animation film critics and artists appreciated Russian auteur-animator Yuri Norstein's folk-influenced work had any impact.[38] It can, however, be seen that the political and ethnically spiritual positioning of Chinese animation and that of the animation produced by the European communist bloc countries were quite different from the openly commercial nature of Japanese animation. Those concerned must have been acutely aware of the distinctions. Artistically speaking, the Studio Ghibli and its collection of animated works were indeed of a higher quality and the directors had carefully selected story narratives that were reflective of Japan's past and contemporary social developments (e.g. *My Neighbor Totoro*, *Grave of the Fireflies*, *Pom Poko*, and *Spirited Away*).

Since then, Japanese animation led by Studio Ghibli has risen to an elevated plane and has enjoyed global success and fame. By comparison, China has ironically decided to adopt a capitalistic path for its economy and studios have been producing mainly commercial animation. Thus, nationally sponsored works like the feature film *Lotus Lantern* (in Chinese, *Baoliandeng*) and the *Journey to the West* television series[39] tend to have a Western flavor despite the selection and adaptation of Chinese well-known folk legends. For example, in the past twenty years or so, animated titles produced by the Shanghai Animation Studio have been described as having "a Western feel" (Hutman, 1996). This is especially so when one notes that the studio has been working diligently on projects subcontracted by Western producers. On the other hand, independent national projects such as the much-promoted animated film *Lotus Lantern* simulates features of Western commercial animation. The use of newly-developed computer techniques of coloring, lighting, filming, and background design creats a strange and unfamiliar ambience that is incongruent to a traditional Chinese tale. In terms of character design, one local film reviewer was critical of the simplistic representation of the evil character Eelangshen who, in the original story, is a handsome god residing in the sky (*Fuzhou Evening News*, September 5, 1999). In the animated version, he looks more like Dracula and dresses like him too. A subsequent collaboration between China and Taiwan, *The Butterfly Lovers* (in Chinese, *Liangshanbo yi Zhuyingtai*), displays picturesque setting and colorful representations of a traditional Chinese folktale. However, it is obvious that director Tsai Ming-chin, in "contemporizing" and "presenting" the tragic love story to the world, has meant to give it a Disney-like treatment by adding supporting animal characters, slapstick humor, spontaneous kissing scenes, and occasional love songs with contemporary Western pop music arrangements (see the article at www.china.org.cn, January 30, 2004).

In order to achieve success quickly (especially in monetary terms), contemporary Asian investors, producers, and animators tend to overidentify with the American commercial influence on Japanese animation. As a result, they gravitate toward that American-influenced direction when planning for their projects. In a number of exchanges between China and Japan in the past (government-sponsored and private), eager young Chinese animators often asked the visiting Japanese how they established a commercial, market-oriented form of animation (see, for example, the quote at the beginning of this section).[40] In recent years, both official and private Chinese establishments have requested the assistance of their Japanese counterparts in setting up animation schools in various parts of China. A report states that shortly after the screening of *Spirited Away*, the Chinese government was alarmed by the fact that in China alone, the sales of anime and its related merchandise reached a staggering amount of over 85 billion yen, despite the stringent regulations and control imposed by the authorities on imported goods.[41]

Could a "gem of the past" be re-appreciated, reconsidered, and re-enacted to accommodate contemporary conditions, given the wealth and technology that China has progressively accumulated over the past two decades? Why should one discard old animated work and its artistic direction and denigrate it as labor-intensive and time-consuming (e.g. the making of ink-and-water-color animation)? Why are they being seen as lacking consumer appeal and métier, when they are simply rare achievements? Would acquiescing to anime or Disney-like production solve the "cultural imperialism" problem? Would replacing the "vacant space" with self-produced and imitative storytelling techniques and formulaic consumer-oriented products suffice? Paradoxically, this "gem of the past" is still held in high regard by an animation kingdom nearby. In praising *Cowherd's Flute* directed by Te Wei, Japanese experimental film artist Aiuchi Keiji writes:

> When the *Cowherd's Flute* was presented, the world was kind of silent, but a deep impact was felt. Through that, the momentous Asian worldview was expressed and metamorphosed moment by moment in progressive water ink paintings. European classical art paints the physical world, but Chinese water ink art expresses the form through the heart. The work portrays a youth playing a flute beside his buffalo; the illusionary world is expressed through the touch of their hearts. The screen shows a water ink world of high mountain, valley, waterfall, and so on; such colored fantastical work overwhelms the world profoundly by the sheer strength of its presentation. (Saitani, 2003: 52; author's translation)

Image-Making, Fantasy, and Reality

In Chapter 3, the subject of "image-building" is discussed in connection to the formation of a national cultural identity. This concluding section re-examines it in light of cultural imperialism. The purpose is to summarize and emphasize the unstated "frames". In fact, there are other factors, practices, and even *non-practices* at work which affect the existence of animation in Asia. We have seen that anime is deeply rooted within a native culture and Japan's experience of modernity. The circumstances and conditions that led to Japan's industralization are partly internally originated and driven. As described earlier in the book, external historical developments also affect the country's awareness of its self-identity which contributes to the nationalistic desire and the vision "to become".

One understated missing frame in the context of anime and, ironically, a telling one, is the stark absence of Japan-based or Japan-sponsored anime productions that feature stories originating from a developing country. While the Disney Studio has occasionally included non-American folktales (for example, *Aladdin* [1992] and *Mulan* [1999]) in its repertoire partly due to its global marketing strategies, on the Japanese side, it is not easy to name any internationally successful anime film or television series that features a non-Japanese story or one that carries no Occidental characteristics (e.g. the geo-ethnic origins of the story, the background design, and the featured characters). The point is, in comparison to Western-based children stories and the many anime adaptations made or remade, the abundance of such one-sided productions portray the understated geo-political dialectical aspects of anime-making and anime consumption. Even Studio Ghibli's latest animated feature films, *Howl's Moving Castle* (2004, adapted from British writer Diana Wynne Jones's work) and *Tales from Earthsea* (2006, adapted from American writer Ursula K. Le Guin's work) attest to this characteristic nationalistic inclination to animate stories originating from bigger powerful Western nations.

While the animated film *Hakujaden* was produced primarily for Western audiences in the 1950s, the *World Masterpiece Theatre* animated television series in the 1970s had an impressive list of children stories adapted from the West. The Japanese passionate courtship of the American market and Western audience was also represented by the animated production of a well-known comic strip, *Little Nemo*, in the 1980s. Within the anime industry in Japan, many are aware of the heartbreaking enterprise story of the late producer Fujioka Utaka (1927–96), who invested much time, money, and labor in his creation of an animated film that would be a "great hit in America" (Otsuka, 2001: 200–218).[42] The resultant work was *Little Nemo: Adventures in Slumberland* and the production period lasted more than ten years during which Fujioka set up a production studio in the heart of California to realize his dream. The animated film was later known as *Nemo/Nimo* in Japan. Although it was eventually marketed as a joint film project, the initiative concept came from Japan, and so were the greater amount of monetary investment and labor effort. The film was screened in Japan in 1989 and in the USA two years later, but it was a box office failure both times.[43] The point I would like to make here is that judging from the breadthless length of animated works produced in Japan, there are very few stories originating from the *other* side (that is, stories from developing countries and lesser known Third World countries) which have been adapted for animation.[44]

To date, there have been only a few exceptions. One is the animated feature film jointly produced by Japan and India, *The Legend of Prince Rama Ramayana* (1987). There was also a co-production with China entitled *Shunmao monogatari taro* (1981). This film is about protection of wildlife and a panda is the main protagonist of the story. A Chinese epic narrative tale, *Romance of the Three Kingdoms*, in Japanese called *Sangokushi*, was also adapted into animated feature films in 1988 and 1989. This spellbinding tale is about chivalry and political intrigues. Another well-known Chinese folktale, *Legend of the Monkey God*, is also an all-time favorite of the Japanese. Tezuka Osamu was the first to serialize the tale in his manga and adapt it into a feature film called *The Enchanted Monkey* (1960). Like the rest of the manga works featuring the Monkey God legend and its subsequent adapted anime narratives that appeared in Japan, the contents were often written in accordance with that particular author's treatment and interpretation of the tale; it did not usually comply with the original Chinese interpretation of the folktale (e.g. the manga-anime TV series, *Dragon Ball* [1984] and *Dragon Ball Z* [1989]). The above-mentioned narrative stories originate from China and India, both of which have a long history and culture. Their adaptations into animation are also partly due to the historical cultural links that had existed with Japan.

What is the primal activity of animating? Essentially, it is a form of image-making, but when it is a voluminous activity that is centralized at a particular place and culture, it cannot help but arouse attention and inquiry. Statistics may give us a sense of the production and consumption fervor of anime in Japan, but they do not tell us precisely what, how, and why this image-making activity reigns so dynamically and popularly within the Japanese context. To produce images is to give life and form to certain visions including unfulfilled desires, internal self-narratives, and fantasies.

But to be energetically involved in picture-making, especially at a higher level, large-scale picture-making becomes a form of image-building and is one activity often instigated by authorities with national and bureaucratic power. Image-making, on the other hand, can be said to work more at the humble plane, within people's spatial existence. Sometimes, images formed are interstitial so as to serve personal and private functions but image-making can be extended to serve higher communal functions. In Japan, anime serves both levels of image production. As seen from the production of *Hakujaden* and a number of manga-adapted anime productions made or remade subsequently (e.g. *Astro Boy*, *Gundam*, *Space Battleship Yamato*,[45] *Doraemon*, and *Sazae-san*), the producers and the consumer-viewers have built an unspoken industrial and social contract to celebrate and honor the *imaginary*, even to the extent of accepting, maintaining, and expanding a transactional capital value of its illusionary status.

With regards to animation, the medium serves as a magnetic field that attracts "stuff" (for example, obsessions, dreams, and desires) that enables one to break out of the ordinary. In studying fantastic texts, Jackson (1981: 77–81) notes the "metamorphic" and "multiple" existence of the subject, and further denotes that "metamorphosis" can in fact function in a frame so as to give teleological meanings. For anime, owing to its pictorialness, fantasies are allowed to present themselves on a frame-by-frame basis, despite the continuous transformation of forms. On the one hand, the acknowledged market and public value of manga and anime carries varying degrees of restraint and self-censorship on the producer(s) as to what extent they can create openly for public consumption. On the other hand, the imaginary is simply perceived to be boundless and can also exist comfortably within private and personal space according to the consumption needs, whims, and fancies of the buyer, reader, and viewer.

The sphere of the imaginary is where fantasy resides. One would have thought that in a modern rationalistic setting where science and technology are the main call of the day and are capable of providing solutions of all sorts, the imaginary may no longer be functional and lies restfully in a redundant state. However, this is certainly not the Japanese situation. The most industrialized nation in Asia and the world's second most powerful industrialized economy still preserves the imaginary realm and values it highly. In fact, without the imaginary Japan would become unimaginable, listless, and even lost. Maybe manga and anime are like drugs to a number of Japanese as cocaine, heroin, and the like are to addicts?[46] This anecdotal remark fails to see the extraordinary "generating energy" of these pictorial media. It is precisely the imaginary, or a semi-religious Shintoist belief in creativity and childlike wonder, that gives birth to both the personal and collective realms of entertainment, which in turn contributes to the Japanese economy. When examining Japan's continuous constitutional effort to preserve the monarchy as head of state after the Second World War, the nation's prolonged attachment to the rituals and rites of such traditional arts and beliefs as *bushidō*, Shintoism, and *chadō* (tea ceremony), as well as its relentless, modernistic drive to industrialize and attain economic superpower status, Lee (1995) laments that the country has chosen to tread between the two worlds of myth and reality. In acknowledging the country's traditional past and its industrialized present, following Lee's line of thought, it can be seen that anime provides a buffer living space in which fantasy, art, and technology can co-exist satisfactorily, benefiting the economic and psychological needs of the nation.

In other words, anime embodies materiality and spirituality and is "mirrorily" reflective of the ontological world of Japanese society in the latter half of the twentieth century. Phenomenally speaking, as this study suggests, the overt phenomenon of the medium-genre bespeaks a covert side of existence while the mental and spiritual aspects of the self found an expressive and existential space to inhabit. Going back to the theoretical propositions discussed in Chapter 3, is Nishida's concept of *poiesis* applicable to postmodern Japan? To him, *poiesis* is the act of forming, "… the formed forms the forming, and that is why I say: from the formed towards the forming. Therefore, here is poiesis …" (1958: 173). That is to say, Nishida is directly vivifying the human individual as the center of the creative world. He is also specific in addressing the kind of individual or subject he is describing. Nishida says,

> Subjects which are not spiritually creative in any way will not persist
> in the history of the world. The idea is essentially the principle of
> "life" of a subject. (1958: 185)

Nishida also refers to "subject," "as a species" (1958: 185) and later, he means "a people" (p. 203). Nishida adds, "we must be creative, from hour to hour" but not according to the traditional way of acting, if not, "the Self" would be mechanized, resulting in "the death of the species" (p. 208).

In light of the intense industrialization of Japan after the Second World War, the "spirit" or *seishin* of Nishida's *poiesis* did permeate postwar Japan and it is visually best expressed through the archetypal sights of millions of salaried employees working long hours for the collective advancement of Japan Inc.[47] In comparative reference to the late German philosopher Martin Heidegger's work on *poiesis*, his concept is tied with the being of the self which he calls Dasein. According to Alexander Ferrari Di Dippo's analysis of Heidegger's concept of *poiesis*, human productive work, for example, a work of art or handicraft manufacture, discloses the Being, offering it appearances; Heidegger "assigns to art the power of an original ontological disclosure" (2000: 41). In other words, the Being can only find meaning in the world by being productive and being involved in the activity of becoming. Heidegger also pre-sites the Being, the Dasein, as having a concealed instability; it is through the experience of *poeisis*, "a bringing forth," that makes the Being existentially valuable and self understanding (Heidegger, 1993: 317). Heidegger's idea of Dasein carries with it the "to be" existence of living, by manifesting becoming, and of persistently sustaining itself in "projection" (Caputo, 1998: 227).[48]

Seen in this angle and in the context of Japan, it may be apt to pose this inquiry: Are anime and its many image projections (as found on television, in cinema, games, graphic posters, and so on) necessary restitutions of a making Self, afraid of its negativity and deficiency, and also, contradictorily, its larger representational Self as seen from the open and the surface? By the latter, I mean the supreme predominant image-Self of a strong industrialized developed nation. This line of inquiry is about the overpowering waves of modernization and Westernization which Japan has faced since the mid-eighteenth century. In retraction, it may also be about the country's early adoption of the Chinese script and aspects of Chinese culture. Linguistically, as discussed in the preceding chapters, the Chinese script is essentially a foreign textual medium; moreover, the realm of the written word is itself a pre-constituted, culturally premediated type of medium. Thinking in the phenomenological-ontological sense, the endless streams of manga-anime productions are likened to a Heideggerian's concept of *poiesis* where "bringing forth" a creative Self constantly regenerates and re-assures its communicative visual entity.

Given the motivation and orientation of anime in the Japanese framework, where do other Asian countries stand in relation to their "social contract" (if any) with the medium of animation, spoken or unspoken? For example, in China, the social contract that bonded the producers, the sponsors and the viewers had occurred for a short period in the past. It was during the Second World War when the Wan brothers made *Princess Iron Fan*, but despite its success among viewers (see Chapter 4), the sponsor was not willing to continue their investment in the animation medium. Disappointed, the Wan brothers proposed their animation development plan to a Hong Kong-based film company, Great Wall Productions, and subsequently moved to Hong Kong and expected that the company would help develop the medium. They were again disappointed because Great Wall Productions was not like Toei, which instinctively saw animation as economically viable (Hu, 2001: 116). When they moved back to mainland China, the Wan brothers' zeal and hard work in animation did not last long as Shanghai Animation Studio to which they returned was soon caught in the political upheavals of the Cultural Revolution.[49]

However, simply pointing to the political and historical misfortunes which, for example, the Wan brothers faced, or the effects on a number of animation studios in such countries as South Korea and Taiwan due to the subcontracted work offered by foreign producers, only simplifies the issue. In a culture or society, there should be in existence an indispensable and persistent collective will (however faint it may be) acknowledging, preserving, and nurturing the dialectical imaginary representations regardless of whatever the political and social conditions there may be. Fables, folktales, myths, and even communal grapevine gossip[50] belong to the realm of the imaginary, and they all tell a kind of "real" that has been somehow marginalized, exiled, or prohibited. The question is whether Asian countries, particularly those aiming to establish an animation industry as dynamic and successful as that of Japan, are ready to harness and nurture this collective storytelling along the imaginary path of animating, given that there are other forms of media which are already in existence and are serving this collective imaginary well. For example, live-action films in India, especially the Bollywood films of song and dance, continue to serve millions of viewers in South Asia and Indian communities worldwide. South Korean live-action films, artistic or non-artistic, romance or horror, gangster or thriller, have in recent years brought much entertainment to home viewers as well as global audiences interested in world cinema. A new cultural phenomenon, *Hallyu*, with its amalgamation of Korean films, television dramas, pop songs, and fashion has taken Asian communities by storm, particularly in East Asia and Southeast Asia, and as a result, brought in much earnings and trading opportunities from abroad to South Korea.[51]

Then, why imitate or recreate an existing dominant foreign medium-genre? It might be more helpful for these Asian countries to reach deeply into their own cultures and look for their innate competence for collective storytelling. It might also be more beneficial for them to accept the fact that the narratives of animation productions do not need to be governed by the predominant standards. Interwoven in this trendy zeal to "match" and to "compete" with those ahead in producing commercial animation abroad is the contemporary availability of new advanced technologies which heightens this development course to follow a familiar formulaic path. The trap lies in the foreign origins of such tools and devices, as in the end their application only contributes and reinforces similar production patterns, methods, and modes of thinking and creating. For example, Malaysian animation teacher Juhanita Jiman (2005) points out various areas to which the animators in her country may have to pay attention. While there is no lack of folklore which animators can use, given the rich multiracial mix and multifaceted lifestyles of Malaysians, the execution process ultimately comprises character design, color schemes, and motifs. Even the calculated animated movements occupy a greater part of the animated storytelling. Hence, the search for an "identity" is no simple matter.[52]

Or, could it be the case that there is "internal imperialism" repressing the imaginary from manifesting in animating forms? If so, where does the repression come from? Is it from the ruling authorities, the cultural agents and sponsors, the community at large, or all combined? In his critique of the discourses of cultural imperialism, Tomlinson (1991:165) summarizes that it is the apparent absence of "collective will-formation" in recording and creating "narratives of cultural meaning." In other words, the onus lies on society itself to "want" to co-participate and co-create narratives despite the presence of locally enacted or foreign obstacles. Moreover, in view of the missing or underachieved liberal modernization conditions in the greater Asian region (with the exceptions of Taiwan and South Korea as political reforms in these two countries since the late 1980s have led to the implementation of new policies and plans for developing the creative industries), other governing status-quo positions, and state arrangements pose hindrances in one way or another in nurturing anime productions that are people-oriented and pro-reflexive. By "reflexive," I refer to a Bourdieu's concept, that is, the ability to be critical and exploratory of societal happenings, which offers independent perspectives unshackled by predominant and predetermined biases and beliefs (Bourdieu, 1973 and 1990). This is so as such productions not only require a great number of talented and committed staff, "enlightened" sponsors, mentors, and experienced art educators, but also a free and tolerant political environment for this unpredictable and energy-motivated medium to thrive. For example, in Japan, manga-anime characters are present in serious newspapers, journals, and other reputable youth publications. Countries in the region has yet to develop their outstanding nationalistic styles as they are still importing indiscriminately a foreign medium-genre without understanding its cultural characteristics and its enterprise intentions.

The Japanese experience of animation (including anime) turns out to be an encompassing kind, fulfilling personal and social needs, spiritually and materially. Cultural theorist Raymond Williams has stressed the "peopleness" of culture; indeed, anime is part of an ethnic people's culture and "is an inseparable part of a complex whole" (1994: 60). It is part of a specific cultural trajectory; therefore, its value is measured by time and generations of evolvement and commitment and a presence of a certain physical and socio-cultural environment. In other words, it is not solely a matter of capital investment and infrastructure building. Nor can it be taken as a homogeneous universal transaction, as if all fans of manga and anime, Japanese and non-Japanese, share the same interests and levels of appreciation of anime. In relation to the studies of anime fandom worldwide, my stance differs from a critic's global view that the *otaku* phenomenon "is not purely Japanese" and has instead become a "transnational" movement (Lamarre, 2004/05: 175),[53] because, to draw a Lacanian analogy, the imaginary has inherent underlying tensions, gaps eccentricities, fantasies, and causes of desires. Also, the imaginary is the "mirror" imagined world, which is capable of reflecting and being reflected upon (Lacan, 1977 and 1988). Hence, the fascination of the medium-genre overseas possibly tells more about the local prevailing cultural circumstances and the dynamics may vary from one place to another.

In short, the particularity with which the Japanese embrace the visual should not be regarded as a common phenomenon and that their experience can be easily transferable and repeatedly produced or re-enacted elsewhere. Theirs is when the conventional word, spoken or written, fails or proves to be insufficient in conveying other realms of meaning or truth. The images also participate in expressing the missing communication gaps and in part allow the gift of creating and imagining to take hold. Hence, anime "is raised to the status of a kind of pictorial ontology," a phrase which Bernhard Waldenfels (1998: 288) uses in espousing Merleau-Ponty's philosophy of perception, and describes how the take-for-granted cognitive linguistic world is trapped by a primordial past and the language of painting offers new visibilities of things (that the painter paints not only what he sees but also "what sees itself in him") (1998: 288). My appropriation of this phrase attempts to channel out more clearly a vital communicative strand in the Japanese perception of truth which includes an experiential world of suggestiveness, nuances, inter-subjectivities, and ambiguities, where the visual realm of expression exists notably well in living up to its operative functions. In other words, the communicative universe in the Japanese context allows more room for visual dialectical exchanges and expressions as compared to other cultures.

In the Mahayana Buddhist tradition, the concepts of *samsara* ("wheel of life") and emptiness or void (in Sanskrit, *shunyata*) are embodied within each other. The latter perceives the phenomenal world as essentially perceptional and it is transmitted or activated by the senses. The former perceives experiences as entrapped in the cycle of flux, especially in birth and death. The world of appearances naturally evokes a reflective mirror. The question is, therefore, whether the mirror is the genesis of emptiness and whether in the end it simply boils down to one hearty laughter of such a phenomenal world and its illusionary existence. Is the average Japanese acutely aware of this transient world of appearances? Or, is the approach to embrace the historical-biological world with all positivity despite the knowledge of its illusionary negative aspect? A follower of Mahayana Buddhism is expected to accept the dichotomous doctrine, that is, acknowledge the floating world (*ukiyo*) of impermanence and pleasure, practice moderation, and tread a middle path of living. However, the Japanese attitude to image-making and image consumption is excessive and particular as seen from the examples of their manga and anime. On the whole, the Land of the Rising Sun not only practices visual-making experiences continuously but also turns them into both leisure and enterprise-based activities.

The virtuosity of the visual as expounded from Japan validates the domain of the illogical, the irrational, the intuitive, and the expressive in the dialectical arc of co-existence. It remains to be seen how other Asian nations take stock of the Japanese "endowment" of image-building and understand the cultural frames of anime and its variable Japanese conditions.

Epilogue

As this book was under preparation, there have already been many publications on anime in the market. A number of them are selected writings or essays written by authors who have been specially solicited. These publications showcase and interpret different dimensions and popularity of the medium-genre. Increasingly, more and more academic-based research on anime is conducted and published. This proves the subject's ongoing appeal and promise. In addition to other fan-inspired publications and numerous websites in English and non-English, there is indeed growing information about anime that celebrates its wide currency.

This book offers new insight and perspective of the medium-genre. Throughout the book there may be some confusion and incongruity as to how anime is defined. In contemporary terms, anime is Japanese animation with distinctive recognizable representations and often with close-knit links to the graphic literary world of manga. From a broader perspective, anime means more and the Western-sounding term speaks of a different Eastern language and culture from which it originates. The "flip-flop" use of the name-terms in the book — "Japanese animation," "anime," and "manga-anime" — is driven and guided not only by a specific culture of what this book is about, but also by the different periods in history from which I chart the visual medium's growth and the socio-cultural context of its development. As I have shown in the preceding chapters, the indigenous repertoire of name-terms for "animation" in Japan are fluid and almost limitless; they testify to the interconnected grid of relationships that animation can offer in the country.

Chapter 1 attempts to highlight the imported aspects of the Japanese language. While the world of words give form and order to a stable civic life, the acceptance of a foreign script understates the exigency of the language issue and its native state. When Japan later faced the advancement of the West and experienced modernization, the country further adopted foreign terms and this proved to be more of a practical matter. What remains as holistically close to the heart of existence is the preference for a visual language that can fill the unspoken and unwritten gaps and express the complexity of life. Chapter 1 also points out that the Japanese inclination toward the graphic and the visual is not necessarily unique as the inadequacy of the word has been expounded in both Western and Eastern thought although in the East, this issue has been addressed much earlier. As the language of the word is not able to articulate wholly the experience of life and its truth(s), the language of the visual prevails as a primordial mode and space to articulate the unsaid, the inexpressible, and the inter-moments. In the Japanese context, as I have suggested, photography and film did arrive at a momentous time that recorded, documented, and even aestheticized the modern era.

As we have seen, the overabundance and fleeting nature of anime works hand in hand with the continual heritage of art in the country. Although it may be argued that the preservation of traditional art in Japan is at times political and ideological, the "contents" of the art forms and their relevance to contemporary Japan cannot be discounted and dismissed especially when we compare them with their Asian counterparts. It has been said that locating and defining anime in the context of Japan's heritage art forms seems too far-reaching and unfounded. What draws our attention is that the technologies may modify the modes of reception and even change the economic aspects of production, but aesthetic sensibilities, artistic perspectives, and narrative stories are continual, recurring, and renewing. So, although Chapters 2 and 6 have different foci, the progressive development of the visual and anime is somehow inseparable from a heritage of ideas, values, and ideological reflections.

The spirit of this book is not guided by a premeditated view of the subject matter. When studying a specific form of animation that comes from a place where its people had achieved modernization within less than half a century and waged a world war with unimaginable consequences, one cannot afford to be fixated on constructing a one-sided reading and understanding. This research, however, has made a deliberate choice to study the subject matter from the soil of its origin, followed by a comparative approach that surveys the region's geo-cultural influences and counter-influences, including historical cultural associations, disengagements, and responses to world developments and events. Chapter 3 exemplifies a native cultural thought and practice that remains active in one of the most technologically developed societies in the world today. The chapter indicates that despite the high-profile presentations and commitments of Zen Buddhism in Japanese culture, the prevalence of a less organized and less dogmatic mass religion, or a set of indigenous beliefs, customs, and practices, continues to dictate and influence the cultural growth of Japan in each era. The chapter also sketches a scenario for alternative thinking in Japan's nearby neighbors, namely China and Korea, and compares their destinies. It discusses the deep-seated cultural frames of anime which explains partly the populace's continual embrace of the fantastic, the visual, and the interstitial.

Chapters 4, 5, and 6 analyze various developments of Japanese animation while mapping them in a chronological time frame. Present and past animation artists and directors, entrepreneurial and institutional patrons, and the unwavering support of the audience-consumers, are discussed. When analyzing Miyazaki's and Takahata's animated works, I take less of the content analysis approach, as many of their works, especially those directed and animated by Miyazaki Hayao, have been frequently highlighted, analyzed, and reviewed. My intention is to explore, describe, and analyze their collaboration in a commercial studio setting. In other words, it is more of a historical-industrial approach that I have adopted while taking stock of the socio-cultural aspects of their artistic and economic contributions. As a substantial number of animated works produced before and after the Second World War have become available for public consumption and study recently, and the current Japanese government regards anime highly as a global "soft power," Japanese scholars have begun various research on the development of anime and its implications in the country and abroad. Hence, Chapters 4 and 5 offer an introductory glimpse of Japan's animated images in the past and their links to history and politics, both locally and internationally. At best, these chapters hope to show the direction of the medium-genre's industrial growth and offer a diagrammatic tour of a much unexplored territory. In other words, there is still room for further discussion and study, which will require lengthy and substantial research.

Chapter 7 wraps up the series of theories and hypotheses for analyzing anime and its presumed links with Asia. It returns to the key issue of a number of Asian countries' efforts to develop their animation industries, which could compete with that of Japan. The anchoring position of my analysis encompasses Japan and Asia and contemplates the difficulties or the lack of "essentials" and "preconditions." The chapter does not intend to discourage or dismiss the idea of developing an animation industry in Asia outside Japan. Rather, as it has been suggested and shown in this book, the anime path somehow requires a natural shaping of various forces that have evolved through years of nurture. It would also need support by a particular tradition of cultural heritage and pre-industrial inclinations. The chapter argues that the labyrinth of anime is more complex and deep-rooted than it seems. When watching an animated film, individual frames of an animated scene or a segment are hardly visible or detected on the surface. Yet, the combination of these layered and hidden frames makes the overall presentation look dimensional, believable, vivid, and rich. In Western art, the frame of a painting is often inseparable from the aesthetic appreciation of the artwork. In fact, it greatly affects the value of the work by its presence and definition. This book is not so much about the external embellishment of any anime frame as it is about the stratum of cultural and historical frames that are buried and hidden in anime as a whole.

In short, animation is not only anime and the capabilities of the medium are endless. The pioneers of animation have already made these clear to us and with the advancement of digital technology, the "craft" of animation has to be understood from the fundamental. It is important to know not only *how* but also *why* the storyteller vis-à-vis the filmmaker adopts animating strategies to advance his or her filmic tale. Last but not least, the role of the specific audience in supporting and appreciating the "believability" of the fantastic elements is also important.

When examining the subject, my analysis does not depend on one discipline. The scope of this study crosses boundaries and its approach may be regarded as eclectic and untraditional. However, one departing point has remained the same throughout this book, that is, geographically, the antenna of inquiry is grounded in Japan and Asia, and my study here seeks to give an exploratory passage to readers from this end. It is my hope that this book will contribute to the understanding of anime and its place of birth, as well as the different experiences and challenges that the region encounters in response to an image-laden-productive kingdom, Japan.

Appendix 1

What follows is the letter from the Wan brothers to film critic, Shimizu Akira. The letter was later published in the film journal, *Eiga Hyōron* (December 1942 issue).

Cartoon

Within the Popular Eastern Fairy Tale
— *Journey to the West, Princess Iron Fan* Production Process[1]

Wan Laiming
Wan Guchan

As we vaguely recall, about 17 years ago we began our research on cartoon art. We went through many difficulties and failures and tried to achieve satisfactory results. This may be due to the many aspects of a career one has to experience and the hardship posed by the environment. After an episode of success, we estimated that we should produce 14 short animated films which would carry educational contents so that we might obtain employment from the Education Ministry and other educational institutions. Although there were recognizable flaws in the technical aspect, it was the beginning of our successful cartoon career.

The greatest problem was that we could not manage an independent business by making short animated films; but this was the only source of income and economic survival. Our initial success encouraged us to further our work. At least, we could work actively in cinema art production with spare funds and continue our hard work. Because we did not have specialist knowledge and senior masters to teach us, we learned by trial and error in the dark. We progressed poorly, how laughable, and it was only after much experimentation that we had the confidence to produce satisfactory results. During that time we also had the help of a company that allowed us to use its facilities for experiments. It eliminated many difficulties. This was also why, in general, artists who adored cartoon art did not dare to try, although there are many who have done so, and have also spent much time and effort; to speak of it, we have been really fortunate.

During that time, film company owners felt that making feature-long animated films was a most risk-taking enterprise; nobody had the courage to try it.

Film is the utmost scientific industrial product in this century. It comprises light, sound, electricity, investment … and has been recognized as one of the eight greatest arts.[2] Besides, cartoon is also a synthesis of all these eight arts with its rich complexity. It is uniquely broad and yet not simple.

In the stillness of Eastern cartoon history unfolded a radiant chapter, that is, film producer Zhang Shangkun, who possesses extraordinary foresight and determination, entrusted us to create China's first feature-long cartoon regardless of any production difficulties. With limitless time, cost, labor, and other material demands, the aim was to nurture the skills for cartoon-making. Ah, we received such care and attention from a significant film producer; it was both gratifying and exciting. Then, we only carried with us a diligent heart and specifically aimed to complete China's first feature-long cartoon, *Princess Iron Fan,* which serves as our grateful repayment to our benefactor.

Now I shall briefly give you a description of our production.

Drama Story

Before we began production, a story had to be selected. The criterion was that it should be an educational Chinese legend or fairy tale. If there were few dialogues and too much action in the story, we had to consider changes as many were either swordfighting stories or meaningless fantastical tales. Even *Journey to the West* could not avoid such storytelling elements. For *Princess Iron Fan* we made changes at various stages, and extracted the purer elements of the story.

Labor

During the drawing process, it was necessary to hire over 200 artists and we had to make sure that they all had knowledge of cartooning. So from these 200 artists, we selected the talented and trained them; we let them have a sense of fulfillment in their work and most sacred of all was that they were all willing and self-sacrificing cartoon art comrades. We saw them work over 12 hours daily and continuously for 3 years. They illustrated about 300,000 drawings and 700 beautiful and sophisticated background art drawings, and accomplished more than what was required. Among these great artists, there were over 12 staff members who suffered from tuberculosis because of this project. Whenever we think of this, we feel very sad. However, they still worked silently and endured the pain and achieved success and received honors for their work in the end.

Finance

The most important part of the drawing process was materials — paper, pencils, colorings, cels, and photographic materials. The estimated cost was more than 600,000 yuan and it broke the financial record of a Chinese Hollywood-type film. The most unforgettable thing was that many people cared and worried about our work; there were also many who thought our work was too risky and success would be difficult. But finally, in early September of last year, in a lovely and cool season, our *Princess Iron Fan* was screened in Shanghai.[3]

During the course of our work:

We always had this notion that the Eastern art of film-making should embody Eastern color and taste, and it should not imitate and follow wholly the style of Hollywood. Thus, based on this creative aspiration, as seen from the characteristics of *Princess Iron Fan*, in the areas of make-up, fashion, action, and line-drawing, they all yield originally to traditional Chinese art. The important working steps were drawing, filming, and sound-recording. Let me explain more in the following sections.

During the drawing stage, there were several sections:

Background Design Section

Research and adapt from both old and new architectural forms, select and improve the strong points and then start to paint and complete the background design.

Mood Design Section

Follow the story script and sketch from life the emotions of happiness, laughter, anger, rebuke, etc.

Model Design Section

For every story character, create solid models for the artist-painters to study and refer to.

Movement Design Section

Work out the timing of movements and dialogue, follow the 24-frame-per-second standard and note the number of drawings that form each filming angle.

Live-action Section

Draw the movable aspects as designed.

Line-drawing Section

Upon receipt of tens of thousands of drawings from live-action section, use pen and color and draw on the cels. This section also holds the responsibility of improving the drawings, and produces exclusively clear and beautiful illustrations.

Coloring Section

This section is in charge of the depth and quality of color usage, and the need of color adjustment as this requires special attention.

Inspection Section

To inspect the draft sketches and ensure that the combined drawings are in order and harmony, according to plan.

Filming

An average film camera is unable to film cartoon. An animation camera requires the special "hand" of a technician to design and set up the equipment. Because of format and speed, it also needs the special skills of a cameraman for designing and planning the camera angles, laying out the batches of work and filming time, adjusting to near, medium, and long shots … filming each frame one by one.

Sound Recording

Among the three parts, we thought that this posed the fewest problems. If it was due to negligence and insufficient efforts in the preparatory stage, the film would seem to have the effect of a silent cartoon and it would waste all our efforts. As it was the last stage of our production process, we worked harder and were determined to complete the film and the credit had to go to the musicians.

The film project from beginning to completion took three years and during this period, the world had encountered many changes. During the making of the cartoon, we were separated from the outside world. Even though our work has reached a milestone, one must not rest on one's laurels. While labor and materials are getting scarce in China, we are still able to experiment and finish China's first feature-long cartoon, *Princess Iron Fan*. Yet, we know that there are many flaws in the film. We hope the Eastern people would at any time give us your comments and advice.[4]

September 13, 1942[5]

(The letter has been translated into English by the author.)

Appendix 2

Table 1: Modernization Developments and the Growth of Anime in Japan

Mid-eighteenth century onward	*Rangaku* (Dutch Learning) and European learning intensified
1853	Arrival of Commodore Matthew C. Perry and his naval fleet
1867	Fall of the Tokugawa shogunate
1868–1912	Meiji period and the delicate balance of Western scientific learning and traditional Eastern learning
1900s onward	Revival of "things" Japanese (e.g., *kabuki* theater, restoration of the use of "brush" in painting, etc.)
1917	Locally made animated films began to appear
1921	The Monbusho (Ministry of Education) designated animation as a children's genre and governmental funds were offered for productions
1930	*Silly Symphonies* was shown (the series was made in America in 1929)
1934	Success of Fuji Film Co. in manufacturing an array of industrial film-related products
1934	Formation of a Motion Picture Control Committee by the pro-war government

(continued on p. 176)

(Table 1 continued)

1934	Short film *Picture Book, Momotarō vs Mickey Mouse* was made
1943	*Momotarō no umiwashi*, Japan's first animated feature film was made
1945	Sequel *Momotarō umi no shinpei* was made
1948–54	Previously banned foreign animated films were publicly screened including *Snow White*, *Bambi*, and *Pinocchio*, etc.
1958	*White Snake Tale*, Japan's first color animated feature film produced by Toei Dōga
1960	Re-signing of the US-Japan Security Treaty sparked off large-scale street demonstrations
1960s onward	Rise of manga-artist Tezuka Osamu and the adaptation of his comic work into animation
1963	*Tetsumu Atomu* (*Astro Boy*) TV series was aired on Fuji Television
1963	Miyazaki Hayao entered Toei Dōga as a trainee animator
1964	Tezuka Osamu met Walt Disney in New York
Late 1970s onward	Anime boom in Japan; Miyazaki directed his first animated feature film *Castle of Cagliostro* in 1979
1981	As many as 45 TV anime series and some 21 animated feature films were made and screened in Japan

Table 2: Developments in Animation in China

1941	*Princess Iron Fan,* an animated feature film, was produced in Shanghai
1949 onwards	Chinese government supported the making of animated films
1950	Formation of Shanghai Animation Studio
1960–63	Appearance of animated films using the ink-and-color technique (e.g., *Tadpoles in Search of Mummy, Cowherd's Flute,* etc.)
1965	Closure of Shanghai Animation Studio and the banishment of staff to countryside labor camps
1976	The Gang of Four fell from power
1977	Shanghai Animation Studio re-opened
1979	*Nezha Shakes the Sea* was one of the animated feature films made

Notes

Introduction

1. Trotsky (1925: 183).
2. Kim (1987: 79).
3. See www.sony.com. The website shows Sony's US businesses include Sony Electronics Inc., Sony Picture Entertainment Inc., Sony Computer Entertainment America Inc. and Sony Music Entertainment.
4. She describes *otaku* as someone "with an obsessive interest in something, a geek. One can be a computer otaku, a fashion otaku or an anime otaku." Linguistically, *otaku* is a slang term and in present-day Japan, an *otaku* is also used to refer to someone who has expert knowledge in a certain field. However, it still carries such derogatory meanings as being anti-social and self-centered in the Japanese context.
5. Conversations with Professor Iwamoto Kenji at Waseda University Division of Cinema and Theater Arts, Tokyo, and Professor Yokota Masao at Nihon University Department of Psychology, Tokyo, in 1999.
6. Foreign students and scholars living in Japan when they found out that I was researching on the subject of anime posed this question to me on several occasions.

Chapter 1

1. The legend dates back to the late fifth century with the publication of a Chinese Buddhist writing called *A History of the Dharma Treasury*. It is said to be a translation from an original Sanskrit text.
2. The approximate number was based on my daily observation of the screening cycles of animated films while living in Japan from 1998 to 2000 and from 2003 to 2004 and my subsequent short trips to Japan. An average Japanese child or parent would tell you his or her expectations of a Japanese holiday season, which would be rendered meaningless without any animated theatrical films to grace the vacation period.
3. The later *Nihon shoki* (*Chronicles of Japan*, AD 720) was written entirely in Chinese characters. Both texts gave accounts of the origins of the Japanese state, but *Kojiki* contained more fragmentary myths and stories that were interwoven into the supposedly chronological narrative; see also Kato (1997: 12–30).

4. The original writing dates back to the late 1920s when Tokieda Motoki gave a series of lectures at the Tokyo Imperial University. He was one of the few *kokugo* scholars who did not support the principle of linking the national language to race and state. See Karatani Kojin, "National and Écriture" in *Surfaces* (1995) for a comparative East-West critique of the late linguist's work.

5. "Barbarian" was used to describe especially the Western imperialists, notably represented by the appearance of the American naval fleet in 1853, led by Commodore Matthew C. Perry who demanded the opening of Japan through the signing of a treaty. Later similar treaties were signed with other Western nations, granting privileges to the foreign powers as demanded.

6. The Edo period is also known as the Tokugawa period, as the Tokugawa shogunate was based in Edo, where present-day Tokyo is located.

7. *Yamato* was the ancient place name of central Japan and it was said to be located in the area surrounding the cities of Nara and Kyoto. It had also been referred to as "the heart of Japan," where the country's first high order of civilization had developed since prehistoric times.

8. *Rangaku* means Dutch Learning, a subject of study during the period 1640–1853 when only a handful of Dutch traders were permitted to live in Japan.

9. Quoted in Kenneth B. Pyle (1998: 101). See also Albert M. Craig, "Fukuzawa Yukichi: The Philosophical Foundations of Meiji Nationalism," in Robert E. Ward (ed.), *Political Development in Modern Japan* (Princeton: Princeton University Press, 1968), 120–1.

10. See note 11 in this chapter. Kume (2002: 341) recorded good impressions of Hong Kong, especially its cleanliness, and praised the British for their law and order control of the territory. What, however, could be in the mind of a Japanese bureaucrat witnessing a Western colonized territory? Indeed, there is a record of a black and white picture in Hong Kong (the photographer is unknown) featuring a pair of samurai officials posing in a salon studio. Both were clad in traditional outfits and accessories complete with samurai knives; their facial expressions and body language revealed a covert sense of mission whatever the specific goals of their visit and stay in Hong Kong were (*Picturing Hong Kong: Photography 1855–1910*, Hong Kong Arts Centre, February 27– March 15, 1998). Perhaps in posing and framing oneself, one could only grasp the fragments of a passing era and feel secure in the momentary space. This "existential space" will be further discussed in the following chapters.

11. Kume (2002, Vol. 5: 313). The Iwakura Embassy visited the United States, various European countries, and also other Asian countries during its onward and return journeys. As early as the 1860s, high-ranking Tokugawa officials visiting countries in the West already had a penchant for having their portraits taken and "brought them home with them" (Iwasaki, 1988: 24).

12. Joseph Nicéphore Nièpce produced the first permanent image by photo-chemical process in France in 1827.

13. This descriptive term of Asia first appeared in Fukuzawa Yukichi's *Datsu a ron* (1885). See also H. Iida (2002), the chapter on "Fukuzawa Yukichi," especially page 82.

Chapter 2

1. There are several cultural periods in Japanese history. In this book, the chronological dates are based on the historical periods of Japanese history. See *"About Japan" Series 11: Japanese Culture* (Tokyo: Foreign Press Center, 1993), 66.

2. Takahata also authored a book, *Jūniseiki no anime-shon* (1999, Tokyo: Tokuma Shoten), to commemorate the art form *emakimono* as a forerunner of Japanese animation.

3. Here, I am not quoting any specific scholar's work. Rather, I am referring to the Chinese traditional appreciation of landscape painting and the general dislike of parts of Chinese pre-modern history when China came under the foreign control of the Mongols and Manchus.

4. Predecessor realist art narratives have already appeared in wood and in color, see Yoshikawa (1976: 118) for a wood illustration of a "catch ball scene" from the ninth century, which is preserved in To-ji, Kyoto. See also p. 119 for other human figures in ink sketches that are stored in temples in Nara and Kyoto.

5. See Swann (1966: 183) and Boger (1964: 42). Contents of *emakimono* were also transferred to screen panel paintings in the fifteenth and sixteenth centuries where they appeared richer in color and decoration.

6. *Doraemon* (1970) is the brainchild of duo manga artists, Fujio-Fujiko. The animated series is still aired on Japan's prime-time television.

7. The picture scroll is about the imperial gate (*Ōu Ten Mon*) fire and the final arrest of Ban Dainagon, the court minister who was accused of masterminding the fire event.

8. The character Hana is one of the three homeless people featured in the animated film. "She" is an ex-drag queen. Ikkyū is noted as an eccentric Zen monk in Japanese Buddhist history. Even the *chinzō* of him captures that "nervous vitality" of his personality (Keene, 1971: 231). Art historian Sherman E. Lee describes the portrait of Ikkyū as a modern "post-Freudian" art-piece especially in relation to its psychological connotations (1983: 126).

9. *Shōhekiga* is a generic term that categorizes paintings on wooden panels, folding screens, and the like.

10. By that I mean the structural design layout of a traditional Japanese tatami room.

11. *Wabi* stresses the simplicity of poverty and the practice to rejoice in its transcendental peace of mind and beauty. Together with *sabi* which stresses loneliness, resignation, and tranquility, the *wabi-sabi* is an aesthetic ideal which rejects the loud and multicolored aspects of urban city life. Images that are favored include weeds, reeds, wild flowers, a weathered hut, a vase that does not have a polished shiny surface, and so on.

12. It is coincidental that both Barthes and Kinoshita produced their works at the same time during the late 1960s. While the *other* saw Japan in a rather Orientalist light, the *subject* tried objectively to self-express his discontentment and existentialist perspective of his society.

13. In analyzing the realist trait of some Momoyama art works, Yoshikawa (1976: 139 and 157) noted that artists belonging to the "The Kano School" preferred the "sensuous" and featured contents with "strong and direct realism" rather than the abstract atmosphere of a Song-inspired Chinese Buddhist form of painting known as *suibokuga*.

14. *Jōruri* (pure crystal) was the title of a puppet tale. Because of its immense popularity, it became synonymous with the genre of puppet theater from the medieval period (AD 1200). *Bunraku* is the later general term for puppet theater in Japan. It is derived from the name of

a famous puppeteer who owned a successful puppet troupe in Osaka during the nineteenth century. See Ortolani (1995: 208) and Kawatake (1971: 44).

15. In particular, the *Tale of Heike Clan*.

16. Manga-animation critic Ono Kosei, interview with the author in Tokyo, December 10, 1999.

17. *Mugen* is a "dream world" essentially and *kaisō* carries meanings of recollection, retrospect, memory and review.

18. *Hanamichi* is a passage where the actor can receive "hana" or flowers from the audience, but it has gradually become an important theatrical space for the actor to enter, exit and act (Kawatake, 1971: 54).

19. This scene seemed to predict the Aum Shinrikyo cult phenomenon and its members' fatalistic activities, including the infamous bombing of subway stations in downtown Tokyo in 1995.

20. Translated as *Treasury of Loyal Retainers*, also known as the *Forty-seven Rōnin*, the play dramatizes the actual hostility between two feudal lords which dates back to the early part of the eighteenth century. It is a vendetta tale of *seppuku* (enforced suicide), fulfillment of duty, revenge, and the inevitable fate of human tragedy and obligation. The samurai moral values of *giri* (obligation) and *ninjō* (human feelings) are emphasized, drawing upon their innate dialectical tensions.

21. See Haraguchi (1996, vol. 1 and vol. 3), pages 67 and 69 respectively.

22. The festival was organized by the Japan Association of Animators (JAA). Most of the members are independent animators.

23. An example of the Japanese aesthetic interest of European history and drama is the Takarazuka theatrical productions in which the visual delights of a European setting are often portrayed and choreographed extravagantly on a glittering stage. This all-female musical theater dates back to 1913 and still attracts millions of audiences in Japan today.

24. Kornicki (1998: 127) gave credit to the Jesuit contribution to the history of printing in Japan although he downplayed the influence of Jesuit contributions to the development of printing in the country as a whole. For example, Needham (1985, Vol. 5, Part I: 341) already noted that, like the Chinese, the Japanese were impressed with the Korean-made movable type of printing. The Japanese themselves imported the Korean-made type after the unsuccessful attempt by the warlord Toyotomi Hideyoshi (1536–98) to conquer Korea in the late sixteenth century.

25. Japanese paintings and woodcut prints drawn from a Western perspective since the seventeenth century are also generally categorized as *uki-e*. Japanese art historian Tamon Miki attributed the influences from Qing China where the Western style of painting had already been adopted. See Tamon (1964: 156).

26. In the later half of the sixteenth century, provinces in the Netherlands joined forces to end the political and religious control of the Catholic Kingdom of Spain.

27. Kaempfer's work first appeared in London in 1727 under the title, *The History of Japan*. The 1999 publication is edited, translated and annotated by Beatrice M. Bodart-Bailey.

28. This illustration can be seen in the introductory page in Keene's book (1969), *The Japanese Discovery of Europe 1720–1830*.

29. I thank retired animator, Oda Katsuya, for showing me video excerpts of this television documentary which he had taped. Oda Katsuya, interview with the author in Tokyo, September 22, 1999. The exact date of recording and the title of this Japanese documentary

are not available. *Utsushi-e* shows and exhibitions are now occasionally featured in city and university museums in Japan. See for example this presented event at http://plaza. bunka.go.jp/bunka/museum/kikaku/exhibition02/english/index-e.html.

30. For a better understanding of traditional Chinese art, see Sickman and Soper (1968: 136, 138–141) in which the authors recount the changing painting styles of Chinese artists, especially those from the Song dynasty onward.

Chapter 3

1. *Hello Kitty* is more of a graphic icon than a cartoon although consumers and fans are equally happy to see the graphic feline "moves" too. Created more than 30 years ago, the feline does not even have a mouth but it has been able to maintain an age-expanding fan base due to the designer's abilities to keep up with times. The sugary innocent world of *Hello Kitty* has a certain *shintō* appeal, which dwells upon the lap of nature in its sweetest wordless presence. See "Longevity-wise, Hello Kitty seems to live 10 lives" in *The Japan Times*, August 26, 2004. The article featured the 30th anniversary of *Hello Kitty* in November 2004 and described it as a successful "brand" series marketed and owned by Sanrio Company.

2. Although it is beyond the scope of this study to examine the extent to which *shintō* thinkers appropriated Daoist thinking from China, writings by these thinkers, at times, showed open contempt of Daoism. Yet, there were attempts to assimilate aspects of Daoist thought. One point is clear: Japanese *shintō* and Chinese Daoism have differences although both share the same Chinese character, *tō* or *dao*. One is, first and foremost, insularly bound to a lineage of imperial gods (see Muraoka, 11–21), the other exists both as a religion and a philosophy which originates from China, and its practices can be divided into two branches, popular Daoism and the philosophical and spiritual Daoism. See *The Texts of Taoism, The Tao Te Ching of Lao Tzu, The Writings of Chuang Tzu, Part I*, trans. James Legge (New York: Dover Publications, 1962) for further readings on Daoist thought.

3. The Anpo protests were a series of demonstrations against the revisions of the US-Japan Security Treaty in 1960. The terms of the treaty entered Japan into close military co-operation with the United States of America, especially in relation to the global protection of American interests. The protests were against the violation of Article 9 of Japan's newly formed postwar constitution which renounced all levels of military involvement. The protestors wanted to rebuild a new democratic Japan devoid of any superpower's interests. See Iida Yumiko (2002: 92– 95). Iida describes the Anpo protests as "the largest democratic movement in Japanese history."

4. Anime is moving pictures compared to old-fashioned prints, and by *momentarily* I mean the frame-by-frame build-up of images that are immaculately calculated to achieve the movements and effects desired.

5. In the English-speaking world, readers can refer to publications such as *The Erotic Anime Movie Guide* (1998) by Helen McCarthy and Jonathan Clements, and Frederick Schodt's pioneering work, *Manga! Manga! The World of Japanese Comics* (1983: 120–137), for accounts of the free-wheeling illustrations of Japanese sexual fantasies.

6. Prince Siddhartha was particularly perturbed by the sights of suffering pertaining to the cycle of birth, old age, sickness, and death, in the realm of the living, and vowed to find a liberation path. He was to become the Shākyamuni Buddha.

7. The Jesuits "gained court positions" in Beijing in the late Ming period during the end of the sixteenth century (Fairbank et al., 1989: 244).

8. For example, Shirane's *Traces of Dreams* (1998: 30–51) gives a detailed analysis of the Western reception of *haiku*, see the chapter on "Bashō Myth East and West."

9. In a series of international meetings (e.g. Paris Peace Conference, 1919) and treaties signed (e.g. Washington Naval Treaty, 1922), Japan did not receive the full privileges of a rising industrialized power and experienced unequal treatment despite its rising military capabilities. See Glenn D. Hook et al. (2001: 25–29).

10. These writings were subsequently published in English in 1960, 1973 and 1958 respectively.

11. *Samsara* means the "wheel of life," that is, the wandering flow of births and deaths intermingles with the flux of desires and wants.

12. We will return to this philosophical term in Chapter 7 where the dire phenomena of manga-anime making in contemporary Japan are examined further.

13. By that, I am referring to the widespread atrocities that occurred during the Second World War in China, Korea, and parts of Southeast Asia.

Chapter 4

1. This is the introductory paragraph extracted from the "Prefatory Note" in *Cinema Year Book of Japan 1936–37* (1937). The yearbook was originally published in English.

2. The most notable awards were given to the Studio Ghibli's productions. For example, Miyazaki Hayao's *Sen to chihiro no kamikakushi* (2001) won the Best Animated Feature Film at the Oscars in 2003.

3. Published in *Asian Cinema*, Tsugata's essay gave a detailed account in English of the three Japanese pioneer animators.

4. See animation historian Tsugata's illustration map (2004: 119) on the institutional genealogical links of Japanese animation from the early 1930s to the founding of Toei Animation Company in 1956.

5. Other Fuji Film Company official records, such as their published yearbooks, claimed that the industry report was the result of a major study (*hiroku kensa*) conducted by the Kodak officials upon the invitation of the Japanese.

6. Ina also reported that among the array of foreign goods on demand, the Japanese government was alarmed when it discovered that photography-related products were ranked high on the list. Thus, the government was determined to build a domestic film industry.

7. The *Silly Symphonies* was a cartoon series made by Walt Disney Productions. The first in that famous series was the *Skeleton Dance* (1929).

8. The translations in English could also mean "The Japan inside Japan, the Japan in the World, the World in Japan" consecutively.

9. See especially the chapter titled "Taishō Culture and Society," which recounts various changes in Japanese life during the period.

10. The first issue of *Shinkō eiga* appeared seven months later in September 1929.

11. It is a collection of essays in memory of *Prokino*'s activities.

12. I am grateful to retired animator Oda Katsuya who showed me a taped copy of a television documentary made in 1987 by NHK about the restoration of this rare film. The title of the documentary is not available.

13. Pan-Asianism or Asianism is an ideology that originated in the early twentieth century. During that period, there was a movement in the West to preserve "things" Eastern, and Japan became the living embodiment of that romantic perspective of the East. "Asia" or the "Orient" became equated with "the East" and intellectuals in Japan also participated in contributing to and defining Asianism (see Morris-Suzuki, 1998: 170–171). Iida Yumiko (2002: 59) clarifies that Pan-Asianism has a certain hegemonic "gaze" situating Japan as a leader in championing the aesthetic and moral values of Asia as opposed to the colonizing, rationalistic and materialistic values of the West.

14. Having been recognized as an industrial power and after gaining victory in two major wars at the turn of the twentieth century, Japan considered itself being treated "unequally" in matters dealing with the arms race (see also note 9 in Chapter 3) and the Western colonial powers' insistence in maintaining the old world order, especially the unanimous decision in keeping China as a free independent country, apart from the already occupied parts of China that had been ceded to the Western powers in the treaties signed in the nineteenth century.

15. P.C.L. and J.O. Company later came under the control of Toho Motion Picture Distribution Corporation in 1936. For background information on P.C.L. and J.O. Company, see Anderson and Richie (1982: 81–83).

16. Schickel (1997: 269–273). The Disney Studio was also called upon by the US government to produce propaganda films during the Second World War.

17. It was not known whether at that time there was such a banal effect on the audiences, as an animated short film was often shown after a news film was screened. But in the recent "A History of Japanese Animation" program held at National Film Center in Tokyo, July 6–August 29, 2004, a number of the animated films shown were made before the end of the Second World War. They had either nationalistic or militaristic themes, and the ideological stance was simply overbearing. Most of the audience were adults and there were also a handful of children present who might have been brought along by their parents. They did not seem to find the animated films appealing. This is very different from, say, an average Japanese afternoon cinema session in which one can encounter the young and old enjoying a light-hearted entertaining piece of animation like *Doraemon*.

    A number of retired animators whom I interviewed had seen such short animated films when they were children or teenagers. They recalled that they, however, did find the films interesting and entertaining as compared to the documentary newsreel films that were included in the screening sessions.

18. Translated as "Manga New Monkeys Crabs Collective War," it is a familiar Japanese folk tale (*nihon minwa*) and the story title is commonly known as *Sarukani kassen*. As the animated film's title suggests, it is meant to have a nationalistic bearing although the original tale carries the universal message of "the big bullying the small" and the latter's final united effort in overcoming their adversary.

19. According to Komatsuzawa (1995: 199–200), although the film was made in 1934, it was part of a series that was dated 1936. The film was made in anticipation of the expiry of the Washington and London military treaties in 1936. Supporting the right-wing military government's views of international politics, the US was depicted as an imminent attacker who attempted to acquire the lands of the Pacific Ocean.

20. Its English title has been given as *Momotarō, the Brave Sailor,* but its literal English translation can be read as *Momotarō and His Sea Eagles.* Another known English title is

Momotarō and the Eagles of the Ocean. Working with only four assistants, director Seo was known to have single-handedly drawn 150,000 animated frames for his ambitious animation project (from the program sheet of *A History of Japanese Animation*).

21. *Momotarō* is a legendary figure in Japanese folk tales. He is known for his inborn muscular strength and kindness toward small animals and ill-treated beings. Kahara Nahoko's paper, "From Folktale Hero to Local Symbol: The Transformation of Momotarō (the Peach Boy) in the Creation of a Local Culture," in *Waseda Journal of Asian Studies* (Vol. 25, 2004), exposes the myth of Momotarō as a cultural creation from the early Shōwa period onward that centers at Okayama Prefecture.

      A number of Japanese folkloric stories and legends originated from China were either appropriated by the ruling authorities or adapted by the commoners. Momotarō means "Peach Boy" and in ancient China prior to the founding of the Early Han dynasty (206 BC–AD 8), the symbol of the peach had already been associated with divine powers, especially the ability to curb evil-doers and devils. To this day, the Chinese consider peaches as symbols of longevity and health. See Yan (2002: 78–91).

22. The American military forces joined the Second World War in December 1941 when the Japanese military forces attacked Pearl Harbor. It officially marked the beginning of the Pacific War. Prior to that, the war was also known as the Greater East Asia War.

23. NHK documentary series on "History of Japanese Animation" in November 1998. The film was first screened in Tokyo in April 1945, according to Yamaguchi (2004: 60), but by mid-August 1945 the Japanese military government surrendered to the Allied Forces. The latter had already begun air raids on Japan in the later half of 1944. *Momotarō umi no shinpei* was said to be ready for public screening by the end of 1944, but its release was delayed due to the increased air raids on Japan.

24. Masaoka might have come across these works in art magazines, although the reference source did not clearly state so. Neither did it reveal how he came to be acquainted with new art developments in Europe.

25. For information about the Wan brothers' early experimentation years, see Lent and Xu, "China's Animation Beginnings: The Roles of the Wan Brothers and Others" (2003).

26. *Princess Iron Fan* was said to be shown in three cinemas in Shanghai when it was released. See Quiquemelle (1991: 178).

27. Until now, I have avoided explaining the multi-name titles that the Japanese have employed for the various types of animation. The terminology may be confusing, but I will discuss this peculiar linguistic aspect in the following chapters.

28. Shimizu Akira was also an employee of the liberal-minded Kawakita Nagamasa (1903–81), a prominent film distributor in Japan and China during that time. It was probably because of Kawakita's friendship with Zhang Shangkun (1905–57), the financial sponsor of *Princess Iron Fan* and the owner of the film company *Xinhua Yingye Gongsi*, that the Wan brothers agreed to write the letter to the Japanese. By then, the Shanghai film industry had come under the administrative control of the Japanese military forces, and Kawakita was appointed as a consultant chair presiding behind the scene.

29. The published article also shows pictures of the Wan brothers and the writer.

30. Examples of such films were included in the filmic series *Anti-Japanese Posters Collection* and *Anti-Japanese War Songs Collection*. See John A. Lent and Xu Ying (2003).

31. See, for example, P. Lim Pui Huen and Diana Wong (eds.), *War and Memory in Malaysia and Singapore* (Singapore: Institute of Southeast Asia, 2000). Until today, ethnic groups

in Malaysia and Singapore still remember the cruel and selective hierarchical treatment of community groups in that order; Chinese, Eurasians, Indians, and Malays. In other regions, from the Philippines to Indonesia, Malaysia, Singapore and so on, the widespread massacre of Chinese was consistently high and rampant. However, the ambivalent attitudes of the Japanese military forces towards the "colonies" could be seen from their less violent activities and legacies in the region of Micronesia. See Ken Hershall's "The Japanese Occupation of Micronesia in the Context of Imperialism," in Roy Starrs (ed.), *Japanese Cultural Nationalism: At Home and in the Asia-Pacific* (Kent, UK: Global Oriental, 2004).

32. Dower (1986: 254) is sharp to observe that the film portrays "the peoples of South Asia" as "generally unclothed" in anthropomorphic outfits and appearing simple-minded, illiterate, and uncouth. In his research on racism and war, Dower (1986: 258; 305) also discovers that despite the surmounting disdain and prejudice with which the Japanese viewed the Western colonial powers, *Momotarō umi no shinpei* illustrations did ultimately present the "Anglo-American enemy" as a "demon with a human face." This means that at least the Japanese did accord a certain amount of respect and equal status to the so-called "white colonists." Whereas in contrast, the Anglo-American graphic images of its "yellow counterparts" were less "diversified" and more "ethnocentric".

33. Yamaguchi and Watanabe (1977: 42) noted that after Singapore was occupied by the Japanese military forces in 1942, many foreign-made films were confiscated and brought back to Japan, among which were *Snow White and the Seven Dwarfs* and *Fantasia* (1940).

Chapter 5

1. Author's translation.
2. Analyzing Japan in the 1970s, Vogel's book praises many aspects of Japanese society including its education, low crime rate, economic success, politics and social welfare. He argues that America has "practical things to learn from Orientals" if Americans continued to have the "desire" to see themselves as number one (1979: ix).
3. According to Dower (1986: 356), the SCAP did order the film *Momotarō umi no shinpei* to be destroyed, but the negatives were discovered in the archival collection of Shochiku in around 1984. Today, the collection of *Momotarō* film series remains more or less intact, including the first animated feature film screened in 1943 and the earlier short films made in 1931 (*Sora no momotarō,* in English *Momotarō of the Sky*) and in 1932 (*Umi no momotarō,* in English, *Momotarō of the Sea*). See also the program leaflet, *A History of Japanese Animation*, July 6–August 29, 2004.
4. The Tokyo War Crimes Trials were presided over by the SCAP and lasted from May 1946 to April 1948. The trials simplified the whole issue of war responsibility and placed the blame on a few individuals who were later sentenced and executed. See Hirano (1992, in particular, Chapter 3, "The Depiction of the Emperor"), in which she details the American policy on Emperor Hirohito in face of pressure from the rightist postwar Japanese government.

      It is interesting to note that, just as in the *Momotarō* film (1945) where the "natives and the oppressed" are absent at the negotiation table during the Tokyo Trials, the real victims of the war and their representatives are also missing. In other words, the rest of

Asia (for example, the Southeast Asian and East Asian regions) also becomes a "third party" observing the trials. See Tanaka (2002) who questions the missing Asian voice in Japanese wartime trials.

5. As discussed in Chapter 1, when Japan began to modernize, the "West" meant Europe, that is, the European civilization was a model to follow.

6. By "anima", I mean the active parts of the soul.

7. In Japanese, "comfort women" means *ianfu*, a term used by the Japanese military forces to highlight the "maternal feminine" role played by groups of women enlisted to serve the Japanese military during the war. In reality, they were sex slaves abducted and forced to give sexual services to the military personnel. See also Yoshimi Yoshiaki, *Comfort Women: Sexual Slavery in the Japanese Military During World War Two*, translated by Suzanne O'Brien (New York: Columbia University Press, 2000).

8. In that interview, director Masaoka also explained that the background scenery was based on a certain scenic spot in Kyoto and the kimono-clad female figure was modeled after a dancer, including her hair make-up and accessories. The interview was originally published in the magazine *Film 1/24*, numbers 23 and 24, on October 1, 1978 under the title "Masaoka Kenzō Interview." It was reprinted in a commemorative exhibition book chiefly edited by Matsunomoto and Otsuka (2004: 20–33).

9. At the beginning, the doll draws him lots of gifts in the form of nicely packaged boxes; in the display are also cakes, sweets, and fruits. She also draws him a big house in which he can live.

10. For example, the SCAP disliked bowing because it was considered feudalistic. Kissing, on the other hand, was encouraged as it was seen as a liberal indication of affection.

11. For a further analysis of Japanese animation produced immediately after the war, see the author's article *Dare ni mukete no anime-shon ka? Shūsen chokugo no anime-shon eiga* ("Animating for *Whom* in the Aftermath of a World War" in *Senryoka no eiga: kaihō to kenetsu*), edited by Iwamoto Kenji (Tokyo: Shinwasha, 2009). The collection of essays focuses on Japanese films made during the Allied Forces Occupation of Japan. In the article, I apply psychoanalytic theory in interpreting the orientalized images found in the two above-mentioned animation films.

12. For example, the animated film, *Hakujaden,* was shown as part of a double bill which included the first live-action film screening of *Isshin tasuke tenka no ichi daiji*, directed by Sawashima Tadashi (1926–), in October 1958. The live-action film was part of a popular period-drama film series featuring a hero called Isshin Tasuke.

13. *Ukare baiorin* is a thirteen-minute color (Konica color stock) animated film, which was directed by Yabushita Taiji. It features an animal farm run by a despotic capitalistic owner. After several mishaps and misadventures, the previously cruel owner learns to appreciate his workers and animals and the communal atmosphere of co-existence. Apart from the socialist narrative elements, the film aims to present an exemplary Disney standard of animation and the human characters all have Western facial features.

14. Other English titles include *The White Snake Enchantress* and *Panda and The Magic Serpent*.

15. Crafton gave a keynote address at the 14th Society for Animation Studies Conference held at the DreamWorks SKG Animation Campus in Glendale, California, in 2002. His paper "Performance in and of Animation" was subsequently published in *SAS Newsletter* in 2003.

16. On the other hand, a discerning eye may find my aesthetic reading of *Hakujaden*'s background artwork too sweeping. For example, Imamura Taihei (1992: 210) praises the traditional aesthetic elements found in *Hakujaden*, citing the exquisite ink painting work and luxurious Momoyama designs as representative of Japanese art. In my own observation, Japanese adaptation of Chinese art and culture has often been imitative, selective, and innovative. In *Hakujaden*, I would argue that the aesthetic attempts to portray a classic Chinese picturesque setting were indeed genuine and amicable.

17. Takarazuka is a highly successful and popular all-female operetta troupe in Japan. See also note 23 in Chapter 2.

18. Until now, Toho has not made available the 1956 live-action film in video; it would be helpful to see and compare the narrative contents.

19. Otsuka Yasuo was one of the key animators involved in the film project. The reasons were never reported in the media and he was unsure of the details as well. Interview with the author in Tokyo, August 11, 2004.

20. Madam White Snake's attraction to Xu Xian is due to remembrance of a past when Xu Xian saved her from a thunderstorm when he was a child. Back then, she was in the form of a snake. Years later, bored with a mundane peaceful life, she wants to live in the human realm in order to repay her debt to her savior, Xu Xian.

21. Pai-nyan is said to be a thousand-year-old snake spirit with special physical and spiritual powers which she has self-studied and attained through the years.

22. For example, Toho co-operated with an Italian film company to make *Madame Butterfly* (1955) and Shochiku co-operated with the French to make *Unforgettable Love* (1956).

23. I thank film specialists Ishizaki Kenji and Matsuoka Tamaki who brought to my attention the existence of this exclusive trade journal.

24. Author's translation.

25. They had experience in producing animation films before the end of the war, and some had worked on animated feature films sponsored by the military.

26. Taylorist principles of management were named after Frederick W. Taylor (1856–1915) who was an engineer and a pioneer in management theory. He advocated scientific management in order to ensure systematic work processes and output.

27. Generally, from an Anglo-American perspective, the war fought against the Japanese has often been termed as the Pacific War (1941–45) which began when Japanese military forces attacked Pearl Harbor in December 1941 and other colonized parts of Southeast Asia. However, to many East Asians, including Koreans, Chinese, and the Japanese, the war was also known as the Greater East Asian War and the Japanese military forces intrusion into continental China dated much earlier at the turn of the twentieth century.

28. In the original *White Snake Tale*, there was an important episode in which Fahai insisted on Xu Xian's becoming a monk, and when he refused and later finally agreed, he was locked up in the monastery.

29. In Jungian psychoanalysis, C. S. Jung stressed the negative imposition of the state's power on individual freedom and expression. The "collective unconscious" plays an important role in shaping the psychic lives of individuals, and the individual (the personal) and the collective are interconnected. See, for example, C. S. Jung, *The Undiscovered Self*, trans. R.F.C. Hull (New York/Toronto: New American Library, 1958).

30. Author's translation.

31. Interview with the author in Tokyo, August 11, 2004. *Hakujaden* has been released in VCD format by Asia Production Limited, a Hong Kong media company. The version maintains its original Japanese soundtrack but Mandarin is included as a second language option and Chinese subtitles are provided.

32. Another reason is that the film distribution network was mainly controlled by Chinese companies. One exception is that Japanese erotic films tended to gain exhibition space in the region and this is partly due to the inability of local film companies to freely film on narratives related to sex and violence. See Benjamin Wai-ming Ng, "Japanese Elements in Hong Kong Erotic Films," in *Asian Cinema Journal* 15(1) (2004): 217–224.

33. The animated film received a Berliner Cultural Award, a Venice International Children Award, and a Mexican government's recognition award, among others. See Toei (1989: 44).

34. Its English name is directly translated from the notes given in the *Eiga nenkan* (1959 and 1960); see pp. 117 and 122 respectively.

35. In reality, by the mid-1970s, the creation of manga-stories in Japan alone was able to sustain the broadcasting media. Without the initial sponsorship of overseas investors, the animation studios in Japan also produced children stories from industrialized Western countries, such as *Alpine Girl Heidi* (1974) and *Anne of Green Gables* (1979).

36. By the later half of the mid-1950s, Toei had become financially stable, as Okawa had successfully expanded its network of cinemas in Japan. *Hakujaden* and a few of Toei's proposed joint projects with Hong Kong producer Zhang Guoli and the Shaw Brothers did not materialize. See Yau (2000: 106).

37. See Hosogaya (2000: 80). The reporter's pen-name was Kitao and his film review was published in *Mainichi shinbun*, October 22, 1958.

38. See Akita (2004: 267) and Yamaguchi and Watanabe (1977: 44–45). Yamaguchi Yasuo, interview with the author in Tokyo, September 17, 2004. Yamaguchi was the former executive producer of the highly popular *Sailor Moon* television anime series and editor of *Nihon no anime zen shi* (2004). He is currently executive director of the Animation Japan Association (AJA, Nihon Dōga Kyōkai).

39. Soon after his *Astro Boy* series was televised in Japan, he visited America in 1964 and met Walt Disney personally in New York (*The Animation Filmography of Osamu Tezuka*, 1991: 103).

40. The character design of Bambi was also used as a model for the Monkey God character in *Saiyūki*, as *Bambi* was one of Tezuka's favorite Disney films.

41. Schodt (1983: 139 and 160) writes that this highly honorific term is given to Tezuka because he is regarded as the "pioneer of the modern Japanese story-comic" and "among the people raised on his comics, he is akin to a national hero."

42. These manga artists are considered to be pioneers of the *gekiga* style (see Yaguchi et al. 1998: 338), it can be said that Tezuka incorporated and adapted *gekiga* elements in his manga.

43. See *Samurai: Dandyism in Japan*, p. 80. For example, the works of *ukiyo*-e artist, Utagawa Kuniyoshi (1797–1861), were among the first to have an extra spark of light painted into the eyes of the characters.

44. The series first began with the title *Kidō senshi gundamu* (1979), known in the West as *Mobile Suit Gundam*.

45. Its full English title is *The Super Dimension Fortress Macross*, in Japanese, *Chōjikū yōsai makurosu*. The series was first introduced to the United States as *Robotech. Macross* is a group project to which various talents contribute the story narrative, character design, special mechanical design, animation, and so on.

46. Based on an exhibition event about the rise of the manga genre in postwar Japan, the publication *Manga no jidai* (1998, edited by Yaguchi Kunio and others) tries to place in chronological order the kinds of manga that had appeared from the early 1950s to the late 1990s.

47. *Tetsuwan Atomu* also means "mighty atom," referring to the super-heroic spirit of robot boy, Astro or Atomu who, despite his robotic body, has human emotions too. He fights for peace and justice in the serialized manga which ran from 1952 to 1968. According to Schodt (1983: 65), the story is a pioneer of the genre and more robot manga stories would come later.

48. It was a known fact that Tezuka "poached" animating staff at Toei in order to begin his own animating enterprise, and at times he even got experienced Toei staff to help him on a freelance basis.

49. *Astro Boy* was able to obtain a television audienceship of above 30 percent when each episode was aired in the early evening despite its limited form of animation (Yamaguchi, 2004: 81).

50. Anime catered for very young children (nursery and kindergarten levels) could start as early as 4 p.m. For example, Nihon Television was (and still is) the screening sponsor for the long-running comic series for younger children, *Soreike! Anpanman*. TV Asahi holds on to two profitable manga-anime series, the highly popular *Doraemon* and *Atashin-chi*, which are aired weekly. TV Tokyo screens new and not-so-new manga-anime series, such as *Cho Robot Seimeitai Transformer Micron Densetsu* and *Tottoko Hamutaro*. All these series begin in the early evening every day.

51. Specifically, Fukushima was researching the impact of manga stories on *shōgekijo* (little theater performance troupes that had risen in postwar Japan) and the appeal of manga among youths.

52. By *anime*, Yonezawa means "full animation," referring to Miyazaki's original training at Toei as an animator, and his talent and ability in converting his serial manga story, *Nausicaä of the Valley of the Wind* (1982), into a full-length animated feature film in 1984.

53. Animation is known as *donghua* in Chinese. *Dōga* and *donghua* are written in the same Chinese characters. The adopted foreign term for animation in Chinese is *katong,* meaning "cartoon." It is interesting to note that in the letter written by the Wan brothers to the Japanese, the term "cartoon" is used to describe the animated film *Princess Iron Fan* (see Chapter 4 and Appendix 1). See also Chapter 7 for discussion on another Chinese term for "animation cinema or film."

54. In *Hokusai manga*, the artist-author depicted people, social customs, plants and animals, buildings, scenery, history, and even ghosts in multifarious expressions. The drawings could be entertaining, informational, and satirical. When viewed today, his works are similar to a preliminary encyclopedia, giving us a glimpse of manga contents and styles in postwar contemporary Japan.

55. The term *manhua* was incorporated into Chinese vocabulary in the late nineteenth century. See Liu's (1995) list of Chinese terms that were of Japanese origin.

Chapter 6

1. Yamamura Kōji, interview with author in Tokyo, October 1, 1999.
2. Their names are Kifune Tokumitsu (husband) and Ishida Sonoko (wife).
3. The first series had 24 episodes and they were filmed in 16 mm in color.
4. *The Snow Queen* (1957) was based on a Hans Christian Anderson tale and was directed by Lev Atamanov (1905–81), who was famous for adapting literary texts into poetic narrative animated feature films.
5. The film was directed by the famous French animator Paul Grimault (1905–94). The film was not completed when it was shown in the 1950s and it was remade in the late 1970s and renamed as *Le Roi et l'Oiseau* ("The King and Mister Bird", 1980).
6. In early 1965, Miyazaki was already making bold creative suggestions to senior staff; he recommended changing the storyline of the feature film *Gulliver's Space Travel*, which was in production at the time.
7. The film's title is abbreviated to *Hols* in this chapter.
8. For details of the film's production background, see my paper, "Usurping the Cinematic Screen: *The Prince of the Sun: Hols Great Adventure*," *The Japanese Journal of Animation Studies* 3(2A) (2002): 21–26. It explains and theorizes the ideological aspects of the film. (The film has also been given another English title, *The Little Norse Prince Valiant*.)
9. Kotabe Yōichi and his animator wife, Okuyama Reiko, interview with the author in Tokyo, December 15, 1999. Takahata Isao, interview with the author in Tokyo, 13 January 2000. (Ms Okuyama is also an experienced animator; she did not leave Toei in the early 1970s and remained as one of the key supervising animators at the studio until she retired.)
10. Monkey Punch is the pen-name of manga artist Katō Kazuhiko (1937–). *Lupin III* first appeared in a weekly manga magazine in 1967.
11. Other series include *Rascal the Raccoon* (1977) and *A Dog of Flanders* (1975).
12. Although *Future Boy Conan* was not a manga-adapted anime television series, its presentation format was in a form of weekly episodes. Though the original manga is not in existence, the appeal of the animated serialized way of telling a story continued to attract audiences; in this case, Miyazaki's animating skills were also an added attraction.
13. One example was the American production, *Little Nemo*. Miyazaki and Takahata were originally involved in the pre-production during the early 1980s. Miyazaki also worked on several episodes of the animated television series *Great Detective Holmes*, produced by an Italian counterpart.
14. Unlike Miyazaki, few animators are successful in attracting investors with manga. The diversion can be rather daunting if one is not a manga artist in the first place. Serial storytelling is a long-drawn-out affair and Miyazaki was painfully aware of it when he tried to conclude his original manga version of the *Nausicaä Valley of the Wind* long after the animated film was completed and screened in cinema theaters (see Miyazaki, 1998: 521–535).
15. It is known that for every major publishing company in Japan, 60 percent of the revenue comes from the sales of manga books and goods. Komatsu Shiro, research director/general manager at Mitsubushi Research Institute Inc., Entertainment and Cultural Business Department, interview with the author in Tokyo, November 10, 1999. Schodt (1983: 13) writes that in 1980, "twenty-seven percent" of the 4.3 billion-plus books and magazines published in Japan were "*manga* — in magazine and book form."

16. Ishizaki Kenji, interview with the author in Tokyo, February 10, 2000.
17. One would suspect that its parent company, Tokuma Shoten, has long wished to establish such a link. In the past, Miyazaki's animated characters, Conan and Lupin III, had been licensed to multimedia companies.
18. Satō Tadao argued that the proliferation of Japanese soft porn films, generally known as "pink movies," was not specific to Japan during that time as he noted that the subject of sex and violence was also prevalent in the works of well-known Western European and American directors (1982: 229). But it could be argued that Japan was indeed the leading Asian nation that produced pink movies during that period. It also led to a distribution demand of these Japanese-made films in other Asian countries.
19. For an analysis of film genres, see Thomas Schatz, *Hollywood Genres: Formulas, Filmmaking, and the Studio System* (New York: McGraw-Hill, 1981).
20. Author's translation. The above comment is part of a feature essay contributed by the late director's daughter, Kurosawa Kazuko, in *Bungeishunjū* (April 1999 issue). Entitled "Kurosawa Akira ga eranda hyappon no eiga" ('100 films Selected by Kurosawa Akira'), it was written in an interesting manner as parts of the essay were penned in the voice of the late director.
21. Miyazaki himself has acknowledged his apprentice days at Toei as a collective learning experience (see also Chapter 5).
22. Dick Wong, interview with the author in Hong Kong, March 1998.
23. Ex-Toei animator and film critic Oda Katsuya, interview with the author in Tokyo, December 7, 1999. Oda was among the first batch of animators recruited by Toei to work on its first color feature animation, *Hakujaden*.
24. The film received good reviews when it was released in America. See the *New York Times*, November 19, 1982 and *Voice*, December 7, 1982.
25. Hara Toru, interview with the author, November 6, 1999, in Tokyo. For example, in the making of *My Neighbor, Totoro* and *Grave of the Fireflies*, both Miyazaki and Takahata wanted the artistic services of the late Yoshifumi Kondō (1950–98) and Hara had to mediate between them.
26. Hara Toru, interview with the author in Tokyo, November 30, 1999.
27. See note 26.
28. See "Japan's Miyazaki Keeps Computers Out of Cartoons," *China Daily*, September 1, 2008.
29. Manga and animation film critic Ono Kosei, interview with the author in Tokyo, December 10, 1999.
30. Hara Toru, interview with the author in Tokyo, November 30, 1999. Miyazaki also complimented Takahata's exquisite musical sensibilities in an essay which is published in Takahata's book (1991: 493–495).
31. Imura Kenji, production manager at Studio Ghibli, interview with the author in Tokyo, February 6, 2000.
32. For example, when the film *Princess Mononoke* was shown in mid-1997, it raked in more than US$50 million in the first month of screening in Japan. It surpassed other record-breaking, profit-earning foreign films in Japanese theaters, such as *Jurassic Park*.
33. Yokota Masao, interview with the author in Tokyo, December 22, 1999.
34. Many have retired from active animation work or have moved on to other artistic pursuits.

35. Oda Katsuya, interview with the author in Tokyo, September 22, 1999.
36. Nihon Television, May 4, 1999. A special program on Studio Ghibli, "From *Princess Mononoke* to *My Neighbors the Yamadas*."
37. See Miyazaki's *Shuppatsuten* (1998): 571–580.
38. Nihon Television, July 26, 1999. Documentary report on the making of *My Neighbors the Yamadas*.
39. Takahata Isao, interview with the author in Tokyo, January 13, 2000.
40. Nihon Television, July 26, 1999. Miyazaki was referring to *My Neighbors the Yamadas* which was six months late in meeting the original schedule. Miyazaki tends to address Takahata as "Pak-san," reminiscent of their *nakama* days in Toei.
41. Takahata Isao, interview with the author in Tokyo, January 13, 2000.
42. Takahata no longer directs any Studio Ghibli films since his last film project was completed in 2000. Miyazaki, on the other hand, continues to direct and produces animated feature films; his most recent productions are *Howl's Moving Castle* (2004) and *Ponyo on the Cliff by the Sea* (2008).
43. Wollen's "unconscious catalyst" has been criticized for its reductive and ambiguous meanings. Here, I am appropriating the term at face level so as to give a position reading of the anime of Miyazaki and Takahata.
44. On a strictly comparative note, Takahata's animated work tends to be down to earth and is concerned with the realities of everyday life, whereas Miyazaki's anime often includes fantastical elements; for instance, his protagonists have the ability to fly and possess other magical powers.
45. The countryside scenery of *My Neighbor Totoro* is an amalgamation of several locations and memories. The latter includes Miyazaki's own and art director Oga Kazuo's memories of his birthplace in Akita Prefecture, see Miyazaki (1996: 485–510).
46. There are regular news reports of this new generation of farmers. See, for example, "Born again farmers," the *Japan Times*, October 18, 1999.
47. See, for example, McCormack (2001: 57; 91), for explanations related to the land-price inflation in Japan.
48. After the war, the new constitution renounced war and stipulated that the country would not engage in military activities and aggression against any other nation. This peace-loving constitution is unique in the world.
49. The Ainu people are regarded as the original inhabitants of Japan; they have gradually been assimilated into mainstream Japanese society since the Meiji period.
50. Takahata Isao, interview with the author in Tokyo, January 13, 2000.
51. "Series Dialogues for Year 2000," NHK Television, December 20, 1999.
52. Among the myths featured in the two state-sponsored literary documents is that of the divine origin of the Japanese Imperial House. The present emperor of Japan is regarded as a direct descendent of the Yamato lineage.
53. It means "cuteness." To understand this aesthetic sentiment from a socio-economic perspective, see Brian McVeigh, "Commodifying Affection, Authority and Gender in the Everyday Objects of Japan," *Journal of Material Culture* 1(3) (1996): 291–312.
54. Author's translation.
55. Ono Kosei, interview with the author in Tokyo, December 10, 1999. See also Ono's article, "Tadahito Mochinaga: The Japanese Animator Who Lived in Two Worlds," in *Anime World Network*, December issue 1999 (www.awn.com).

56. Kinoshita Sayoko, interview with the author in Tokyo, January 20, 2000. In the interview, I asked Sayoko why there was a lack of more penetrating work by her husband after his masterpieces such as *Made in Japan* and *Pica Don* (1978). She explained that, among other reasons, the time and energy devoted to running the Hiroshima Festival was enormous; to say the least, they needed to deal with the daily expenses of their own animation studio and Renzo had to work on other animation projects to support their voluntary work at the festival. (*Pica Don* is a short animated film that commemorates the atomic bombing of Hiroshima.)

57. Kotabe Yōichi and his animator wife Okuyama Reiko, interview with the author in Tokyo, December 15, 1999. Kotabe also cited another reason for the rejection by the Swedish author; that is, the Japanese were stereotyped as "economic animals" in the West particularly after the war. (*Pippi Longstocking* is a series of children's books and was first published in 1942. Though later, several live-action films including a television series were made, an animated version was not produced until 1997.)

58. While watching these programs when I was young, I remember feeling surprised and slightly disoriented when I saw that the credits at the end of each episode were full of Japanese names. The theme song was also sung in a language incongruent to the Occidental characteristics of the cartoon characters and the background setting.

59. It literally means, "the way of the warrior." I do not use the term here to refer to the negative, militaristic aspects of *bushidō* that were found in the history of Japan during the late nineteenth and early twentieth centuries. Rather, the distinctive aspect is the sense of duty to one's work or "lord." Studio Ghibli mourned the loss of Kondō Yoshifumi, the young and talented animator who had been designated to be its "third" star-director. A dedicated colleague of Miyazaki and Takahata, Kondō was one of the chief animators who worked on a number of television series and feature films that Miyazaki and Takahata directed. He was the director of *Whisper of the Heart* (*Mimi wo sumaseba*, 1995). He passed away in 1998.

60. *Kinema Junpō* (1995: 26–31). Oshii Mamoru was once invited to work with Miyazaki and Takahata on a film project called "Anchor" but the project never materialized due to ideological differences.

61. Tsuchida Isamu, interview with the author in Tokyo, January 24, 2000. He retired from Toei in the early 1990s.

62. This chapter covers mainly the common elements of Miyazaki and Takahata's anime cinema in the context of a "collective audience" at which they aim. I do not analyze the different fantastical approaches of the auteur-pair. While their works deserve further analyses, it is not the intention of this chapter.

Chapter 7

1. Thai animated film, *Khan Kluay* (2006).
2. See *Korean Animation* (2004: 5).
3. Hara Toru, interview with the author in Tokyo, November 30, 1999.
4. Yamaguchi Yasuo, executive director of AJA (Nihon dōga kyōkai), interview with the author in Tokyo, September 17, 2004; Yoshioka Osamu, senior managing director of Toei Animation Company, interview with the author in Tokyo, August 11, 2004.

5. These include, for example, *Japanese Animated Films: A Complete View from Their Birth to "Spirited Away" and Beyond,* held at the Tokyo Museum of Contemporary Art, July 15–August 31, 2004, and *Nihon anime no hishōki wo saguru*, which was held at the Ustunomiya Art Museum, June 11–July 15, 2001. The latter was a rotating exhibition that lasted more than 18 months and was held in several parts of Japan.

6. Yamaguchi Yasuo, executive director of AJA (Nihon dōga kyōkai), interview with the author in Tokyo, September 17, 2004.

7. Arisako Toshihiko, interview with the author in Tokyo, September 16, 2004. Toei has a long history of collaborating with the West on animation projects.

8. N. P. Palabrica, general manager of Toei Philippines, interview with the author in Manila, March 15, 2004. Also Ivan C., CEO and president of CGCG Inc., interview with the author in Taipei, March 19, 2004. Both revealed in their interviews that although the Japanese animation studios might pay less than their Western counterparts, the amount of subcontractual work given was often consistent and tended to be on a long-term basis. However, the subcontractual work from their Western partners might not be on a regular basis.

9. As Tsui Hark enlisted the consultation services of a Japanese animation studio, it is not known how the final character designs differ from the original Hong Kong submissions. Nor is it known how much "anime-ization" was requested by the Hong Kong counterparts. One can imagine the difficulties faced by the animation director when he tried to amalgamate the two-dimensional instructions faxed in by the Japanese with his improvised three-dimensional graphics in Hong Kong. Andrew Chen, animation director of *Chinese Ghost Story,* interview with the author in Hong Kong, April 9, 1998.

10. *Princess Mononoke* was in fact the first Studio Ghibli production that made use of three-dimensional graphics.

11. Asian film critic and scholar Matsuoka Tamaki, interview with the author in Tokyo, July 1998. She thinks that in fact Siu Sin, the main female protagonist, is pretty and by native anime standards, she would appeal positively to Japanese audiences.

12. From the 1980s onward, after video production facilities reached broadcasting standards for the cassette market, OVA or OAV ("original video anime" and "original anime video" respectively) has become increasingly popular among anime fans who crave for anime productions that are not screened publicly.

13. For example, *My Beautiful Girl Mairi* (2001) received the Grand Prize for Best Animated Feature Film at the Annecy International Animation Festival in 2002. *Oseam* was awarded the same prize at Annecy in 2004.

14. At the Annecy International Animation Festival in 2004, there was a special focus on contemporary South Korean-made animation. As a result, audiences were exposed to the similarities between South Korean animation and anime.

15. Both animated films are regarded as "otaku" films in Japan, which were made to satisfy their respective manga fans, as compared to other family-based animation produced for a wider market. In the West, they are, however, viewed as extraordinary due to the violent graphics set against a futuristic background. Subsequently, Ōtomo's *Steamboy* and Oshii's *Ghost in the Shell II* were produced in response to demands from fans abroad, but the films did not do well in Japan. Both animated stories did not have an original manga story to base on and *Ghost in the Shell II* was an improvised animated story chiefly directed and created by Oshii Mamoru.

16. Nelson Shin is an experienced animator and has worked on animation projects including *Pink Panther*, *The Simpsons*, and *The Transformers*. See http://www.imdb.com/name/nm0793802/filmoyear.

17. Recently, Korean television dramas have taken the lead in attracting viewers in Asia.

18. Depending on the contractual agreement, some anime productions prefer not to show the overseas credits. This is because there may be several layers of subcontractual work involved. For example, a Filipino or a Taiwanese animation subcontractor may be asked to further subcontract the animation project to another Asian country due to lower labor costs. For this reason, they would tend to conceal the identity of the lead Japanese producer. N. P. Palabrica, general manager of Toei Philippines, interview with the author in Manila, March 15, 2004.

19. "Indonesia no anime wo miru kai," a seminar presentation organized by Toei Animation Kenkyū Sho, Embassy of Indonesia, Japan and The Japan Foundation, February 12, 1999, Tokyo.

20. Frankie Chung, interview with the author in Hong Kong, April 9, 1998. Incidentally, he was also the chief character designer of the animated film *A Chinese Ghost Story*. See Hu (2001).

21. For example, *Khan Kluay* was funded by several business corporations apart from gaining support from the Thai Ministry of Communications Technology (*Animation World Network*, June 12, 2006). In South Korea, the government has sponsored a number of animated works. For example, the US$6 million production budget of *Empress Chung* was sponsored by the Ministry of Culture and Tourism for Feature Films. See the promotion booklet, *Korean Animation* (2004), distributed at the Annecy International Animation Festival in 2004.

22. Nomura Research Institute, a well-known research organization in Japan, gave the details of the report.

23. News reports on the Internet have recently referred to the *otaku* phenomenon as a form of "pop cult fanaticism."

24. Allison focuses on the role of the mothers in mediating sexuality and desires in modern Japan.

25. *Lolita* (1955) is a book written by Vladmir Nobokov. The tale is about a middle-aged man who becomes sexually obsessed with a 12-year-old girl.

26. Anzai Masayuki was a panel speaker at the Information Society Models and the New Everyday Life Finnish-Japanese Information Society Conference, October 6–7, 2003, Tokyo.

27. For example, one television variety show reported that as many as 300,000 people were at the August event in 1999.

28. The creator of this manga was Yūki Masami but the animated version was directed by Oshii Mamoru.

29. Seven people were killed in broad daylight in Akihabara on June 8, 2008. It was reported that the killer mimicked murderous acts from various 3-D games; see http://kotaku.com/5015348/akihabara-killing-to-cause-japanese-internet-regulation and http://www.cnn.com/2008/WORLD/asiapcf/06/08/japan.stabbing.spree/index.html.

30. Lin Elie, conversations with the author in Tokyo, January 21, 2004, and in Taipei, March 18, 2004.

31. At the "Asia in Comics 2004: Comics by Asian Women Forum" on February 21, 2004, presentation by Kim Young-joong, editor-in-chief of Seoul Cultural Publishers Inc.

32. The author is not sure how many foreign animation artists, film critics, and producers were invited to participate in the survey; judging from the section, "Unveiling result of qualification" (pp. 110–157), a great number of them were Japanese.

33. Author's interviews with ex-Toei staff members, particularly those who worked at Toei from the late 1950s to the 1960s, in Japan, July 1998–March 2000. See also Imamura (1992), Miyazaki (1998) and Takahata (1991, 1999).

34. Yamaguchi Yasuo, interview with the author in Tokyo, September 17, 2004. Yamaguchi was executive producer of the highly popular *Sailor Moon* TV anime series.

35. Ginzburg (1960: 3–4). I am unsure whether there is an English translation of this book. The translation here is mine. Veteran animators and producers whom I had interviewed in Japan cited this book in their private collections.

36. The studio eventually reopened in 1972 but only became active again after the fall of the Gang of Four in 1976. In that year, experienced animators such as Te Wei and others returned and began working on new animation projects (Bendazzi, 1994: 402).

37. With the support of the management at Toei, the production team of the feature film included experienced animators Kotabe Yōichi and Okuyama Reiko, producer Yamaguchi Yasuo, and art director Tsuchida Isamu. It was also supervised by live-action director Urayama Kirirō (1930–85), who was known for directing films that tackled society's issues and problems.

38. Yuri Norstein (1941–)'s masterpiece *Tale of Tales* (1979) has a distinctively Russian flavor, and to this day his works are admired by many commercial and non-commercial animators in Japan. See Takahata (1991: 225–250). See also Hu (2005) for an account of his directorial privileged position in the making of *Fuyu no hi* (2003) when Norstein was given the lead role to animate the linked poetry.

39. The *Journey to the West* animated television series consists of 52 episodes. They have been aired repeatedly in the "Cartoon City" section of the Children Channel, China Central Television (CCTV). The Children Channel (*xiao er pin dao*) was established in 2003.

40. The quote has been extracted and translated from a survey questionnaire conducted by the Japan Foundation in November 1993 at the end of a month-long seminar on Japanese animation at the Beijing Film Academy led by veteran producer Hara Toru and animator Oda Katsuya. I thank them for sharing the information with me.

41. See http://www.japandesign.ne.jp/KUWASAWAJYUKU/information/anime.html. A series of seminars were held between October 22 and December 4, 2004 at Kuwasawa Design Research Centre, during which the overseas reception of Japanese manga and anime was discussed.

42. Fujioka Utaka was the chairman and founder of Tokyo Movie Company which produced successful animated works such as the *Mumin* television series (which was based on the *Moonmintroll* book series by Finnish writer, Tove Jansson), the *Rupan sansei* television series in the 1970s, and the *Meitantai Hōmuzu* (Sherlock Holmes) television series in the 1980s.

43. It is said that while the Japanese audiences found the film too "American" for their taste, the American audiences experienced the opposite "unAmerican-ness" of the film. The actual reasons for its failure may be multifold and may involve inadequate marketing planning, especially in the US.

44. The above observation refers mainly to commercial productions. Recently, there have been a few productions sponsored by non-profit organizations featuring comic stories from Southeast Asia. For example, Malaysian artist Lat's comic characters have been adapted into an educational animation series sponsored by UNESCO. The project is led by veteran Japanese animator-director Suzuki Shinichi. The series, which is primarily distributed to Third World countries, focuses on themes such as literacy, adult continuing education, and environmental protection.

45. Known as *Uchū senkan yamato* in Japan, it began in 1974. Several of its animated television series depict a science-fiction world with undercurrent memories of Japan's defeat at the end of the Second World War and a new postwar, indomitable and collective spirit to continue the "Japanese mission." Only this time, it is in outer space with advanced technology that is comparable to Western standards. Its various English titles include *Star Blazers*, *Space Cruiser Yamato*, and *Battle of the Planets*.

46. This remark was posed to me by a retiring American professor who had lived in Japan for many years. He recalled how drugs became a "hip" item among youths and adults in North America during the 1960s.

47. "Japan Inc." was a nickname that Japan acquired in the early 1980s. The name was alluding to the close working relationship between the government and the private business sector in expanding Japanese economic influence overseas (see Introduction).

48. To be precise, the concept "Dasein" refers to the state of the Being. See Heidegger's "Being and Time" (1993: 41–87) in which he states that the "concept of Being is undefinable" (43). See also David F. Krell's explanations of Heidegger's concept of Dasein (3–40).

49. The height of the Cultural Revolution occurred between 1966 and 1969 as China continued to search for a modern path that would free the country from its old ideological thinking, customs, and habits. It led to power struggles among the leaders and widespread contempt for bureaucrats, professionals, artists, and their alleged entrenched bourgeois practices and privileges.

50. Such a communicative network usually occurs in authoritarian and dictatorial political systems where the media suffers from tight censorship and the populace relies on oral transmission of information.

51. While the popularity of manga and anime in parts of Asia has been interpreted as a form of Japan's successful cultural imperialism, the recent popularity of *hallyu* faces the same criticism. Its critics include those from Japan. It has led to the publication of a comic book, *Hyom-hallyu,* meaning "Anti-Korean wave," which has sold at least 300,000 copies in Japan alone (Park, 2006). See also Onishi (2006), "A Rising Korean Wave: If Seoul Sells it, China Craves it."

52. Malaysia's first full-length animated film, *Silat Lagenda,* was made in 1998. It did not receive good reviews and it was hardly screened outside the country.

53. Lamarre's insightful essay, however, exposes the circulative perspectives from which we view anime and its essentialist links with "things Japanese"; he tends to see the *otaku* phenomenon as a global one, vis-à-vis its significant link with American global culture and Japan's destined modernity connections with the Western world.

Appendix 1

1. This is the title of the letter. The letter can also be read as a form of letter-article. Since the tone of the writing is quite personal at times and having seen the original writing in Chinese, I would classify it as a letter-article. Kadokawa Culture Promotion Foundation now owns a collection of the late Shimizu's archival film notes from which the writings by the Wan brothers can be found.

2. The other seven art forms are: painting, sculpture, architecture, music, literature, dance, and drama.

3. The film was screened in China in 1941. *Princess Iron Fan* was screened in Japan a year later, with a specially prepared Japanese soundtrack.

4. In the letter, the Wan brothers politely addressed the Japanese people as the "Eastern people".

5. The original letter was not dated. However, Shimizu's article dated it as above. It seems that the letter was written soon after Shimizu had met the Wan brothers in Shanghai. See Chapter 4 for a discussion of the letter and its historical context.

Glossary

Chinese Terms

chuanqi 傳奇
dangfeng 擋風
dongfang 東方
dongfang renshi 東方人士
fengshui 風水
jiaren 假人
junzi 君子
katong 卡通
lizhi de qingchun donghua 勵志的青春動畫

manhua 漫畫
meishu dianying 美術電影
qingdiao 情調
riben renshi 日本人士
shanshui hua 山水畫
tanci 彈詞
tao (dao) 道
tongxin 童心
yijing 意境

Japanese Terms

amerika kessaku manga matsuri アメリカ傑作漫画祭り
anime アニメ
anime-shon アニメーション
anime-ta アニメータ
anime-shon no kamisama アニメーションの神様
anpo 安保
asobi 遊び
atarashii jidai 新しい時代

bideo ge-mu anime ビデオ ゲーム アニメ
bijutsu 美術
biwa 琵琶
bunka eiga 文化映画
bunka katsudō 文化活動
bunmei kaika 文明開化
bunmei no riki 文明の利器

bunraku 文楽
bushidō 武士道
byōbu 屏風
byōga eiga 描画映画

chadō 茶道
chanoyu 茶の湯
chinzō 頂相
chiyogami eiga 千代紙映画

daimyō 大名
daishu no mono 大衆の物
*datsu – A– 脱亜
dōga 動画

e-den 絵伝
e-kotoba 絵言葉
eiri jigyō 営利事業

emakimono 絵巻物
e monogatari 絵物語
engi 縁起

fuan 不安
fūdosei 風土性
fukoku kyōhei 富国強兵
furusato 古里、故郷
fusuma 襖
fūkei 風景

geki 劇
gekiga 劇画
gentō 幻燈
geta 下駄
giri 義理

haiku 俳句
ha-moni-shori ハーモニー処理
hanamichi 花道
hiroku kensa 広く検査

ianfu 慰安婦
idō de aru 移動である

jidaigeki 時代劇
jijitsu 事実
jiyū minkan 自由民間
jojishi 叙事詩
jōmi 情味
jōruri 浄瑠璃

kabuki 歌舞伎
kaiga eiga 絵画映画
kaigai chishiki 海外知識
kako no nihon geijitsu 過去の日本芸術
kami 神
kamishibai 紙芝居
kanbun 漢文
kanji 漢字
kanji 感じ
kannen tekina 観念的な
karakuri-e からくり絵
katakana 片仮名
katei no yūgu 家庭の遊具
kawaii かわいい（可愛い）

kenro 顕露
kimono 着物
kioku 記憶
kiroku-ga 記録画
kodama 木霊
kōiteki chokkanteki 行為的直観的
kokoro 心
kokugaku 国学
kokugo 国語
kokusaika 国際化
kokutai 国体
kokyō 故郷
komikku eiga コミック映画
kongō eiga 混合映画
korō 固陋
kūsō no geijutsu 空想の芸術
kūsōka no hōhō 空想化の方法
kyōgen 狂言
kyōiku eiga 教育映画

ma 間
manga 漫画
manga eiga 漫画映画
manga fuirumu 漫画フイルム
manga no kamisama 漫画の神様
matsuri 祭り
megane-e 眼鏡絵
minkan no yūgu 民間の遊具
minshu 民主
misemono 見せ物
mono 物
monogatari-emaki 物語絵巻
mono no aware 物の哀れ
mugen-kaisō-hō 夢幻回想法
mura 村
musubi 産霊

naichi 内地
nakama 仲間
namban byōbu 南蛮屏風
namban bunka 南蛮文化
nanpō eiga kōsaku 南方映画工作
nidai kyōkoku 二大強国
nihonga 日本画
nihon minwa 日本民話
nihon ni tekichinashi 日本に適地なし

nihon shikō 日本志向
nihon teki 日本てき
ninjō 人情
nikki-emaki 日記絵巻
nō 能
nōgaku 能楽
nozoki のぞき
nyū Ō 入欧

okashi お菓子
ongaku eiga 音楽映画
onkochishin 温故知新
otaku おたく
o tonari no chūgoku お隣りの中国

rangaku 蘭学

sainō 才能
sakka shūdan 作家集団
sakuhin 作品
seinenmuki 青年向
seishin 精神
seishōnen eiga shingikai 青少年映画審議会
seiyō 西洋
sekai meisaku gekijō 世界名作劇場
senga eiga 線画映画
senkai 仙界
seppuku 切腹
shamisen 三味線
shashin heiki no chūmon 写真兵器の注文
shijō ga semaku 市場が狭く
shikaku bunka 視覚文化
shina 支那
shinjō 心情
shintō 神道
shiroi ten 白い点
shite シテ(仕手、為手)
shoin 書院
shomin-geki 庶民劇
shōgekijō 小劇場
shōhekiga 障壁画
shōji 障子
shōjo 少女
shōnenmuki 少年向
shōshimin 小市民
shūdan sagyō 集団作業

shunga 春画
sogai 阻害、阻碍
sonnō jōi 尊王攘夷
sōshi-emaki 草紙絵巻
suibokuga 水墨画

teikoku shugi sen niwa hantai shiro 帝国主義
　　戦には反対しろ
terebi manga テレビ漫画
tōyō de hatsu no daichōhen manga 東洋で初
　　の大長編漫画

udon 饂飩(うどん)
ugoku manga 動く漫画
ugoku take 動くたけ
uki-e 浮絵
ukiyo 浮世
ukiyo-e 浮世絵
utsushi-e 写し絵
uran ga tame 売らんがため

wabi-sabi 侘び寂び
wakon yōsai 和魂洋才
warui kuni 悪い国
wasei eishaki 和製映写機

yakuza やくざ
yamato damashii 大和魂
yamato-e 大和絵
yamato kotoba 大和言葉
yomihon 読み本
yume 夢
yūmei 幽冥
yūyake 夕焼け

zen 禅
zenei eiga 前衛映画

Animated Works Cited*

A Chinese Ghost Story (1997)
A Dog of Flanders (1975)
Akira (1988)
Aladdin (1992)
Anne of Green Gables (1979)
Astro Boy (1963)
Atashin-chi (2002)
Atama yama (2002)
Bambi (1942)
Cho Robot Seimeitai Transformer Micron Densetsu ("The Transformers," 1984)
Cinderella (1950)
Confusion in the Sky (Part I and II, 1961, 1964)
Cowherd's Flute (1963)
Doraemon series (1970, *Doraemon* film, 2004)
Dragon Ball series (1984)
Dragon Ball Z series (1989)
Dumbo (1941)
Eigaenzetsu: Seji no ronrika (1926)
Empress Chung (2004)
Entotsuya pero (1930)
Evangelion series ("Neon Genesis Evangelion," 1995)
Fantasmagorie (1908)
Frosty's Winter Wonderland (1976)

Future Boy Conan (1978)
Fuyu no hi (2003)
Gertie the Dinosaur (1914)
Ghost in the Shell (1995)
Ghost in the Shell 2: Innocence (2004)
Gōshu: The Cellist (1982)
Grave of the Fireflies (1988)
Great Detective Holmes ("Sherlock Hound," 1981)
GTO-Great Teacher Onizuka (television anime series, 1999)
Gulliver's Space Travel (1965)
Gundam series (*Mobile Suit Gundam*, 1979)
Hammerboy (2003)
Heidi: Girl of the Alps (1974)
History of Japanese Animation Part I and II (1970, 1972)
Howl's Moving Castle (2004)
Hustle Punch (1965)
It Was the Night before Christmas (1974)
Jarinko Chie (1981)
Journey to the West series (1996)
Khan Kluay (2006)
Kiki's Delivery Service (1989)
King Kong (1967)
Kojira (1927)
Kumo to chūrippu (1943)

---

* Where the official English title is not available, the original title is listed. Some of the animated works have several English titles but only one English title is listed here. Readers should refer to the main text for other published titles.

Land before Time (1988)

Laputa: The Castle in the Sky (1986)

Lion King (1994)

Little Nemo: Adventures in Slumberland (1989)

Lotus Lantern (1999)

Lupin III series (1971)

Lupin III: Castle of Cagliostro (1979)

Macross series (*Super Dimension Fortress Macross*, 1982)

Made in Japan (1972)

Mahō no pen (1946)

Manga shinsarukani kassen (1939)

Minna no uta (series dates back to 1961)

Mobile Police Patlabor (1988)

Momotarō vs. Mickey Mouse (1934)

Momotarō and the Eagles of the Ocean (1943)

Momotarō – Divine Troops of the Ocean (1945)

Mulan (1999)

Mūmin series (1969)

My Beautiful Girl Mairi (2001)

My Neighbor Totoro (1988)

My Neighbors the Yamadas (1999)

Nausicaä of the Valley of the Wind (1984)

Nezha Shakes the Sea (1979)

Omochabako shiri-zu daisanwa (1934)

Once Upon a Time in Japan series (from 1975)

Only Yesterday (1991)

Oseam (2003)

Panda kopanda (1972)

Panda kopanda amefurisa-kasu no maki (1973)

Pica Don (1978)

Picture Book, Momotarō vs. Mickey Mouse (1934)

Pinocchio (1940)

Pippi Longstocking (1997)

Ponyo on the Cliff by the Sea (2008)

Prince of the Sun: The Great Adventures of Hols (1968)

Princess Iron Fan (1941)

Princess Mononoke (1997)

Rascal the Raccoon (1977)

Rats on the Mayflower (1968)

Rose of Versailles (television anime series, 1979)

Sailor Moon (television anime series, 1992)

Sakura (*Haru no gensō*, 1946)

Sangokushi (1988, 1989)

Sazae-san series (television anime series since 1969)

Shōnen sarutobi sasuke (1959)

Shunmao monogatari taro (1981)

Silly Symphonies series (*Skeleton Dance*, 1929)

Space Battleship Yamato (1974)

Snow White and the Seven Dwarfs (1937)

Sora no momotarō (1931)

Soreike! Anpanman (1988)

Spirited Away (2001)

Steamboy (2004)

Tadpoles in Search of Mummy (1960)

Tales from Earthsea (2006)

Tale of Tales (1979)

Taro, the Dragon Boy (1979)

The Butterfly Lovers (2004)

The Curious Adventures of Mr Wonderbird (1952)

The Doggie March (1963)

The Enchanted Monkey (1960)

The First Easter Rabbit (1975)

The Little Mermaid (1989)

The Last Unicorn (1981)

The Legend of Prince Rama Ramayana (1987)

The Raccoon War ("Pom Poko," 1994)

The Snow Queen (1957)

The Stingiest Man in Town (1978)

Three Thousand Miles in Search of Mother (1976)

Tokyo Godfathers (2003)

Tōkyūniku dansen (1943)

Tom Thumb (1967)

Tottoko Hamutaro (*Hamtaro*, 1990)

Ukare baiorin (1955)

Umi no momotarō (1932)

Whisper of the Heart (1995)

White Snake Tale (1958)

Wonderful Days (2003)

World Masterpiece Theater series (from 1974)

Bibliography

Akita, Takahiro. "Manga eiga no warai to eiyū 'momotarō' to sensō" [Laughter and hero in manga film: Momotarō and war]. In *Eiga to daitō a kyōei ken* [Film and the Greater East Asia Co-Prosperity Sphere], edited by Iwamoto Kenji, 255–267. Tokyo: Shinwasha, 2004.

Allan, Robin. *Walt Disney and Europe: European Influences on the Animated Feature Films of Walt Disney*. London: John Libbey, 1999.

Allison, Anne. *Permitted and Prohibited Desires*. Boulder, CO: Westview Press, 1996.

Anderson, L., Joseph, and Donald Richie. *The Japanese Film: Art and Industry*. Princeton: Princeton University Press, 1982.

Azuma, Hiroki, ed. *Mōjōgenron efu kai: posutomodan otaku sekushuariti* [Postmodern otaku sexuality]. Tokyo: Seidosha, 2003.

Banta, Melissa. "Life of a Photograph: Nineteenth Century Photographs of Japan from the Peabody Museum." In *A Timely Encounter: Nineteenth-Century Photographs of Japan*, edited by Melissa Banta and Susan Taylor, 11–22. Cambridge, MA; Wellesley, MA: Peabody Museum and Wellesley College Museum, 1988.

Barthes, Roland. *Empire of Signs*. Toronto: McGraw-Hill Ryerson, 1982.

Beasley, W. G. *Japan Encounters the Barbarian: Japanese Travelers in America and Europe*. New Haven and London: Yale University Press, 1995.

Bendazzi, Giannalberto. *Cartoons: One Hundred Years of Animation*. London: John Libbey, 1994.

Blocker, Gene H., and Christopher Starling, I. *Japanese Philosophy*. Albany: State University of New York Press, 2001.

Boger, Batterson H. *The Traditional Arts of Japan*. New York: Bonzana Books, 1964.

Bourdieu, Pierre. "Cultural Reproduction and Social Reproduction." In *Knowledge, Education and Cultural Change: Papers on the Sociology of Education*, edited by Richard Brown, 71–112. London: Tavistock Publishing, 1973.

———. *In Other Words: Essays Towards a Reflexive Sociology*, translated by Matthew Adamson. Stanford: Stanford University Press, 1990.

Boxer, Ralph C. *Papers on Portuguese, Dutch and Jesuit Influences in 16th and 17th Centuries Japan*. Washington DC: University Publications of America, Inc., 1979.

Buscombe, Edward. "Ideas of Authorship." In *Theories of Authorship: A Reader*, edited by John Caughie, 22–34. London and Boston: Routledge, Kegan Paul and British Film Institute, 1981.

Caputo, John D. "Heidegger." In *A Companion to Continental Philosophy*, edited by Simon Critchley and William R. Schroeder, 223–233. Oxford: Blackwell Publishers, 1998.

Carlson, Marvin. *Performance: A Critical Introduction*. London: Routledge, 2004.

Cholodenko, Alan, ed. *The Illusion of Life: Essays on Animation*. Sydney: Power Publications and Australia Film Commission, 1991.

Coaldrake, William H. "Edo Architecture and Tokugawa Law." *Monumenta Nipponica,* 36 (3) (1981): 235–284.

Conrad, Sebastian. "Perceptions of 'Europe' in Japanese Historiography." In *The Japanese and Europe: Images and Perceptions*, edited by Bert Edström, 58–76. Surrey: Japan Library, 2000.

Crafton, Donald. *Before Mickey: The Animated Film 1898–1928*. Chicago: University of Chicago Press, 1982.

———. "Performance in and of Animation." *Society for Animation Studies Newsletter* 16(1) (2003): 8–13.

Craig, Timothy J., ed. *Japan Pop! : Inside the World of Japanese Popular Culture*. London: M.E. Sharpe, 2000.

Dale, Peter N. *The Myth of Japanese*. New York: St. Martin's Press, 1986.

Desser, David. *Eros Plus Massacre: An Introduction to Japanese New Wave Cinema*. Bloomington: Indiana University Press, 1988.

Di Pippo, Alexander F. "The Concept of Poiesis in Heidegger's An Introduction to Metaphysics." *Thinking Fundamentals, IWM Junior Visiting Fellows Conferences* vol. 9 (2000): Vienna.

Dillion, Martin C., ed. *Merleau-Ponty vivant*. New York: State University of New York, 1991.

Dower, John W. *War Without Mercy: Race and Power in the Pacific War*. New York: Pantheon Books, 1986.

———. *Embracing Defeat: Japan in the Wake of World War Two Defeat*. New York: W. W. Norton, 1999.

Drazen, Patrick. *Anime Explosion! The What? Why? And Wow! Of Japanese Animation*. Berkeley, CA: Stonebridge, 2003.

Edström, Bert, ed. *The Japanese and Europe: Images and Perceptions*. Surrey: Japan Library, 2000.

Enrlich, David. "Interview with Te Wei" *ASIFA News,* 6(2) (1993): 8–11.

Fairbank, John K., Edwin O. Reischauer, and Albert M. Craig. *East Asia: Tradition and Transformation*. London: George Allen and Unwin, 1989.

Fan, Jian-you. "Riben donghua de lailong qumai" [Origin and development of Japanese animation]. In *Donghua dianying tanshu* [Explorations of animation cinema], edited by Wong Yu-shan and Yu Wei-zheng, 114–152. Taipei: Yuan Liu, 1997.

Faure, Bernard. "The Kyoto School and Reverse Orientalism." In *Japan in Traditional and Postmodern Perspectives*, edited by Charles Wei-Hsun Fu and Steven Heine, 245–282. Albany: State University of New York Press, 1995.

Fukushima, Yoshiko. *Manga Discourse in Japanese Theater: Location of Noda Hideki Yume no Yūminsha*. London: Kegan Paul, 2003.

Furniss, Maureen. *Art in Motion: Animation Aesthetics*. Sydney: John Libbey and Company Ltd., 1998.

G. B. Co. Ltd. *Betsusaku takarajima 638 nihon no anime: All About Japan Anime* [Special issue treasure island on 638 Japanese animation: All about Japan anime]. Tokyo: Takarashimasha, 2002.

Ginzburg, Sergeevich S. *Dōga eiga ron: eiga geijutsu no hōhō to ninshiki* [A study on animated films: Methods and understandings of film art], translated by Kawagishi Teiichiro. Tokyo: Rironsha, 1960.

Goodman, Grant K. *Japan: The Dutch Experience*. London and Dover: Athlone Press, 1986.

Halas, John. *Film Animation: A Simplified Approach*. Paris: UNESCO, 1976.

Hane, Mikiso. *Modern Japan: A Historical Survey*. Boulder, CO: Westview Press, 1986.

Haraguchi, Masahiro. *Archives of Studio Ghibli*, vols. 1–4. Tokyo: Studio Ghibli, 1996.

———. *Archives of Studio Ghibli*, vol. 5. Tokyo: Studio Ghibli, 1997.

Harris, Kathryn. "Mr. Sony Confronts Hollywood What They're Talking about in the Media Biz", *Fortune 500 Magazine,* December 23, 1996. See also http://money.cnn.com/magazines/fortune/fortune_archive/1996/12/23/219858/index.htm.

Heidegger, Martin. *Basic Writings: From Being and Time (1927) to the Task of Thinking (1964),* edited by David Farrell Krell. San Francisco: Harper Collins, 1993.

Hirano, Kyoko. *Mr. Smith Goes to Tokyo: Japanese Cinema Under the American Occupation, 1945–1952*. Washington and London: Smithsonian Institution Press, 1992.

Hook, Glenn D., Julie Gilson, Christopher W. Hughes, and Hugo Dobson. *Japan's International Relations: Politics, Economics and Security*. London and New York: Routledge, 2001.

Hosogaya, Atsushi, ed. *Nihon anime no hishōki wo saguru* [Exploring the development of Japanese animation]. Tokyo: Yomiuri shibunsha and Bijutsukan renraku kyōgikai, 2000.

Hu, Tze-yue G. "The *Art* Between Frames in Hong Kong Animation." In *Animation in Asia and the Pacific*, edited by John A. Lent, 105–121. Sydney: John Libbey and Company Ltd., 2000.

———. "Japanese Independent Animation: *Fuyu no hi* and its Exclusivity." *International Journal of Comic Art* 7(1) (2005): 389–403.

Huizanga, Johan. *Homo Ludens: A Study of the Play Element in Culture*. New York: J. & J. Harper Editions, 1970.

Huss, Ann L. "Qingshe: A Story Retold." *Chinese Culture Journal* XXXVIII (1) (1997): 75–94.

Hutman, Kenneth. "Sinomation: Shanghai Animation Studio: Yesterday, Today and Tomorrow." *Animation World Magazine*, April issue 1(1) (1996). See http://mag.awn.com/index.php?ltype=search&sval=sinomation&article_no=179.

Iida, Harumi. *Meiji wo ikiru gunzō: gendai nihongo no seiritsu* [To live in Meiji group: Formation of modern Japanese language]. Tokyo: Ōbū, 2002.

Iida, Yumiko. *Re-thinking Identity in Modern Japan: Nationalism as Aesthetics*. London: Routledge, 2002.

Imamura, Taihei. *Manga eiga ron* [Manga film theory]. Tokyo: Iwanami shoten, 1992.

Ina, Nobuo. "Bunka no atarashii suishinsha" [A new agent of culture]. In *Yakudō suru takakuka e no michi* [A path to pulsing diversification], 10–17. Tokyo: Fuji International, 1963.

International Cinema Association of Japan. *Cinema Year Book of Japan 1936–37*, edited by Tadashi Iizima, Iwasaki Akira, and Uchida Kisao. Tokyo: Sanseido, 1937.

Iwamoto, Kenji. *Gentō no seki: ega zenya no shikaku bunkashi* [The century of magic lantern: A history of pre-film visual culture].Tokyo: Shinwasha, 2002.

———. ed. *Nihon eiga to nashonarizumu 1931–1945* [Japanese films and nationalism]. Tokyo: Shinwasha, 2004.

Iwasaki, Haruko. "Western Images, Japanese Identities: Cultural Dialogue between East and West in Yokohama Photography." In *A Timely Encounter: Nineteenth-Century Photographs of Japan*, edited by Melissa Banta and Susan Taylor, 23–38. Cambridge, MA; Wellesley, MA: Peabody Museum and Wellesley College Museum, 1988.

Jackson, Rosemary. *Fantasy: The Literature of Subversion.* London: Methuen, 1981.

Jansen, Marius B. *The Making of Modern Japan.* Cambridge, MA; London: Belknap Press of Harvard University Press, 2000.

Jiman, Juhanita. "Malaysian Animation Industry: The History, Development and Collective Efforts to Set up Global and Recognizable Animation Standard." *International Journal of Comic Art,* 7(1) (2005): 422–431.

Kaempfer, Engelbert. *Kaempfer's Japan: Tokugawa Culture Observed,* edited, translated and annotated by Beatrice M. Bodart-Bailey. Honolulu: University of Hawai'i Press, 1999.

Kamei, Takeshi, ed. *Nihon shashinshi e no shōgen* [Testimony of a history of Japanese photography], vols. 1 and 2. Tokyo: Tokyo Metropolitan Museum of Photography, 1997.

Karatani, Kojin. "Nationalism and Écriture." *Surfaces,* vol. (201) (1995): 4–25. http://www. pum.umontreal.ca/revues/surfaces/vol5/karatani.pdf.

Kasdan, Margo A., Christine Saxton, and Susan Kasdan Tavernetti. *The Critical Eye: An Introduction to Looking at Movies.* 2nd edition. Iowa: Kendall/Hunt, 1993.

Kato, Shuichi. *A History of Japanese Literature from the Man'yōshū to Modern Times,* translated and edited by Don Sanderson. New abridged edition. Surrey: Japan Library, 1997.

Kawatake, Toshio. *A History of Japanese Theater II: Bunraku and Kabuki.* Yokohoma: Japan Cultural Society, 1971.

Keene, Donald. *The Japanese Discovery of Europe 1720–1830.* Stanford: Stanford University Press, 1969.

——. *Landscapes and Portraits: Appreciation of Japanese Culture.* Tokyo: Kodansha International Ltd., 1971.

Kim, Hee-Jin. *Dōgen Kigen: Mystical Realist.* Tucson: University of Arizona Press, 1987.

Kinsella, Sharon. *Editors, Artists and the Changing Status of Manga in Japanese Society 1986–1995.* PhD Thesis, Oxford University. The British Library: British Thesis Service, 1996.

Komatsuzawa, Hajime. "Toybox Series 3: Picture Book 1936 (Momotarō vs. Mickey Mouse)." In *The Japan/America Film Wars: World War II Propaganda and its Cultural Contexts,* edited by Abe M. Nornes and Fukushima Yukio, 198–200. Chur, Switzerland: Harwood Academic Publishers, 1994.

Komparu, Kunio. *The Noh Theater Principles and Perspectives.* New York/Tokyo: Weatherhill/ Tankosha, 1983.

Kornicki, Peter F. *The Book in Japan: A Cultural History from the Beginning to the Nineteenth Century.* Leiden and Boston: Brill, 1998.

Koyasu, Nobukuni. *Kanjiron* [Kanji theory].Tokyo: Iwanami shoten, 2003.

Kristeva, Julia. *Revolution in Poetic Language.* New York: Columbia University Press, 1984.

Kuhn, Annette, and Susannah Radstone, eds. *The Women's Companion to International Film.* London: Virago Press, 1990.

Kume, Kunitake, ed. *The Iwakura Embassy 1871–73: A True Account of the Ambassador Extraordinary and Plenipotentiary's Journey of Observation Through the United States of America and Europe, Continental Europe, 3; and the Voyage Home,* vol. 5, translated by Graham Healey, Eugene Soviak and Chushichi Tsuzuki. Chiba: The Japan Documents, 2002.

Kurosawa, Kazuko. "Kurosawa Akira ga eranda hyappon no eiga" [100 films selected by Akira Kurosawa]. In *Bungeishunjū,* April issue, 262–283. Tokyo: Bungeishunjū, 1999.

Lacan, Jacques. *Écrits: A Selection,* translated by Alan Sheridan. New York: W.W. Norton, 1977.

———. *The Seminar of Jacques Lacan*, edited by Jacques-Alan Miller. New York and London: W.W. Norton, 1988.

Lamarre, Thomas. "An Introduction to Otaku Movement." *Entertext* 4(1) (2004/5): 151–187.

Lee, Khoon-choy. *Japan: Between Myth and Reality*. Singapore: World Scientific, 1995.

Lee, Sherman. *Reflections of Reality in Japanese Art*. Cleveland and Bloomington: The Cleveland Museum of Art and Indiana University Press, 1983.

Lent, John A. "The Animation Industry and Its Offshore Factories." In *Global Productions*, edited by Gerald Sussman and John A. Lent, 239–254 Cresskill, NJ: Hampton Publishing, 1998.

Lent, John A., and Xu Ying. "China's Animation Beginnings: The Roles of the Wan Brothers and Others." *Asian Cinema* 14(1) (2003): 56–69.

Levi, Antonia. *Samurai from Outer Space: Understanding Japanese Animation*. Chicago and La Salle: Open Court Publishing, 1996.

———. "The New American Hero: Made in Japan." In *The Soul of Popular Culture: Looking at Contemporary Heroes, Myths and Monsters*, edited by Mary Lynne Kittelson, 68–83. Chicago and La Salle: Open Court Publishing, 1998.

Li, Yan. *Zhonghan wenxue guansi shilun* [A history of Chinese and Korean Literature relationship]. Beijing: Shehuixue wenxian chubanshe, 2003.

Liu, Lydia H. *Translingual Practice: Literature, National Culture and Translated Modernity – China, 1910–1937*. Stanford: Stanford University Press, 1995.

Lu, Feng. "Bianhua duoduan de yazhou yingzhan" [The many transformational phases of the Asian Film Festival]. In *Dianying pinglun* [Film review journal], December 8, 197–237. Taipei: Zhongguo yingpinglun xiehui, 1980.

Markus, Andrew L. "The Carnival of Edo: *Misemono* Spectacles from Contemporary Accounts." *Harvard Journal of Asiatic Studies*, 45 (2) (1985): 499–541.

Matsunomoto, Kazuhiro, and Yasuo Otsuka, eds. *Nihon manga eiga no zenbō* [Japanese animated films: A complete view from their birth to *Spirited Away* and beyond]. Tokyo: Nihon manga eiga no zenbōten jikkō iinkai, 2004.

Matsuzaki, Keiji. "Entotsuya Pero" [Pero, the Chimney Sweeper]. *Shinkō Eiga,* June issue (1930): 18–19.

McCarthy, Helen. *The Anime Movie Guide*. London: Titan Books, 1997.

———. *Hayao Miyazaki: Master of Japanese Animation*. Berkeley, CA: Stonebridge Press, 1999.

McCarthy, Helen, and Jonathan Clements. *The Erotic Anime Movie Guide*. London: Titan Books, 1998.

———. *The Anime Encyclopedia: A Guide to Japanese Animation Since 1917*. Berkeley, CA: Stonebridge, 2001.

McCormack, Gavan. *The Emptiness of Japanese Affluence*. Armonk, NY: M.E. Sharpe, 2001.

Merleau-Ponty, Maurice. *Signs*, translated by Richard C. McCleary. Evaston: Northwestern University Press, 1964a.

———. *The Primacy of Perception*, edited by James M. Edie. Evanston: Northwestern University Press, 1964b.

———. *The Visible and the Invisible,* edited by Claude Lefort, translated by Alphonso Lingis. Evanston: Northwestern University Press, 1968.

Miller, Roy. A. *Japan's Modern Myth: The Language and Beyond*. New York: Weatherhill, 1982.

Miyazaki, Hayao. *Shuppatsuten (1979–1996)* [Starting point]. 10th edition. Tokyo: Studio Ghibli, 1998 (1996).

Monet, Claude, Gary Hickey, and Virginia Spate. *Monet and Japan: An Exhibition Organized by the National Gallery of Australia*. Canberra: National Gallery of Australia, 2001.

Mori, Takuga. "Nihon anime-shon eigashi no hitobito" [The various people in the history of Japanese animation]. *National Film Center Newsletter* 10 (2) (2004): 13–15.

Morris, Meaghan. "Banality in Cultural Studies." In *Logics of Television: Essays in Cultural Criticism (Theories of Contemporary Culture)*, edited by Patricia Mellencamp, 14–43. Bloomington: Indiana University Press, 1990.

Morris-Suzuki, Tessa. *Re-inventing Japan: Time, Space, Nation*. Armonk, NY: M.E. Sharpe, 1998.

Munsterberg, Hugo. *The Arts of Japan: An Illustrated History*. Tokyo: Tuttle Publishing, 1957.

Muraoka, Tsunetsugu. *Studies in Shintō Thought*, translated by Delmer M. Brown and James T. Araki. Tokyo: Yushodo, 1964.

Najita, Tetsuo, and H. D. Harootunian. "Japan's Revolt against the West." In *Modern Japanese Thought*, edited by Bob T. Wakabayashi, 207–266. Cambridge: Cambridge University Press, 1998.

Napier, Susan. "Panic States: The Japanese Imagination of Disaster from *Godzilla* to *Akira*." In *Contemporary Japan and Popular Culture*, edited by John W. Treat, 253–264. Honolulu: University of Hawai'i Press, 1996.

———. *Anime from Akira to Princess Mononoke: Experiencing Contemporary Japanese Animation*. New York: Palgrave, 2001a.

———. "Confronting Master Narratives: History as Vision in Miyazaki Hayao's Cinema of De-assurance." *Positions* 9(2) (2001b): 467–493.

Natsume, Fusanotsuke. *Tezuka Osamu no bōken: Sengo manga no kami* [The adventure of Osamu Tezuka: God of postwar manga comics]. Tokyo: Tsukuma shobō, 1995.

Needham, Joseph. *Science and Civilization in China, Volume 5, Chemistry and Chemical Technology, Part 1: Paper and Printing*. Cambridge: Cambridge University Press, 1985.

Nishida, Kitarō. *A Study of Good*, translated by Valdo H. Viglielmo. Tokyo: Yushudo Co. 1960.

———. *Art and Morality*, translated by David A. Dilworth and Valdo H. Viglielmo. Honolulu: University of Hawai'i Press, 1973.

———. *Intelligibility and the Philosophy of Nothingness: Three Philosophical Essays*, translated by Robert Schinzinger in collaboration with I. Koyama and T. Kojima. Westport, CT; Tokyo: Greenwood Press and Maruzen, 1958.

Nishiyama, Matsunosuke. *Edo Culture: Daily Life and Diversion in Urban Japan 1600–1868*, translated and edited by Gerald Groemer. Honolulu: University of Hawai'i Press, 1997.

Noake, Roger. *Animation: A Guide to Animated Film Techniques*. London: MacDonald and Company, 1988.

Okada, Emiko, Suzuki Shinichi, Takahata Isao, and Miyazaki Hayao. *Anime no sekai* [World of anime].Tokyo: Shinchōsha, 1988.

Onishi, Norimitsu. "A Rising Korea Wave: If Seoul Sells it, China Craves it." *International Herald Tribune*. January 10, 2006. http://www.iht.com/bin/print_ipub.php?file=/articles 2006/01/02/news/korea.php.

Ortolani, Benito. *The Japanese Theatre: From Shamanistic Ritual to Contemporary Pluralism*. New Jersey: Princeton University Press, 1995.

Otsuka, Yasuo. *Sakuga asemamire* [Creating pictures is sweat work]. Tokyo: Tokuma Publishing and Studio Ghibli, 2001.

Ozawa, Takeshi. "The Samurai: Photographs from the Last Days of the Tokugawa Shogunate and the Meiji Period." In *Samurai: Dandyism in Japan*, iv. Tokyo: Tokyo Metropolitan Museum of Photography, 2003.

Park, Chung-a. "Hallyu Phenomenon Faces Backlash in East Asia." *The Korea Times*, January 16, 2006. http://www.times.hankooki.com.

Petrov, Vsevolod. *Russian Art Nouveau: The World of Art and Diaghiliev's Painters*. Bournemouth, England: Partstone Press, 1997.

Piovesana, K. Gino. *Recent Japanese Philosophical Thought 1862–1962: A Survey*. Tokyo: Enderle Bookstore, 1963.

Plato. *The Republic of Plato*, translated by Francis C. MacDonald. Oxford: Clarendon Press, 1966 (1941).

Poitras, Gilles. *The Anime Companion: What's Japanese in Japanese Animation?* Berkeley, CA: Stone Bridge Press, 1999.

———. *The Anime Companion 2: More What's Japanese In Japanese Animation?* Berkeley, CA: Stone Bridge Press, 2005.

Pollack, David. *The Fracture of Meaning*. Princeton: Princeton University Press, 1986.

Pyle, Kenneth B. "Meiji Conservatism." In *Modern Japanese Thought*, edited by Bob T. Wakabayashi, 99–146. Cambridge: Cambridge University Press, 1998.

Quiquimelle, Marie-Claire. "The Wan Brothers and Sixty Years of Animated Film in China." In *Perspectives on Chinese Cinema*, edited by Chris Berry, 175–186. London: British Film Institute, 1991.

Read, Herbert, ed. *The Thames and Hudson Dictionary of Art and Artists*. Revised, expanded and updated edition. London: Thames and Hudson, 1994.

Robertson, Jennifer. "It Takes a Village: Internationalization and Nostalgia in Postwar Japan." In *Mirror of Modernity: Invented Traditions of Modern Japan*, edited by Stephen Vlastos, 110–129. Los Angeles: University of California Press, 1998.

Routt, William D. "Stillness and Style in *Neon Genesis Evangelion*." *Animation Journal*, 8(2) (2000): 28–43.

Russell, Mark. "Movies: 'Empress' Draws Koreas Together." *International Herald Tribune*, August 30, 2005. http://www.iht.com/articles/2005/08/29/opinion/chung.php.

Saitani, Ryo, ed. *Sekai to Nihon no anime-shon besito 150* [Best 150 world and Japanese animation films selected by professionals]. Tokyo: Fusion Product Inc., 2003.

Sano, Akiko. "Manga eiga no jidai: to-ki ikōki kara taisenki ni okeru nihon anime-shon" [Manga film era: Japanese animation from the Talkie Period to the Great War Time]. In *Eigagakuteki sōzōryoku: shinema sutadei-zu no bōken* [Imaginative power of cinema studies: Cinema studios' adventures], edited by Katō Mikirō, 96–126. Kyoto: Jimbun Shoin, 2006.

Sano, Midori. "Heian jidai II (kōki)" [Heian period II (late period)]. In *Nihon bijutsushi* [A history of Japanese art], 18th edition, edited by Tsuji Nobuo, 69–84. Tokyo: Bijutsu shuppansha, 1999.

Sansom, B. George. *A History of Japan 1615–1867*, vols. 1–3. Kent: Dawson and Sons, 1963.

———. *Japan A Short Cultural History*. Tokyo: Charles Tuttle, 1983 (1931).

Satō, Tadao. *Currents in Japanese Cinema*, translated by Gregory Barrett. Tokyo: Kodansha International, 1982.

Schechner, Richard. *Performance Studies: An Introduction*. London and New York: Routledge, 2002.

Scheiner, Irwin. "The Japanese Village: Imagined, Real, Contested." In *Mirror of Modernity: Invented Traditions of Modern Japan*, edited by Stephen Vlastos, 67–78. Los Angeles: University of California Press, 1998.

Schickel, Richard. *The Disney Version: The Life, Times, Art and Commerce of Walt Disney*. 3rd edition. Chicago: Elephant Paperbacks, 1997.

Schodt, L. Frederick. *Manga! Manga! The World of Japanese Comics*. Tokyo: Kodansha International, 1983.

Seckel, Dietrich. *Emakimono*. New York: Pantheon Books, 1959.

Shibaguchi, Yasuko. *Anime-shon no iro shokuni* [A color designer of animation].Tokyo: Tokuma Publishing, 1997.

Shimizu, Akira. "Dōwa 'saiyuki' ni shuzai seru: chōhen manga 'tetsusen kōshu' seisaku hōkoku" [Obtaining legendary tale *Saiyuki* material: Feature-length animated film, *Princess Iron Fan* production report]. *Eiga Hyōron,* December issue, 1942.

Shirane, Haruo, ed. *Early Modern Japanese Literature: An Anthology 1690–1900*. New York: Columbia University Press, 2002.

———. *Traces of Dreams: Landscape, Culture Memory and Poetry of Bashō*. Stanford, CA: Stanford University Press, 1998.

Sickman, Laurence, and Alexander Soper. *The Art and Architecture of China*. 3rd edition. Harmondsworth, Middlesex: Penguin Books, 1968.

Siegel, Mark. "Foreigner as Alien in Japanese Science Fantasy." *Science Fiction Studies*, 12(37) (1985): 252–263.

Slaymaker, Douglas, ed. *A Century of Popular Culture in Japan*. Lewiston, NY: Edwin Mellen Press, 2000.

Soothill, William E. *The Analects of Confucius*. 2nd edition. New York: Paragon Book Reprint Corporation, 1968.

Standish, Isolde. "Akira, Postmodernism and Resistance." In *The Worlds of Japanese Popular Culture: Gender, Shifting Boundaries and Global Cultures*, edited by Dolores P. Martinez, 56–74. Cambridge: Cambridge University Press, 1998.

Sutton, Florin G. *Existence and Enlightenment in the Lankavatara Sutra*. New York: State University of New York, 1991.

Suzuki, Daisetz T. *The Lankavatara Sutra: A Mahayana Text* (translation with an introduction). London: Routledge and Kegan Paul, 1932.

Swann, Peter C. *The Art of Japan from the Jomon to the Tokugawa Period*. New York: Crown Publishers, 1966.

Takahata, Isao. *Eiga wo tsukuri nagara kangaetan koto 1955–91 I* [What I was thinking, while making a film].Tokyo: Tokuma Publishing, 1991.

———. *Eiga wo tsukuri nagara kangaetan koto 1991–99 II* [What I was thinking, while making a film]. Tokyo: Studio Ghibli, 1999.

Takakiba, Tsutomu "Kaiga eiga no tokushusei: chūka no sakuhin *Saiyūki* wo mite"[Art film special characteristics: Viewing Chinese work, *Saiyuki*]. *Bunka Eiga,* October Issue (1942): 50–52.

Tamon, Miki. "The Influences of Western Culture on Japanese Art." In *Acceptance of Western Cultures in Japan from the 16th to the Mid-nineteenth Century*, translated by John Blewett, 152–160. Tokyo: Center for East Asian Cultural Studies, 1964.

Tanaka, Yuri. *Japan's Comfort Women: Sexual Slavery and Prostitution during World War II and the US Occupation*. London: Routledge, 2002.

Tanner, Ron. "Mr. Atomic, Mr. Mercury and Chime Trooper: Japan's Answer to the American Dream." In *Asian Popular Culture,* edited by John A. Lent, 79–102. Boulder, CO: Westview Press, 1995.

Taylor, Richard. *The Encyclopedia of Animation Techniques*. London: Quarto Publishing, 1996.

Tezuka Productions. *Tezuka Osamu gekijō: Tezuka Osamu no anime-shon firumogurafi-* [The animation filmography of Osamu Tezuka]. Tokyo: Tezuka Productions, 1991.

Thompson, Kristin, and David Bordwell. *Film History: An Introduction*. New York: McGraw-Hill, 1994.

Toby, Ronald P. "Carnival of the Aliens: Korean Embassies in Edo Period Art and Popular Culture." *Monumenta Nipponica*, 41(4) (1986): 415–456.

Tomaru, Ryūzo. "Shashin ryūtsū gyōkai no chōrō" [A senior of photography business]. In *Nihon shashinshi e no shōgen* [Testimony of a history of Japanese photography], vol. 2, edited by Kamei Takeshi, 125–147. Tokyo: Tokyo Metropolitan Museum of Photography, 1997.

Tomlinson, John. *Cultural Imperialism: A Critical Introduction*. Baltimore: John Hopkins University Press, 1991.

Treat, John W. "Introduction: Japanese Studies into Cultural Studies." In *Contemporary Japan and Popular Culture*, edited by John W. Treat, 1–14. Honolulu: University of Hawai'i Press, 1996.

Trotsky, Leon. *Literature and Revolution*, translated by Rose Strunsky. New York: International Publishers, 1925.

Tsugata, Nobuyuki. "Research on the Achievements of Japan's First Three Animators." *Asian Cinema* 14(1) (2003): 13–27.

———. *Nihon anime-shon no chikara* [Power of Japan animation]. Tokyo: NTT shuppan, 2004.

Tsunoda, Ryūsaku, William Theodore deBary, and Donald Keene, eds. *Sources of Japanese Tradition*. New York: Columbia University Press, 1958.

Tsurumi, Shunsuke. *A Cultural History of Japan 1945–80*. London: KPI, 1987.

Twine, Nanette. *Language and the Modern State: The Reform of Written Japanese*. London and New York: Routledge, 1991.

Vernal, David. "War and Peace in Japanese Science Fiction Animation: An Examination of *Mobile Suit Gundam* and *The Mobile Police Patlabor*." *Animation Journal*, 4(1) (1995): 56–84.

Vogel, Ezra F. *Japan as Number One: Lessons for America*. Cambridge, MA: Harvard University Press, 1979.

Volosinov, V. N. *Marxism and the Philosophy of Language*, translated by Ladislav Matejka and I. R. Titunik. New York: Seminar Press, 1973.

Wakabayashi Bob T., ed. *Modern Japanese Thought*. Cambridge: Cambridge University Press, 1998.

Waldenfels, Bernhard. "Merleau-Ponty." In *A Companion to Continental Philosophy*, edited by Simon Critchley and William R. Schroeder, 281–291. Oxford: Blackwell Publishers, 1988.

Walthall, Anne. *Peasant Uprisings in Japan: A Critical Anthology of Peasant Histories,* edited by and translated by Anne Walthall. Chicago: University of Chicago Press, 1991.

Wells, Paul. "Hayao Miyazaki Floating Worlds, Floating Signifiers." *Art and Design,* No. 53 (1997): 22–25.

———. *Understanding Animation*. London: Routledge, 1998.

Westermann, Mariet. *The Art of the Dutch Republic 1585–1718*. London: Laurence King Publishing, 2004.

White, Livingston A. "Reconsidering Cultural Imperialism Theory." *Transnational Broadcasting Studies Journal,* No. 6 (2001), Spring/Summer Issue. http://www.tbsjournal.com/Archives/Spring01/white2.html.

Whorf, Benjamin Lee. *Language, Thought and Reality*. Cambridge: MIT Press, 1962.

Williams, Raymond. "The Analysis of Culture." In *Cultural Theory and Popular Culture*, edited by John Storey, 56–64. Hemel Hempstead: Harvester Wheatsheaf, 1994.

Wollen, Peter. *Signs and Meanings in the Cinema*. London: Secker and Warburg, 1972.

Yaguchi, Kunio, ed. *Manga no jidai: Tezuka Osamu kara evangerion made* [The manga age]. Tokyo: The Museum of Contemporary Art, 1998.

Yamaguchi, Katsunori, and Watanabe Yasushi. *Nihon anime-shon eiga shi* [The history of Japanese animation]. Osaka: Yubunsha, 1977.

Yamaguchi, Yasuo, ed. *Nihon no anime zenshi* [A whole history of Japanese animation]. Tokyo: Ten-Books, 2004.

Yan, Shao-dang. "Riben gudai xiaoshuo de chansheng yi Zhongguo wenxue de guanlian" [The emergence of ancient Japanese fiction and its relationship to Chinese literature]. In *Zhongri bijiao wenxue yanjiu zhiliao huipian* [A compilation of Sino-Japanese comparative literature research], edited by Wang Zhuo, 78–91. Hangzhou: Zhongguo meishu xueyuan chubanshe, 2002.

Yau, Kinnia S. T. "Hong Kong and Japan: Not One Less." In *Border Crossings in Hong Kong Cinema*, 104–110. Hong Kong: The 24th Hong Kong International Film Festival, 2000.

Ye, Lang. *Zhongguo meishushi dawang* [General outline of Chinese aesthetics]. 7th edition. Shanghai: Shanghai renmin chubanshe, 2003 (1985).

Yokota, Masao. "A Master Animator: Yasuji Mori's Works for Children." *International Journal of Comic Art*, 6 (2) (2004): 376–391.

———. *Anime-shon no rinshō shinrigaku* [Clinical psychology of animation]. Tokyo: Seishinshobō, 2006.

Yonezawa, Yoshihiro. "Manga to anime to Miyazaki Hayao" [Manga and anime and Hayao Miyazaki]. In *Bamboo Mook Series: Miyazaki Hayao no sekai: kurieitazu fairu* [The world of Hayao Miyazaki: A creator's file], 156–164. Tokyo: Takeshobō, 2005.

Yoshikawa, Itsuji. *Major Themes in Japanese Art*. New York and Tokyo: Weatherhill and Heibonsha, 1976.

Yoshinobu, Inoura. *A History of Japanese Theater I: Noh and Kyogen*. Yokohoma: Japan Cultural Society, 1971.

Yuasa, Shino. "Animators Battle Poverty, Chinese Rivals: Careers Undone by Pitiful Salaries, Competition from Asian Neighbors." *The Japan Times*, June 25, 2004, p. 3.

Zhao, Qingge. *Baishechuan: The Legend of the White Snake*. Bilingual edition. Beijing: New World Press, 1998 (1956).

Newspapers, Periodicals and other Publications without Author's Names:

"Animated Lovers." www.china.org.cn, January 30, 2004. http://www.china.org.cn/english/culture/85722.htm.

"Animation Trade Continues to Grow." *Macroview Weekly,* November 15, 2006, p. 2.

Eiga Nenkan 1954–1960 [Motion picture almanac]. Tokyo: Japan Film Producers' Association.

Imidas (Innovative multi-information dictionary annual series). Tokyo: Shueisha, 2000.

The Japanese Film Heritage: From the Non-film Collection of the National Film Center. Tokyo: National Museum of Modern Art, 2002.

"*Khan Kluay* Hopes to Ignite Thai Animation Industry." *Animation World Network,* June 12, 2006. http://news.awn.com/index.php?ltype=date&newsitem_no=17145&dir=2.

Kinema Junpō (Special edition on Miyazaki Hayao and Takahata Isao). July 16, No. 1166. Tokyo: Kinema Junpō Sha, 1995.

Korean Animation: Heats up the Senses. 28th Annecy International Animated Film Festival Honoring Korea, June 7–12. Seoul: Seoul Metropolitan Government, Korean Film Council, Seoul Animation Center, Ministry of Culture and Tourism, 2004.

"Manga Mamas Japanese-Style Comic artists in Jakarta? Yes, Thanks to Expatriate Wife Machiko Maeyama's 'School for Aspiring cartoonists'," *The Straits Times,* April 20, 2003.

"Manga *Saiyūki* gappyō" [Manga *Saiyuki* picture book], *Eiga Gijutsu,* October Issue (1942): 64–66.

Otaku ni narenai anime suki no hon [Book for animation fans who cannot become nerds].Tokyo: KTC, 1997.

"Otaku shijō 2,600 oku yen" [Otaku market, 260 billion yen]. *Asahi Shinbun,* August 24, 2004.

Overseas Chinese Figures in Cinema. Hong Kong: Urban Council, the 16th Hong Kong International Film Festival, 1992.

Samurai: Dandyism in Japan. Tokyo: Tokyo Metropolitan Museum of Photography, 2003.

Shōwa shoki sayoku eiga zasshi betsukan [Left-wing film magazines in the early Showa era special issue]. Tokyo: Senkifukkokuban kankōkai, 1981.

Sōgyō nijūnen no arumi [Steps of 20 years' establishment]. Tokyo: Fuji Film, 1960.

Sū-pa-robotto gahō: kyodai robotto anime sanjūgonen no arumi [The super robots chronicles: The history of Japanese super robots animations, 1963–1997]. Tokyo: B Media Books, 1997.

"Tantan *Baoliandeng.*" *Fuzhou Evening News,* September 5, 1999. http://www.66163.com/Fujian_w/news/fzwb/990905/8_12html.

Toei Animation Yearbook. Tokyo: Toei Animation Company, 1989.

Index